Robert Pringle

The Power of Money

How Ideas about Money
Shaped the Modern World

Robert Pringle

ISBN 978-3-030-25893-1   ISBN 978-3-030-25894-8   (eBook)
https://doi.org/10.1007/978-3-030-25894-8

Cover illustration: © Colin Anderson Productions pty ltd / DigitalVision / Getty

This Palgrave Macmillan imprint is published by the registered company Springer Nature Switzerland AG.
The registered company address is: Gewerbestrasse 11, 6330 Cham, Switzerland

To the memory of my father

Acknowledgements

Two individuals are owed a special debt of gratitude: Brendan Brown and Alessandro Roselli. Without their encouragement, this book might have been begun but would never have been completed. I have benefitted greatly from an almost continuous dialogue with each of them over many years. I should also thank them for reading chapters of the book in draft form and for their enlightening comments.

My former colleagues Graham Bannock and Alan Doran provided the spur to a much-needed 'reality check' at an early stage in the writing process. Michael Bordo similarly provided helpful comments and suggestions. Peter Urbach read most of the book in draft and not only highlighted logical flaws in my reasoning at several points but also suggested numerous stylistic improvements in the text. My long-standing friendship and dialogue with Haruko Fukuda, another former colleague, has yielded many insights into recent changes in the world of banking and investment, not least its weird remuneration practices.

A special thanks to my interlocutors in an informal email study group on international monetary issues—Warren Coats, Joseph Potvin, Leanne Ussher and Larry White. Our exchanges over the past ten years have been a constant source of stimulus and delight.

Among other people from whom I have learnt much in the wide variety of fields covered in this book are the following: Claudio Borio, Forrest Capie, John Chown, Lyric Hughes Hale, Steve Hanke, David Harrison, Keith Hart, Ikuko Hiroe, Geoffrey Ingham, Tom Jupp, Martin Klosterfelde, Andrew McNally, Robert Mundell, Margaret O'Neill, Hiroto Oonogi, Will Pringle, Hugh Sandeman, Judy Shelton, Andrew Sheng, Masaaki Shirakawa, Robert Spicer, Toshikazu Takei, Marc Uzan, Frank Vogl, Ryo Watabe, William White, Toyokuni Yamanaka and members of the Austerity Club. I honour the memory of the late Allan Meltzer, a great mentor and friend with whom I corresponded for many years and the late David Henderson who, over long lunches in Hampstead, supplied a brilliant, occasionally caustic yet always witty and constructive commentary on my evolving ideas.

The far-flung network of monetary economists, central bankers and commentators built up by Central Banking Publications has been invaluable. I have benefitted also from my regular contacts with Nick Carver, the publisher and Chris Jeffery, the editor, as well as other members of the staff and of the company's editorial advisory board.

A big 'thank you' to Simon Blundell, Reform Club librarian, for maintaining a great library, for his skill in obtaining any book at lightning speed and for suggesting works that might be relevant to my research.

I inherited from my father, John Pringle, OBE, not only a passionate interest in civilisations past, present and future but also an unpublished manuscript outlining his reflections on 'science and human survival'. I have drawn on this for the discussion of liberalism in Chap. 20.

Books tend to be written by relatively successful people for relatively successful people. But that risks biasing the whole analysis. My father's work at Rethink Mental Illness, the mental health charity that he founded in 1972, gave him special insight into the distress experienced by sufferers from severe mental illness and their families. Many sufferers are not simply relatively unsuccessful, by worldly standards, but may be quite unable to meet the demands of modern life. I hope that some sections of the text, notably in the discussion of Outsiders, benefit from his insights.

Contents

1

Introduction

The following essays are about wars, revolutions, social breakdown, the clash of cultures, socialism, delusional behaviour, technology, the arts, history, sociology and many other topics—each viewed through the prism of money. They illustrate how money is interwoven with almost every aspect of our lives. Money, like marriage, is a social institution but also an intensely personal matter. People tend to have strong attitudes towards it. Parents pass on certain attitudes, values and ways of managing money to their children. At the personal level, money forms one dimension of everybody's lives. As a social institution, it is often contentious. The arrangements that societies have made to regulate money have varied widely. At least over the past 100 years, such arrangements have seldom stayed settled for long. Diverse philosophies of money have been influential in many of the great conflicts, key historical developments and turning points of the twentieth and early twenty-first centuries. In many ways, they have helped to shape the modern world.

Understanding money's power as well as its limitations is especially important now. This is because people are linked together through complex monetary and technological networks. We live in a global money 'space'. Increasingly, we also share a common global outlook (see below for definitions of these terms). The global takeover by this outlook is among the most significant developments of the past 120 years. We are staking the future of our societies on an assumption that its benefits far outweigh its disadvantages. We had better be right, for this is a high-risk strategy.

© The Author(s) 2019
R. Pringle, *The Power of Money*, https://doi.org/10.1007/978-3-030-25894-8_1

The Power of Money Illustrated

Historical instances and episodes illustrate the power of money from 1900 to the present. They show, for example:

- The remarkable influence of a few German thinkers not only in shaping the twentieth century's ideas about money but also on what actually happened—on history—despite Germany losing two wars;
- The role of monetary innovation in creating a modern, mass consumer society, starting in America and the emergence of the newly enfranchised, powerful, middleclass, female shopper in the 1920s;
- The monetary bungles that brought about the fall of the Weimar Republic and the rise of Hitler; these included excessive Allied demands for war reparations, hyperinflation, the withdrawal of American loans after the Wall Street crash and the refusal to reflate the economy in a timely manner;
- The important lessons German thinkers learnt from the failure of Weimar about the need for stable prices; these had a lasting influence on post-war (West) Germany and on the design of the European Central Bank; an important lesson they could also have drawn from the war reparations debate (but failed to) was how to treat a sovereign debtor country (e.g. Greece in 2015);
- The enormous, futile efforts that were made essentially to eliminate money not only in the Soviet Union but also in other states, at the cost of millions of human lives;
- The *agreement* among economic historians that money mismanagement was the major cause of the Great Depression of the 1930s, coupled with the *disagreement* about whether the mismanagement consisted of fuelling the pre-crisis boom by creating *too much* credit and money or rather consisted in *not creating enough* credit and money when the depression hit and banks started collapsing;

Other chapters look at the reasons behind events, for example:

- How the genius of a few economists rescued capitalism—but only when society was ready to receive their messages;
- Why two global conflicts were needed for the Western idea of money to triumph;
- How America used its money power after World War II to make the world safe for its idea of capitalism and build a new world order—and how China

is following 70 years later with the most aggressive use of money power the world has ever seen;

- How a social consensus on the relative unimportance of money in life and low social status of bankers supported controls on money and suppression of interest rates and markets, curbing the power of money for a generation;
- How private sector financial innovation put pressure on governments to free money and capital flows in the 1970s and 1980s, resulting in the formation of a global money space—a space within which money moves easily and at low cost;
- Why a rising tide of new money eroded the walls erected around the economies of the Soviet Bloc, contributing to the collapse of Communism;
- How Western triumphalism and the 'end of history' narrative in the 1990s led to *hubris* and Money Delusion that in turn caused over-borrowing and financial crises;
- Why the launch of the euro was a project typical of the Money Delusion of the late twentieth century;
- Why the dominant forms of capitalism are its most corrupt forms, such as state capitalism, crony capitalism and surveillance capitalism;
- Why anti-capitalist and anti-money messages still have power to move people;
- How central banks learnt to control the value of money reasonably well in terms of preventing excessive inflation or deflation and why this came at a high cost of multiple asset bubbles and rising inequality of wealth.

One conclusion is that societies can and do change their money quite rapidly. Monetary rules and procedures do not form a static, hard, inflexible system. Yet this is often how they appear. We may feel that we have to accept them blindly—an image carefully cultivated by the powers that be. But appearances are deceptive. People can reform money—not only the official arrangements, such as the exchange rate system and central banks but also informal habits, norms and standards of ethical behaviour. What is needed to make change happen? Not primarily economic expertise but rather imagination, determination and an awareness of the priorities and needs of society (I refer here to democratic societies where the use of force to impose a system is out of the question).

Aims

More broadly, the essays in this book have three main aims: first, to describe and explain the emergence of a global money space and society; second, to show the wide-ranging implications of these developments, including the downsides; and, third, to make the case for deep-seated change in our outlook. I suggest that we can look to fields ranging from sociology to philosophy and the visual arts for ideas to support the needed change in outlook. Ideas, beliefs and attitudes play critical roles. I shall argue that ideas—in this case, ideas about money—have had as great an influence on events as material interests. Now we need new ideas more than ever.

It is true that money is, in many ways, just another technology. It is, however, more than a tool. It gives holders of money potential command over all other tools. It can come to play such a big role in our lives that it exercises undue influence over us, shaping our futures in ways we may not really want. This is, I believe, the case at present. This is a dangerous moment. As individuals we can reclaim autonomy. The same goes for our societies. But it will need a deeper understanding of how these forces shape our world.

Compare the world of 1900 with our own. Then, as now, evidence of social improvement was all around: people saw progress in fighting diseases, in access to clean water, cleaner city streets, electric light, railways connecting places hundreds or even thousands of miles apart, and rapid intercontinental communications enabled by a complex web of telegraphic cables. Almost every day, it seemed, saw some fresh technological miracle. They could expect such progress to continue.[1] We know their world was about to be shattered by World War I. This conflict also destroyed their monetary order, a pillar of their civilisation. It would take 100 years and many social experiments before a viable global money linking people all over the world through technological networks would re-emerge. Are we, like our ancestors, heading towards disaster without being aware of it? Will the world we have built with our money and our imagination also prove to be unsustainable? Cracks have appeared in the facade, as they did before World War I.

In a world tied together by markets and monetary networks, there is a sense that something is fundamentally wrong, that our societies are heading in the wrong direction. But we should not despair.

A Distinctive Global Culture

The emergence of 'the global money space' followed by a widely shared culture were world-changing developments. Arising in the heartlands of capitalism in Western Europe and North America in the latter part of the twentieth century, they acquired their present (2020) form and global reach in the decade following the financial crash of 2007–09. They were the unintended result of actions by states and the private sector over preceding decades. Many elements can be traced back to specific episodes and innovations of the past.

I show that almost every decade since 1900 left an impact. The innovations, theories and practices that form the present system were, when first introduced, sometimes shocking and controversial. Conditions that people at the time took for granted as natural and normal are often revealed to have been unstable and evanescent. As regards our global culture, history suggests that a few elements of it will endure, but we cannot know which.[2] We cannot know, either, what forms ideas of money will take in the future.

The scope and global reach of our culture are unprecedented. It is true that a mercantile spirit has flourished in many ages of history—think of Venice in the late Middle Ages, the city states of the Renaissance, the Dutch Golden Age, the United States in the time of the Robber Barons. But there is a big difference between those times and ours. In former times, mercantile values existed alongside other values, customs and beliefs. Groups had different ways of life. These included the military, the clergy, the landowning aristocracy, farmers, craftsmen, artisans, and professional bodies and guilds (and, indeed, after the industrial revolution, traditional working-class culture). Each had its distinct standards of ethics. Now all these competing outlooks and ways of life are giving way to a single, unitary approach. Also, this approach is attached to a financial, industrial and commercial system vastly greater in scope and power than any witnessed before.

Global E-commerce

Global e-commerce is among the pervasive influences inducing participants to adopt an outlook on the world with shared features. I know some of the challenges involved from personal experience.[3] Yet many make the effort and succeed. Entrepreneurship is thriving; at any one time hundreds of millions of individuals are involved in start-ups, and many of them source and/or deliver their products and services across national borders. Governments everywhere foster welcoming conditions for start-ups as well as more mature enterprises.

The question for them is: how to survive and prosper in the knowledge economy.[4]

The Effects and Dangers of These Developments

There is much to welcome in all this. For many millions of human beings, the spread of the money space has come as a liberation. One venture that tracks and celebrates the onward march of the enterprise spirit strikes describes itself as 'an ever-growing community of believers in the transformative benefits of entrepreneurship' (Global Enterprise Monitor 2019).

'Transformative benefits'? Indeed. However, look at the downsides as well as upsides of these changes. These include a liability to the mentality I term Money Delusion, as well as undesirable manipulation of money by public and private interests that in turn contribute to unprecedented levels of financial crime, kleptocracy and corruption. The whole system has become deformed. Then there are the effects of the new culture on the individual psyche; many people depend almost totally on monetary and technological networks. This is a source of continual strain and anxiety. Also, our global culture splits society into Insiders and Outsiders. This is much more than simply a question of wealth and income inequalities. I shall argue that such deformations are not just undesirable by-products of the culture that will be eliminated over time but, rather, typical manifestations of it.

Reforms

This approach explains why neither the Left with its usual cries for more state action (support for the disadvantaged, tougher anti-monopoly drive, regulation to prevent exploitation, a minimum wage and new social contract as well as tight regulation) nor the Right with its nationalist fantasies offers credible remedies. They are both in the grip of the same culture and mindset. Indeed, one of the devices of the money virus—a metaphor for the way monetary influences infiltrate society and the body politic—is to politicise every issue. This splits the Resistance to it. While the dogfight between Left and Right drags on, the debate gets bogged down and no effective reforms are implemented. Meanwhile, communities and other supportive social structures dissolve, along with their distinctive myths, ethics and outlooks.

Thesis: Ideas Matter

Another major claim of this book is that ideas about money and the roles it plays—and should play—in social life have been among the most powerful ideas impelling change, including revolutions, wars and other features, good and bad, of global history over the past 120 years. Of course, people as well as classes and nations also follow their interests, and the outcome is determined by a complex interplay between ideas and interests. As Max Weber, a founding father of sociology, put it, ideas may act like points on a railway line: 'very frequently the "world images" that have been created by ideas have, like switchmen, determined the tracks along which action has been pushed by the dynamic of interest' (Weber 1922). Even when it comes to money, the very stuff people use to realise their demands, the influence of ideas is often as important as material interest.

Money should be viewed in its social, political and ideological context. It has usually been only an element in a broad political, economic and social philosophy. The era of liberalism, free trade and free capital movements of 1900 was succeeded by the various 'isms' of the twentieth century ending in 'neoliberalism'. But that ideology took a battering in the crash of 2007–09. This cut the link between money and an underlying political philosophy. One important strand running through the period is a specific idea of money and a theory about how it gains value. This is the state theory of money. Starting from late nineteenth-century Germany it was adapted to serve the needs of many governments, was adopted by leading economists and formed the backbone of the official monies of the period.

The future of money as a social institution is always open. What we deem to count as money, the beliefs we hold about it, the values we assign to it and the arrangements we make to govern it are subject to continual change. This may be imperceptible at any one time, lending money a monolithic air. In reality, it is constantly adjusting to changing pressures. Whatever arrangements we have can be challenged. Attempts to close down discussion are often made, typically by people who are doing well out of the existing system. They should be resisted.

The way forward follows naturally from the analysis: change our idea of money (again) as part of a change in our culture. Going straight for a technical fix is unlikely to succeed. Neither religious faith nor conventional moralities are sufficiently strong as constraints on behaviour. However, there are places where we can look for insights and suggestive ideas. One is in recent work by sociologists. We can also seek lessons from studying cultures that hold to a different idea of money's place. From contemporary art we may hope to gain a new way of 'seeing' money. Such a cultural approach to reform fits in with the idea of money advanced in this book—one that links it to broad social trends. Once society has discovered new ways of seeing money, economists can figure out how to put them into practice.

Outline by Chapter

Each of the chapters is self-contained and can be read separately, but they contain a unifying idea; this is approached from several angles that are brought together in the concluding essay. In the historical survey, *Time Past* (Part I), ten periods are selected, arranged in chronological order to illustrate my aims. These are designed to show how ideas about money shaped the modern world and how each period left a legacy, in many cases contributing vital ingredients to our current outlook and distinctive monetary arrangements. That discussion comprises Chaps. 2–11.

Time Present (Part II), explores the effects and implications of the global outlook, focussing on the past twenty years. It discusses how modern money and its culture gradually wash away local, regional and national communities and family ties. Survival in the global marketplace is tough and likely to absorb a person's time, intelligence and energy. Economist and former central bank governor Raghuram Rajan has called for 'community' to be built as the third pillar of capitalism alongside the state and the market (Rajan 2019).

Part II starts with a recapitulation: how, in the light of the analysis offered in Part I, this astonishing modern global society and the prominent role accorded to money and monetary ties emerge. It then outlines typical features of this new society and outlook. It was seriously affected by the financial crisis of 2007–09, which, I argue, resulted from Money Delusion, a natural outgrowth of the outlook (Chap. 13). Money has become a weapon in the international tug of war. Yet modern money leads to such outcomes. Is it compatible with financial stability? (Chap. 14).

The amazing gambles that modern societies are willing to take on money are illustrated by the euro, the most ambitious official experiment with money ever made. It is typical of our age in showing the confidence political leaders can have in an imaginary money. They promise to realise a particular monetary dream and assume it will lead to the construction of the necessary political and institutional framework required to make it work (Chap. 15). Despite the attempts to provide price stability through commitment to inflation targets, modern money is 'unanchored'. Escaping from social control, money easily runs wild. This helps to explain the growth of several disturbing modern phenomena, such as crony capitalism, widening inequality, the rise of populism, and political shocks such as the election of Donald Trump and Brexit. For many people money is desired mainly for its political (rather than purchasing) power (Chap. 16). Money always has two sides: heads and tails—the sovereign and the market—collective and individual—unifying and divisive—with all their potential, positive and negative. Now its negative potential has come to the fore. It inevitably produces Outsiders and generates Resistance (Chap. 17).

Time Future (Part III) starts with the dilemma we face in responding to the coming of virtual money. A cryptocurrency asset such as Bitcoin has given rise to a classic asset bubble, and seems (to traditional ways of thinking about money) to have no economic basis of value. However, many feel that it holds out hope that society can reclaim money from 'them', the elites that allegedly control and abuse it. So-called stablecoins such as libra are a more effective challenge to prevailing arrangements. Private cryptocurrencies face numerous obstacles. The modern state is a jealous god. It combats obstacles to the scope of its powers, as seen in its campaigns against cash, gold and cryptocurrencies (Chap. 18). The following chapter reports recent work by sociologists that has added to our understanding of the nature of money. This work has investigated important topics such as the power relationships between the state, financial interests and the wider society in the production of money; why money is often used (and misused) as an instrument of social progress; and why modern money seems often to hold us in thrall (Chap. 19). The following chapter discusses the influence of the liberal intelligentsia, which facilitated the rise of the money culture by their onslaught on classical liberalism, which had legitimated money as an instrument of ownership. They bear some of the responsibility for present discontents (Chap. 20).

A reset of our money arrangements requires a deep-seated change in social attitudes and outlook. Society should set the direction of travel: what we want money, as a social institution, to be for. We can learn something by studying societies that have, in the past, enabled people to keep money in a given place; the example of Japan is discussed (Chap. 21). Turning to a completely different field, the following essay explores possibilities of learning new ways of 'seeing' money through contemporary art. John Berger was a pioneering art critic who helped us to 'see' art in new ways. We need a John Berger to help us into new ways of 'seeing' money (Chap. 22). Resorting to the unlovely but expressive and somehow indispensable German word, *Weltanschauung*, that is what needs to change. We should, however, take care. A global ideology aiming at the maximisation of monetary returns, for all its faults, is much to be preferred to the often horrific and cruel ideologies of the twentieth century when nationalism, communism and fascism were the principal means to control money's power (Chap. 23).

Future Money: Each of the chapters in Part III discusses ways in which we might refresh our money with new ideas, learning from other societies as well as through monetary innovations. Is the state theory of money compatible with, or an obstacle to, needed reform? I argue that the harms done by current attitudes to money are potentially as damaging socially as those inflicted by global warming. They are harder to see, but they affect citizens just as much. We need a sea-change in our ideas, values and beliefs about money. Money can and should be part of a broad effort to improve the human condition. We should aim to give money a new, natural habitat and anchor.

Definitions, Limitations and Method

Broad definition of money: In the following accounts of various episodes in the past 120 years, we will come across many diverse characterisations of money as a social institution. Given these diverse associations, it is necessary to broaden the usual economic definition of money. Economists define money as a unit of account (the numeraire for measuring and communicating values), means of payment and store of value. That is fine for the purposes of economic analysis. It is a thin concept of money—necessary for economists' particular method of analysis and for economics to hold its claim to be a science but one that squeezes out much of the contents—and I would argue also the meanings—that money carries. Money comes thick with moral and symbolic associations. It is rich and varied in possibilities and potential. I believe its significance in a specific time and place can only be understood by examining how the word is used. If money is a social contrivance, a convention, it is also an idea being continually re-defined. Is its appearance of concreteness illusory? Seen from one angle it is; yet from another it is a reality with which we must all deal. Such complications make it necessary not to restrict the term unduly.

Indeed, unless where specified to the contrary, this book uses the very broadest concept of money. It is, indeed, sometimes shorthand for the monetary system, the monetary regime and other such terms.[5]

Money space and *money culture*: For the sake of clarity, I now introduce two concepts that play major roles only in Part II but are also mentioned on a few occasions in Part I: *money space and money culture*. Money space is defined as an area within which individuals, companies and governments (including official agencies like central banks) can make and receive payments of money easily and at relatively low cost. In short, an area within which money is expected to flow easily and swiftly; n.b. I do not use it to refer to the room for fiscal and monetary policy manoeuvres or manipulation. Money culture is the mix of beliefs and values about, and attitudes towards, money. It is about the roles it plays or should play in society and in an individual's life.

Broad scope of relevant ideas: linked to the above, the ideas about money include but are not limited to the ideas of economists. Indeed, a key argument is that ideas and sentiments circulating in the wider society and especially its intellectuals and opinion leaders often exert a strong influence on events. These sometimes infuse mass movements, as in the case of socialism, but in other cases often just provide a background ideological 'mood'. They filter the ideas of economists and financial experts. Policy-makers are influenced by the climate of opinion.

Caveats: Several warnings are in order. First, this is not an attempt to write a potted financial history of the twentieth century. It is about the various ways that humans have looked at money. Secondly, it is not an intellectual history nor a history of ideas; readers will not find detailed accounts of the monetary theories propounded by the leading economists nor of economists' debates about them (although brief summary accounts are offered where appropriate, with references to relevant literature). Histories of ideas usually focus on their supply; these essays investigate rather the demand side—what society wants from its money, given its changing needs, priorities and values. Thirdly, many debates about monetary issues that might have been important at the time but that were quickly solved without affecting the broad sweep of events are omitted.[6] I do refer to the fact—surprising to many non-economists—that money does not matter in the models economists use to explain capitalism.[7] This is a relevant sociological fact. The abstract debate about whether money in theory is merely a veil is not such a fact.[8]

Multi-disciplinary and multi-cultural: The analysis draws on several disciplines, notably economics, sociology, and history as well as literature, contemporary art and other cultural products from diverse cultural traditions. This eclectic mix may be uncongenial to some. I apologise in advance for my blunders—I cover such a wide area I have doubtless made errors of fact and interpretation. I invite readers to favour it as they would a poem (or indeed money!), with a 'willing suspension of disbelief'.

Evidence: Various nations and social classes have traditions of thought about money that guide their daily behaviour and relationships and also form part of their identities, of their ways of existing in the world. To find out what money meant for people in such respects in specific times and places, I use the evidence of novels, plays, poetry, social and political writings, and occasionally the visual arts and music. By such methods one may hope to bring to life what people had in mind at the time, their concerns and hopes and especially what symbolic meanings they attached to money. Obviously, the selection has to be highly personal. Indeed, I occasionally invoke my experience as a financial and economic commentator and as an entrepreneur (often relegated to footnotes that can be skipped easily).

Three Themes

The chapters in each part are loosely connected by a common thesis or theme. Each of these can be expressed in three words.

The thesis of Part I is that *ideas drive actions*, that is, the values, beliefs and attitudes that people hold at any one time have powerful influences on their actions, and thus on historical developments. Even money, the instrument by which we pursue our material aims, satisfy our need for nourishment, and use in planning our futures at communal as well as personal level, is shaped by ideas. This is tested by examining a wide range of ideas about money. The twentieth century was a laboratory in which many different ideas—some mad, some bad, some great, some just so-so—were tried out. The theme of Part II is that *actions have consequences*. These may be direct and visible; others are indirect and hard to discern. Some are intended; others unintended; some are merely short term in the effects; others go underground and exert consequences that become visible years or decades later. It is no simple matter to identify longer term consequences of actions. The theme of Part III is that *consequences breed new ideas*. Actions have effects, long and short term, that people in the present have to respond to, yet they may have very different ideas about the responses they should make from those who initiated the actions that led to such effects. For people in the present always face a new situation. Money and the monetary system confront people as objective facts—a reality they have to come to terms with. Yet every part of this analysis shows money, how it functions and the ideas, symbols and values associated with it, to be continually changing. If that is the case, society cannot disown responsibility for its money any more than can an adult shrug off his or her responsibility not only for their money but for their part in shaping other people's money as well. The message is that, rightly interpreted, history should inspire change and renewal. Whether money works well or badly is in the end down to us.

A brief summary of the results of each part's test of the hypothesis is given at the conclusion of Part I in Chap. 11, Part II in Chap. 17 and Part III in Chap. 22.

Such somewhat philosophical issues arise because of money's special characteristics. Money exists at the intersection of the individual and the social, the personal and the impersonal, nature and artifice, subject and object, the abstract and the concrete, art and science; and of past, present and future.

Notes

1. The atmosphere of the age is brilliantly evoked by Stefan Zweig in his memoirs (1942).
2. In this book I use the term 'culture' both in its sociological and in its artistic senses, that is, to denote the values, beliefs, attitudes and practices of a society, social class or group and/or its creative output. I trust that it will be clear from the context which meaning I intend to convey in referring to it. When I refer to the outlook or culture of a society in its broadest, most philosophical terms I use the German expression, *Weltanschauung*.
3. I launched Central Banking Publications Ltd, a business targeting a worldwide community (a business now 30 years old and still growing) at a time that coincided with the coming of the World Wide Web and of email. The business was buoyed by the new ease of communication and global audience created by these stunning innovations.
4. A good guide to the state of entrepreneurial activity is provided by the annual reports of the Global Enterprise Monitor (GEM), founded in 1999 as a joint project between Babson College (USA) and London Business School (UK). Based on GEM data, about 10% of the world's working age population of some 4.5 billion is trying to start a business or has started and run one in the past 3 years or so; many of these will also source and/or deliver their products and services across national borders.
5. Economists would be guilty of disciplinary imperialism if they insisted that money must accord with their definition of it and that any broader use is illegitimate. This is going far too far. It assumes money is an identifiable thing with certain essential features, like a table. But money is not like that. It has no irreducible, unchanging, nature. It does not have to be a means of payment; according to many authorities its key feature is as a unit of account and it served as such probably hundreds or even thousands of years from ancient Babylon on without necessarily being used as a means of payment. Moreover, the economic definition of it, seemingly so clear, is full of unresolved complexities. Take the idea of a 'store of value'. What does that mean? Does it mean, for example, that if I do not buy a cup of coffee when offered one now but keep my money, I can buy that same cup of coffee later, when I choose? Obviously not. So, I can store the equivalent of this cup of coffee. But what does that actually mean? It turns out that the three features of money that make up the

economic definition are, in combination, a value-free, utopian, almost mystical idea. See Hadas (2018). There is no reason why every form of money, what passes for money, should conform to this abstract idea. To pluck money as an abstract idea out of its social context, to examine it as a specimen under the microscope, is even to do violence to it, to begin the process by which it becomes a force of short-termism, of alienation.

Discussion of the 'nature' of money is reminiscent of that between two schools of German historical thought at the end of the nineteenth century. The question was this: Was the classical Greek economy the same as ours or different? Max Weber dismissed the argument by pointing out that we wouldn't be interested in the Greeks unless they were different and we couldn't understand them unless they were the same as us.

6. I omit, for example, any extended treatment of the debate on so-called threatened shortage of international money in the 1960s, the 'Triffin dilemma', the creation of special monetary asset in the International Monetary Fund, the SDR, the massive effort to make this artificial unit the centre of the international monetary system, the worries concerning 'global imbalances' that erupt from time to time, and much of the debates about 'reform of the international monetary system'—all these have been ideas that failed (and often deserved to fail), or problems that turned out to be non-problems.

7. Or in the models used by central banks to set interest rates. Indeed, some central bankers are keen to downplay the role of money in their work further on the grounds that a perception that central banking is 'all about money' might deter some women from applying for employment.

8. See Chap. 19 for a further discussion of this.

Bibliography

Global Enterprise Monitor (2019). *2018–19 Global Report*. London: GEM.

Hadas, E. (2018). 'Three Rival Versions of Monetary Enquiry: Symbol, Treasure, Token'. A lecture given at Las Casas Institute, Blackfriars Hall, Oxford University on May 29. New Blackfriars (forthcoming).

Rajan, R. (2019). *The Third Pillar: How Markets and the State Leave the Community Behind*.

Weber, M. (1922–1923). 'The Social Psychology of the World Religions', in Gerth, H. H. and Mills, C.E. *From Max Weber Essays in Sociology*. London: Routledge & Kegan Paul, 1948.

Zweig, S. (1942–2011). The World of Yesterday: Memoirs of a European (German title, *Die Welt von Gestern: Erinnerungen eines Europäers*), trans. Anthea Bell. London: Pushkin Press.

Part I

Time Past: How Ideas Drove Actions

2

Europe's Money and Culture Before 1914

The Victorians were highly inventive in monetary matters. They not only created a myth of an ideal, global money (the international gold standard) but also came up with revolutionary ideas challenging the prevailing role of money and the class-based society that supported it. People would spend much of the twentieth century in bitter and often murderous conflicts over both aspects of this legacy. This illustrates how an idea of money shaped events and also provoked a reaction against it.

Money, in the form of the gold standard, was regarded as the natural accompaniment to a broad, humane, progressive political philosophy—classical liberalism. Money should be embedded in a strong, ethical, faith-based culture. Though important, money's place was limited, well defined and well understood. In Britain, the City of London was powerful, but did not dictate policies to the government of the day. Many bankers and merchants became wealthy but they vied for esteem with other groups—notably the aristocracy, professional classes and top scholars and scientists. To be sure, Victorian society had many faults but these were dwarfed by its achievements.

The ruling concept of money embodied a clear doctrine. As taught by John Locke, the philosopher, in the late seventeenth century, money should be an invariant standard—its value should not be eroded by inflation. Experience had shown that only the precious metals could provide the basis for such a standard—indeed, they were the standard.[1] This had to be above the government or state and was best viewed as part of the order of nature. The state had no right to tamper with it. For Locke, money had moral value insofar as it

© The Author(s) 2019
R. Pringle, *The Power of Money*, https://doi.org/10.1007/978-3-030-25894-8_2

enabled property that would otherwise lie idle to be put to work. By using money, men could exchange a surplus of perishable goods for goods that would last longer. Gold and silver do not decay and thus may be hoarded 'without injury to anyone'. He understood, remarkably, that the introduction of money with a fixed gold value would lead to greater inequality as people had both the incentive and capacity to accumulate it.

That is why, Locke maintained, men had 'by general consent' made the common 'pledge' which assured users that they would receive equally valuable things in exchange for money (Locke 1695). Writing or printing words on a bill, or on paper money, cannot give that intrinsic value to money, even if decreed by law, that is conferred by gold and silver. He attacked proposals to weaken the coinage through depreciation (e.g. when the state raised the official price of a given weight of gold or silver). This action would mean, for example, that landlords should be forced to accept a smaller amount of gold in settlement of a contract than they had originally contracted for—which would be to defraud them. Locke acknowledged that the value society initially placed on a given weight of silver or gold coins was imaginary—in a sense, arbitrary. But he argued that this did not matter so long as, once having set a value, society maintained it. This was necessary to protect society from the threat posed by the exercise of arbitrary power by the state or sovereign. That is why money could not be a mere creature of the state, to be altered in value according to the whims of governments, but had to inhabit a higher realm— the realm of nature (Martin 2013). Money was harnessed to an underlying political philosophy. This link was revolutionary in its time but would endure as the monetary basis for the greatest advance in economic well-being the world had ever seen.

Locke's theory of money was accepted until the end of the nineteenth century—the first Palgrave Dictionary of Economics in 1896 approved of it. But on the continent of Europe different ideas were gaining ground. In 1905, Friedrich Knapp (1842–1926), a German economist, published *The State Theory of Money*, in which he declared that money gains its value from being issued by the government, not from its gold/silver content (Knapp 1905). Clearly, this theory elevated the state to a much more central role in providing society with money than did Locke's concept of money as a thing, a commodity, grounded in Nature. Changing ideologies and attitudes opened up a major divergence between the Continent and Great Britain. Many subsequent chapters in this book refer to the state theory of money, the twentieth century's dominant theory of how money gains value, as it took on different guises in its journey through the century.

Victorian money culture had its contemporary critics, such as Charles Dickens, whose 1854 novel *Hard Times* was a scathing indictment of the social effects of capitalism, and Matthew Arnold, a prominent social critic. Arnold's book of 1869, *Culture and Anarchy*, popularised the term 'Philistine' to describe people obsessed with a mechanical form of living directed at the accumulation of money. It was commonplace to observe that people are always apt to regard wealth as a precious end in itself, but culture helps us to see it differently:

> Now, the use of culture is that it helps us, by means of its spiritual standard of perfection, to regard wealth as but machinery, and not only to say as a matter of words that we regard wealth as but machinery, but really to perceive and feel that it is so.

This is Culture as Salvation from money:

> If it were not for this purging effect wrought upon our minds by culture, the whole world, the future as well as the present, would inevitably belong to the Philistines. (Arnold 1869)

The German Romantics

Nineteenth-century German philosophers drew on an earlier tradition of German economics to develop an alternative to the classical idea of money. As the philosopher, Isaiah Berlin (1909–97), pointed out somewhat sardonically in a 1965 lecture on romanticism, 'There is even such a thing as Romantic economics, particularly in Germany'. Men like the philosopher Fichte (1762–1814) and List (1789–1846), a founder of the German historical school of economics, believed in the necessity of creating an 'isolated' state, *der geschlossene Handelsstaat*. In such a state, 'the true spiritual force of the nation can exercise itself without being buffeted by other nations.' For these German economists, 'the purpose of economics, the purpose of money and trade, is the spiritual self-perfection of man, and does not obey the so-called unbreakable law of economics…' (Berlin 1999, 146).

What Berlin called German *romantic* economics opposes laissez-faire and Locke's cold idea of money. There are no iron laws of economics resembling the laws of nature. On the contrary, economic and monetary institutions should promote ideas of people living together in a spiritually progressive manner. In such ways, different approaches to the role of economics and the state challenged the British concept. Karl Marx (1818–83) held to a somewhat traditional *theory* of money, but in the 1840s spoke out as a *moralist* against the money cult:

> Money debases all the gods of mankind and turns them into commodities…
> Money is the estranged essence of man's work and existence; this alien essence dominates him and he worships it. (Marx 1843)

Thus were introduced concepts that would be debated and fought over throughout the twentieth century and into the present. 'Estranged essence' or *alienation* points to man's separation, detachment, and isolation from his work and his true nature and from the society round him. Alienation became the theme of countless academic studies and journalistic commentaries. Although it degenerated into a catch-all phrase to describe any state of which the analyst disapproved—a term of abuse—it had enduring power. According to Marx and his innumerable followers, money destroys true value. It transforms the real powers of man and nature into abstract concepts and therefore imperfections—into 'tormenting chimeras'. Money makes us think not of our real needs but of how to get more money. Marx argued that the individuals who make capitalism work had ceased to be fully human (see Kahan 2010). Money is the great dehumaniser. At the origin of commercial society is the de-humanisation of what ought to be under human control—all because of money. Money destroys the community. Marx blamed Judaism and Christianity for spreading the gospel of wealth. But where a Medieval priest would have called on his congregation to give up the worship of Mammon (Hebrew for money) and return to God, Marx called on humanity to give up both God and Mammon as illusions to make a revolution. He sneered at the British economist Jeremy Bentham (1748–1832) for assuming that the modern shopkeeper, especially the English shopkeeper, is 'the normal man'.

Look at how German culture treated money. Inheriting such a tradition, the composer Richard Wagner (1813–83), who opposed Christianity, also hated monied property. The distribution of wealth was violently unjust and arbitrary: for Wagner, 'Life was made hard and painful, sometimes impossible, for people who had nothing' (Magee 2000). It was wrong that money determined almost everything about a person's life. The fat cats 'will continue to rule the world as long as money remains the power to which all our activities are subjugated'. The *Ring of the Niebelung* is, among other things, one of the greatest condemnations of the love of money (gold) as a driving spring of human action ever written. This common theme, of desperate protest, links Marx, Wagner, Nietzsche and, as we shall see, even the more level-headed Max Weber.

How Germans Saw Themselves

During the later nineteenth century and the first decade of the twentieth, as rivalry between the great powers increased, so did different philosophies become more entrenched. While trying to avoid the danger of stereotyping, there was a difference in the ways different nations saw their identity—what they 'stood for', the values they cherished and the contribution they could make to the progress of humanity. If the British were proud of their Empire, the rule of law, spreading Christianity, science and technology, Germans portrayed themselves as concerned with spiritual ends, culture, profound poetry and music and freedom. Opposed to dominance by finance, Germany's scholars saw themselves as guardians of Germany's special character. As historian Paul Kennedy remarks, English and French social science was, to German commentators, 'simply another manifestation of an atomistic and materialistic view of mankind' (Kennedy 1988). British Germanophiles admired Germans because of their own distaste for 'economic man'—following in the tradition of Coleridge and Arnold. They accused England of cultural shallowness. All sides claimed to be fighting for freedom, but had different ideas of what freedom meant. Many cultured Germans shared the romantic longing for a past where 'community' prevailed over 'society'. The classic expression of this is by German sociologist Ferdinand Tonnies (1855–1936) in his book *Community and Society* (1887) where he exalts the organic community of pre-industrial Europe as held together by 'feminine' emotion; whereas under man-dominated, industrial society, women were being alienated from their true nature. A woman indoctrinated by such ideas becomes 'enlightened, cold, knowing': 'nothing is more alien to her original character, nothing more harmful'.

Another influential thinker in developing the German idea of money was Georg Simmel (1858–1915). In his essay 'On Social Differentiation', he distinguished between what he called objective and subjective culture. The former was the world of philosophy, books and art, the latter the more impoverished world of bankers and businessmen. In 1900 he published *Die Philosophie des Geldes* (The Philosophy of Money). Simmel saw money as 'disintegrating and isolating' but also as unifying in bringing together elements of society that 'would otherwise have no connection whatsoever'. Tellingly, Simmel compared money to prostitution: 'The indifference as to its use, the lack of attachment to any individual because it is unrelated to any of them, the objectivity inherent in money…which excludes any emotional relationship…produces an ominous analogy between money and prostitution' (see Simmel 1900; Watson 2010). Money, he argued, tends to restrict creativity, favour impersonal objects, and flatten the rich variety of individual experiences. Watson comments that Simmel's sociology, especially in his later works with their diatribes against big cities, was a theme taken up in Weimar Germany, paving the way for the ideology of National Socialism. However, Simmel's contribution to the sociology of money remains influential.

Attitudes were also no doubt influenced by envy of British ascendancy, much like the anti-Americanism in Europe after World War II, but there is no denying the depth of the cultural divide marked by the English Channel. German writers depicted German culture as bearing the highest traditions of European thought and idealism, showing hostility towards British ideas of money and economics. After the defeat of France in 1871, in particular, Germans started to assert their distinctive idea of culture. They appealed to German cultural leaders such as Goethe, Fichte, and Kant against what they called the shallow, atomistic society of Gladstone's England. The philosopher Hegel and historian Ranke had evoked the idea of a slow unfolding of the idea of German identity and superiority. Walter Rathenau, a highly cultivated Jewish industrialist and politician (he was to be foreign minister under the Weimar Republic) longed for 'The Empire of the Soul': *Now capital dominates society; one day society will dominate capital* (see Fritz Stern: 'Einstein's German World' 2001). On the outbreak of war in 1914, Rathenau remarked: 'A holy joy lifted German hearts'. The Anglo-Saxons had placed the crude culture of individualism at the centre of their worldview. Germans would champion 'Bildung'—spiritual emancipation. Looking to the image of Germany as a nation of poets and thinkers, many German public intellectuals affected a superior attitude to Britain and the United States (see Radkau 2005). As late as 1918 Friederich Meinecke, a great historian, decried the 'bestial' greed of Germany's enemies.

In the 1890s Max Weber (1864–1920), an Anglophile, had supported the expansion of German navy as naval power would decide 'each nation's share in the economic control of the planet and therefore the earnings of its people'. He did not see at the time that this would push Germany into collision with Britain. Later, he regarded the war as inevitable, given that Germany was being boxed in by imperialist powers. By 1914 he considered Germany's whole existence as a nation was at stake. Though he privately advocated compromising with France on the Alsace Lorraine question, when war came, Weber, then aged 50, said that 'regardless of eventual success, the war is great and wonderful'. Weber had a passionate sense of Germany's national identity, going back to the Middle Ages. It had nothing to do with race, but was based on culture, which reached its highest development in small German provinces and in Switzerland. He defined the nation as the bearer of honour and the highest values. The differences between Germany and England were due to religion, not race.

The hunger for spirituality should be conceptualised as a response to what Weber characterised as the 'disenchantment of the world' (Weber 1918). Modern capitalist society had rationalised everyday life to the point where values seemed to be dominated by economic calculation alone. In such circumstances, finding a language to express the human spirit preoccupied groups of influential artists and intellectuals, as well as religious figures. Not all were touched by this mood of estrangement, but it was widely noted that material security coexisted with spiritual and moral confusion. During the late nineteenth and early twentieth centuries, the themes of fragmentation, estrangement and alienation acquired significant influence over the Western cultural imagination. To many young people it seemed as if bourgeois society 'had lost its spirit'.

For many artists, intellectuals and religious leaders, the war appeared to provide an opportunity to recover something of this lost spirit. Church leaders embraced the war as an instrument of religious revival. Weber, too, was attracted by the promise of solidarity achieved through the experience of war (so, by the way, was Sigmund Freud). Weber argued that a community of solidarity created on the battlefield provided meaning and motivation comparable to the experience of religious brotherhood. He stated that a 'war does something to a warrior which, in its concrete meaning, is unique', because 'it makes him experience a consecrated meaning of death which is characteristic only of death in war'. In a rationalised world, by contrast, death has no meaning. 'It would be shameful', said Weber in a speech at Nuremberg in August 1916, 'if we lacked the courage to ensure that neither Russian barbarism, English monotony nor French grandiloquence rule the world. That is why the war is being fought' (Radkau 2005).

During the first phase of the war, German academics generally agreed that Germany was protecting the values and culture of Europe against the barbarism of Russia and the materialism of the west. Such support, that appears to us as nothing more than thinly disguised propaganda, reached a low point with the *Manifesto of the Ninety-Three*. This was a statement issued on October 4, 1914, about two months after the start of the war, endorsed by 93 prominent German scientists, scholars and artists. It declared their unequivocal support of Germany and its military actions up to that point. It denied that Germany had started the war or that it had treated Belgium brutally, and pointed to the butchery conducted by Russian troops to the East. It defended the German army:

> Were it not for German militarism, German civilisation would long since have been extinguished. For its protection it arose in a land which for centuries had been plagued by bands of robbers as no other land had been.

The Manifesto inspired support for the war by German schools and universities. However, some of its signatories later regretted signing it.

Why Thomas Mann Defended the War

Novelist Thomas Mann supported the war in defence of German traditions of 'culture, soul, freedom, art'. He believed that its 'will to power and worldly greatness (which is less a will than a fate and a world necessity) remains completely uncontested in its legitimacy and its prospects'. He attacked democracy, or 'politics' in favour of an authoritarian state (Thomas Mann, *Reflections of a Nonpolitical Man* 1918; he later repudiated these views).

I feel it is really important to understand this point of view, as it dictated a completely different conception of society and of money from that which has become so ingrained in us as to make any other idea incomprehensible. Thomas Mann, one of Europe's greatest novelists, insisted that Germany's role was indispensable to upholding culture. In his own text, Thomas Mann, who had not signed this manifesto, went even further by (1) praising the war as a purifying and necessary experience and (2) by claiming that the German position was the reflection and defence of a higher culture. According to Mann, Germans had to defend themselves against a shallow Western civilisation, which stood for 'reason, enlightenment, moderation, moralisation, skepticism, dissolution—and mind' as well as affluence and acquiescence, while German cultural values were concerned with a certain organisation of the world. War is thus celebrated by Mann as a highly welcome departure from the lures of civilisational affluence, a return to mystical life values, and a preservation of national characteristics.

The scope of the *Reflections* is even broader, while continuing to follow the same ideological goals. Thomas Mann stressed the special geographical situation held by Germany, which did not share Western values, the tradition of Protestantism (with its religious and political connotations) and, finally, German cultural traditions, especially in music and philosophy. As a 'spiritual people', Mann considered Germans to be apolitical or even anti-political, which is also how he saw himself. Mann vehemently attacked the concept of the so-called *Zivilisationsliterat*, namely, a literature advocating progressive or democratic values, as an unpatriotic or anti-German concept. This was because it betrayed the foundations of truly German art.

Part of a Wider Cultural Split

In sum, many Europeans quite apart from the Marxists were repelled by the effects of industrial growth in turning society into a materialist machine driven by nothing else than money-grubbing, isolated, individualistic, egotistical, spiritually empty people. (This was viewed as a British disease, although the distaste was shared by many British novelists and social critics.) I might mention here that this attitude outlasted World War I, even in France. Francois Mauriac (1885–1970), a celebrated French writer, said: 'I do not understand and I do not like the English, except when they are dead….' In the interwar period also, French books hostile to England were far more numerous than the favourable ones. The French thought of England as out of date, with little or nothing to contribute to the solution of modern problems. Even during World War II, many were indifferent as to whether England or Germany won. Britain was seen as a country of millionaires amidst poverty, a country that 'always showed the most profound contempt for the colonial peoples it conquered', said a manifesto of March 1942 signed by well-known writers.

Many French intellectuals and upper bourgeoisie, by contrast, saw Germany, as a country that 'would liberate France from materialism in philosophy' (Zeldin 1980). Here was a country where minds were free: why, almost every peasant was musical! Even humble villages had people who loved literature and philosophy. Marx, Hegel and Nietzsche were all major sources of inspiration. Germany's contribution to French philosophy was pervasive, much more important than that of the English. Although fear and hatred of the Germans was widespread, many educated people stuck to Flaubert's view that Germans were a nation of dreamers even after France's humiliating defeat by Bismarck in the war of 1870. Victor Hugo said: 'No nation is greater'. German idealism alone had saved France from English empiricism—the English who reduced everything to miserable calculations of utility and pleasure, where the value of everything was measured in money. Despite even the bitterness resulting from the Versailles settlement of 1918, and the animosity between the two countries, some French people advocated reconciliation and spiritual union with Germany. On a personal note, my grandmother, who was French, treasured her piano transcription of Wagner's Tannhäuser, and would often play it, despite losing a much-loved brother, aged only 17, to a German sniper's bullet in the closing weeks of the war.

Was World War I caused by a culture clash over different ideas of money? No. However, aversion to the money-driven materialism seen by many Continental intellectuals as central to British economic success helps in my opinion to explain the otherwise surprising degree of sympathy and even support for Germany among educated classes of Continental Europe. It may even explain why Germans fought as if their survival was at stake, as if Germany alone could uphold Europe's core values.

Note

1. In Locke's time, the standard was silver. 'Silver is the instrument and measure of commerce in all civilized and trading parts of the world.' It is 'the measure of commerce by its quantity, which is the measure also of intrinsic value' (Locke 1695). The reasoning behind Locke's position continued to be accepted after gold replaced silver as the standard. The value of the pound sterling, set by Isaac Newton in 1717 at £3. 17s and 10 1/2p an ounce of pure gold, became sacrosanct, the basis of British policy for 200 years.

Bibliography

Arnold, M. (1869). *Culture and Anarchy*.
Berlin, I. (1999). The *Roots of Romanticism: The A. W. Mellon Lectures in the Fine Arts* (ed, H Hendry). Princeton: Princeton University Press.
Dickens, Charles (1854). *Hard Times*.
Kahan, A.S. (2010/2017). *Mind Vs. Money: The War Between Intellectuals and Capitalism*. Oxford: Routledge.
Kennedy, P. (1988). *The Rise and Fall of the Great Powers*. London: Unwin.
Knapp, F. (1905/1921). *Staatliche Theorie des Geldes* (The State Theory of Money), München u. Leipzig, Duncker & Humblot, 1905. 3rd edition 1921.
Locke, J. (1695). Further Considerations Concerning Raising the Value of Money, Wherein Mr Lowndes's Arguments for it in his late Report concerning an Essay for the Amendment of the Silver Coins, are particularly examined'. London: A. and J. Churchill.
Marx, K. (1843). 'On the Jewish Question', In *Karl Marx: Early Writings* trans. R Livingstone and Gregor Benton, Penguin Books 1974.
Magee, B. (2000). *Wagner and Philosophy*. Penguin Books.
Mann, T. (1918). *Reflections of a Nonpolitical Man*.
Martin, F. (2013). *Money: The Unauthorized Biography*. London: The Bodley Head.
Radkau, J. translated by Camiller, P. (2005). *Max Weber: A Biography*.
Stern, F. (2001). *Einstein's German World*. Princeton: Princeton University Press.

Simmel, Georg (1900). *Die Philosophie des Geldes* (The Philosophy of Money).
Toennies, Ferdinand (1887). *Community and Society.*
Weber, M. (1918). 'Science as a Vocation' in Gerth, H.H. and Mills, C.E., *From Max Weber Essays in Sociology.* London: Routledge & Kegan Paul, 1948.
Watson, Peter (2010). *The German Genius.*
Manifesto of Ninety-Three (October 4, 1991, New York: HarperCollins.4).
Zeldin, T. (1980). *France 1848–1945: Intellect and Pride.*

3

The 1920s: Lessons from Weimar

Germany in the 1920s is notorious for its experience of hyperinflation and the dispute over war reparations. Important lessons were drawn from both experiences. They did not come in time to save Germany from its descent to Hell. And they did not measure up to the scale of the challenge posed by the breakdown of the old monetary order in World War I. But the lessons learnt would have a major impact, especially after World War II. They continue to influence policy. There were also lessons that could have been drawn from the time but were not.

World War I delivered a body blow not only to several old empires such as those of Russia, Austro-Hungary and the Ottoman but to the whole idea of a self-regulating economy and its money. It turned Great Britain into a massive debtor country. It also brought to the fore social and political forces that would make it very difficult for any country to follow the rules of the old system. These included the rise of trades unions and labour parties, universal male suffrage plus a measure of female suffrage, and popularly elected governments. The war weakened support for free trade. Farmers demanded protection from food imports. With the rise of labour movements, working class leaders were in a stronger position to demand tariffs on manufactured imports. Once unshackled from gold, central banks could reduce interest rates to encourage domestic demand and output even if that risked depreciation in the external value of the currency. But nobody knew how to run such a discretionary policy.

Should money still be seen as part of the natural order and put beyond the reach of meddling politicians, or should it be used as a tool to promote full employment and finance state spending? In this way the war opened a debate

© The Author(s) 2019
R. Pringle, *The Power of Money*, https://doi.org/10.1007/978-3-030-25894-8_3

that has continued ever since. Also, observers realised that monetary as well as economic and political power had shifted across the Atlantic. The new Federal Reserve (founded in 1913) had different ideas about money than the Bank of England or the Banque de France. The Fed had been set up precisely to provide an 'elastic' supply of money and to counter financial crises. During the war the United States had seized world monetary leadership from London. What would it do?

In retrospect, over the long sweep of history, one can view World War I as marking the end of one century-long global money cycle, and the start of another. This would also last for 100 years. The first was based on metallic money, with participants constrained by ethical principles and self-regulation linked to ethical rules; the second was founded on state money and financial regulation. The money of the first period was consistent with the spirit and motivating ideas of the time: a long-term perspective, an assured predictable value, the maximum liberty for the individual consistent with public order, a small public sector, a state subject to law and to monetary rules, a degree of separation of the state from finance, individual moral responsibility, self-regulation of the professions, and a rigid code of financial conduct. The second 100-year cycle was to see, after many monetary disasters, the surprising birth of a global monetary space. This would be the first in history to encompass the entire world and link most of its inhabitants and would preside over a staggering rise in living standards, along with progress in health, leisure time, tolerance, rights of minorities and women. It would be based on the state theory of money.

In this transition, Europe between 1918 and 1939 was to be the crucible in which ideas, new and old, would clash and mix with events under extreme pressure to force recognition of the need for a new regime, a new kind of money. We look first at Germany's experience in the 1920s. Although good new ideas did not come along in time to save it from the Nazis, the period was to be an important stage in the transition from one order to the next. A little history is needed to see how the experience of Weimar Germany relates to issues relevant to this study—the practical influence of ideas about money on the course of history and the emergence of a global money space and culture.

Weimar Not Predestined to Fail

In 1918 the world desperately needed a period of peace to allow reconstruction to take place and trade to resume. But signs of trouble were everywhere. Former foes were determined to punish the losers. So, instead of focussing on reconstruction, peace talks focussed on how much money the allies could extract from the defeated Germans. War reparations and the Allied insistence that Germany accept responsibility for all the damage caused by the war created a burning sense of injustice in Germany. Then hyperinflation showed how wrong beliefs about money could destroy a society. These factors undermined confidence in the new republic, which had been set up in the small town of Weimar, in 1919, with a democratic parliamentary constitution. It would need good luck, economic recovery and steady government to have a chance to survive. In its 14 years, the Weimar Republic faced numerous problems, many of them stemming from monetary challenges, notably war reparations, hyperinflation, currency stabilisation and a huge inflow of capital, mainly from the United States in 1927–29. But the victory of Fascism was by no means inevitable until more blunders about money unleashed the Wall Street Crash—after which Americans pulled their money out of Germany— and the onset of the US Great Depression in 1929 spread to Europe, causing high unemployment. This strengthened the Nazi party, and in 1933 Hindenburg appointed Hitler as Chancellor. His seizure of power brought the Weimar republic to an end.

The story had some happier consequences. As described below, a few social scientists rose to the challenge posed by Marxism and the troubles of the 1920s by reflecting more deeply on the conditions needed for free markets and capitalism to survive. The lessons that some thoughtful people drew from these experiences helped Germany to develop a basis for the restoration of sound money and thus for the West German 'economic miracle' after World War II, which in turn was a basic ingredient contributing to Europe's later prosperity. From this perspective, the catastrophes contributed indirectly to the construction of a global monetary society in the later twentieth century. It was crucial that some thinkers drew the right lessons from the catastrophe— many other countries in the twentieth century were destined to experience hyperinflation without drawing the right lessons from it.

Reparations and Guilt

The Versailles Treaty required Germany to accept responsibility for causing all the loss and damage during the war. The treaties forced Germany to disarm, make substantial territorial concessions and, under article 231, later known as the War Guilt clause, pay reparations to the Allies. Much of North-East France had been devastated by the war and Germany's 'scorched earth' policy—systematically destroying industry and agriculture, including whole towns and villages, as they retreated. Germany itself had not been invaded and thus suffered little direct material damage. The United States insisted on being repaid the money it had lent to the Allies to help them prosecute the war; the Allies insisted on Germany paying them. But Germany could not pay any substantial sum unless its economy was allowed to recover. At the time economists, notably Maynard Keynes, argued that the treaty was too harsh and the reparations figure was excessive and counter-productive. Yet Prussia had exacted reparations from France after its victory in 1870, which were paid quickly; and Germany had made clear it expected its enemies to pay for the cost of the war on their defeat. Some blame Keynes for encouraging Germans to feel justified in not paying, and thus possibly contributing to the grievances that would fuel the rise of Nazism.

In any case, the Allies lacked the political will and consensus to make Germany to pay by armed force, as shown by the US and UK condemnation of the French occupation of the Ruhr in 1923. If Germany was reduced to chaos, that is, by occupation of parts of its territory or a sea blockade, how could it pay the sums it had been forced to promise? Thus, the former allies were obliged to resort to carrots rather than sticks; in effect, Germany was offered the chance to rejoin the community of nations if Allied demands were fulfilled. The Dawes Plan of 1924 moderated Allied demands and provided for a loan to Germany to be financed by bond issues on the New York market. This gave confidence to US investors and initiated a boom in US private lending to Germany. The economy recovered quickly. However, the underlying problem remained—Germans saw the obligations under the plan as temporary while the Allies feared that, once Germany was accepted back, it would immediately be the most powerful nation in Europe. In all, Germany paid about 21 billion marks, about 2.1% of national income, compared with a sum initially set at 132 billion. Germany borrowed abroad more than it paid in reparations, and later defaulted on the loans. So, in the end Germany received more money than it paid out.

The period saw the rise of the political lie in democracies; to fool their newly enfranchised voters, politicians lied about reparations. The maximum claim for reparations was intended to trick public opinion in France and Britain into believing that Germany was being punished severely, when in fact the Allies had no intention of collecting the full amount. But this of course backfired. The unrealistically high claim was taken seriously in Germany, stoking up hatred and resistance, thus making it more difficult to collect even a much smaller amount. Indeed, some economic historians, such as Alessandro Roselli, question whether the Allies ever really expected to collect even the basic amount of 50 billion, which was still 123% of German estimated GDP (Roselli 2014).

Germany could have paid more, if France had been patient. In fact, there is almost no limit to how much a country can pay, given enough time. Assuming that over time world trade would resume, and that German traders would not be barred from full participation in it, Germany was bound to recover. There is ample evidence that they were willing, indeed anxious, to pay quite large reparations if they could either by expanding their exports or by borrowing or indeed by taxation. But they were not given the time, and when France became impatient, she occupied the Ruhr, making it less possible for Germans to pay any reparations and less likely that they would have the political will to do so. Greed lost the creditors everything.

Hyperinflation

Inflation had been building up since Germany suspended the gold standard on the outbreak of war in 1914. However, this was true of other belligerent countries as well. Wholesale prices in Germany, Britain and France at the end of 1918 were respectively 2.4, 2.3 and 3.5 times their pre-war level (Graham 1930). In the United States, which had experienced a massive economic boom, prices had doubled. The situation was not hopeless. After a fall in the exchange rate in the immediate post-war period, the mark's value against foreign currencies was relatively stable from March 1920 to May 1922. But to cover its obligations, including war reparations, the German government increasingly resorted to money creation, printing more banknotes. Prices rose by 20 times in the last half of 1922; by the end of that year they were 1000 times their pre-war level. Hyperinflation (defined as prices rising 50% or more a month) then took hold, as people in a frenzy tried to get rid of notes as quickly as possible. This process reached its crazy climax in August–November 1923, with prices ending up 1400 billion times the pre-war level.

Despite the colossal rise in the issue of bank notes, people experienced a severe shortage of currency. The central bank thought it was their duty to print as many notes as possible to meet demand. It apologised for its inability to provide enough notes. By 1923 the mark was worthless. Without access to foreign currency, it became impossible to purchase imports. Several authors have vividly described the effects. Everyday items such as a loaf of bread or a postage stamp cost 100 billion marks. Here was a new monetary phenomenon made possible by paper money (setting aside such experiments as were conducted in China under the Yuan Mongol dynasty and in France during the revolution). According to Adam Fergusson, the effect was magnified by the increasing materialism of society: 'the more materialist that society is, the more cruelly it hurts': the collapse of the recognised, traditional, trusted medium of exchange, the currency by which all values are measured, 'unleashes such greed, violence, unhappiness and hatred, largely bred from fear, that no society can survive uncrippled and unchanged' (Fergusson 1975). Certainly, it brought catastrophe to the German and Austrian middle classes, although the real economy did not suffer as much as might be expected. Unemployment was lower than in Great Britain or France. German state finances benefited in the longer run by the wiping out of debt, even while those who had invested in government debt lost everything.[1]

Controversy continues on the causes. While accepting the economic consensus that increases in the money supply and in the velocity of circulation are involved, and nearly all hyperinflations also stem from governments printing money to pay for budget deficits, the question remains: why did the Weimar government and central bank choose such means of financing the deficit? Why did they not cut the budget deficit while there was still time or find a non-inflationary way to finance it? Again, mistaken but strongly held beliefs about money played a role. The Reichsbank board of directors thought it was the duty of the central bank to promote business though an active monetary policy and to keep a competitive exchange rate: 'many of the leaders of business were convinced that inflation was necessary to the rehabilitation of the German industrial organization....' Thus, inflation was combated half-heartedly at best.

As at many points later in the twentieth century, sectional interests were at work. Some groups benefited from inflation, especially those with large debts including enterprises financed by bank loans, farmers with mortgages, the provinces and central government, and these groups put pressure on the government/central bank to print money. Inexperience was also a factor: never had Europeans managed a paper money standard (with the singular exception of the ill-fated and short-lived experiments with *assignats* during the French Revolution). A hundred years on, the answer to Germany's dilemma seems obvious: stop the money presses! Yet have we not ourselves felt 'compelled' into risky monetary experiments with unconventional monetary policies such as quantitative easing (see Chap. 14)? They have been deployed on a scale that would have surprised even the central bankers of the Weimar republic.

Could Germany have avoided hyperinflation? Roselli concludes cautiously that although it might have been possible for the government to pay for reparations out of taxation, it 'refused to follow this alternative out of the probably justified fear of social unrest and of an almost certain grave recession'. The government preferred to resort to monetary financing of the budget deficit: 'It was probably confident that inflation might be contained, and in this, the government was not alone: speculative foreign investment in paper marks was widespread.' He discounts the conspiracy theories; plausible domestic policy objectives lay behind the government's policies. Indeed, 'perhaps for a while the inflationary policies saved the Weimar Republic' (Roselli 2014).

Recovery Followed by Another Crash

The inflation stopped immediately the authorities stopped printing money. Following stabilisation in 1924 the economy expanded strongly. Investment opportunities in the new Germany were soon spotted in Wall Street, and a massive flow of capital from the United States began—both short and long term. This buoyed up the German economy for a few short years until the inflow of capital was brought to a halt and then put into reverse by the Great Depression in America. US investors and bankers called in their loans, cashed their investments, and this pulled the rug out from under the German economy and banking system. Deposits at German banks shrank from early in 1930 onwards, and capital outflows accelerated after the elections in September that substantially increased the Nazi party's representation. The Credit-Anstalt Bank of Austria failed in May 1931—traditionally seen as the symbolic start of the financial panic. Germany in effect abandoned the gold standard in July and August 1931. Yet the German government under Chancellor Brüning, in a portentous decision, maintained its deflationary policy rather than devalue or let the currency float.

There were close links between the failures of German banks in the summer of 1931 and the Nazi party's rise to power. The financial shock increased support for anti-Semitism. The Nazis successfully blamed Jews for the people's misery: The bank at the centre of the crisis, Danatbank, was led by a prominent Jewish banker, Jakob Goldschmidt. A recent study shows that these effects of the monetary crisis were crucial in explaining political radicalisation. Customers suffering losses as a result of the failures of Danatbank and Dresdner Bank (DD) strongly increased support for the Nazi party in the city or region where such firms were located. Moreover, higher exposure by local firms directly increased Nazi voting above and beyond its direct effect through falling incomes:

> With the financial crisis, the Nazis had seemingly incontrovertible proof for their misguided theories of Jewish domination and destruction. As in many other countries, Jews were vastly overrepresented in 1930s German high finance. (Doer et al. 2019)

The above brief outline of events shows how several distinct ideas of money came to the fore in the 1920s. These included the use of money as punishment; money as an agent of self-destruction; monetary control as a stabiliser—how to end hyperinflation and resume growth; money as an agent of destruction from outside—the fall of the Weimar Republic following the Wall Street Crash and the failure of the Brüning government to use monetary policy to slow the downward spiral of the Great Depression. There is also a continuity with the anti-money philosophy of pre-1914 German intellectuals and the sociology of George Simmel (as noted in the previous chapter).

Democracy Under Money's Thumb

There was debate also about another aspect of money's role with twenty-first-century resonance: would the power of money always come to dominate democracies? In the *Decline of the West* (1918–22), a book that won global notoriety, Oswald Spengler argued that democracies are inevitably manipulated by the media. The penetration of money's power throughout a society marks the shift from Culture to Civilisation. All democracies are plutocracies. The 'tragic comedy' of the world-improvers and freedom-teachers is that they simply assist money-power to be more effective. Freedom of the press requires money, as it entails ownership, thus serving money at the end. Elections are dominated by donations to political parties. The ideologies espoused by candidates, whether Socialism or Liberalism, are set in motion by, and ultimately serve, only money. In a comment with resonance for the twenty-first century, Spengler also observes that the greater the concentration of wealth, the more the struggle for political power revolves around money. This is neither corruption nor degeneracy, he argues; it is the necessary end of mature democracies.

I return to this theme in the discussion of crony capitalism in the era of presidents Trump, Xi and Putin in Chap. 16 and in the Introduction to Part Three. Although Spengler's historical sweep has little credibility with historians, any more than those other 'end of history' prophets Karl Marx, Arnold Toynbee and Francis Fukuyama, all of them answer to our need to find meaning in history. Sometimes current events take a turn that seems to prove one of them to have been on the right track. Maybe it is now Spengler's turn with his forecasts of democracy inevitably falling prey to plutocracy due to make a comeback?

Germany's Lasting Contribution

Let us step back for a moment and consider the broader picture. Why does Germany feature so prominently in the twentieth century's story of money? There seem to be several reasons for this. The introduction of the *mark* in 1873 was a decisive step in unifying Germany. In Britain and France the nation state and money grew up together. German political and monetary theory was founded on the paramountcy of the state over individuals. As mentioned in the previous chapter, it was not by coincidence that German writers pioneered the theory and practice of the state theory of money. Such a centralised system answered to the dominance of the nation state. No wonder it would replace the decentralised, semi-automatic mechanism of the gold standard. The state theory of money introduced by Friedrich Knapp, as mentioned in Chap. 2, turned out to be better suited to the large-state, high-tax era that got such a boost from the two world wars and remains dominant in the twenty-first century. Knapp's theory was explicitly aimed at overturning traditional theories of money, which saw money as the product of a natural evolution. Once it had proved its value as a tool of nation states, people were quick to abandon the former idea of money as imposing a monetary standard that disciplined its users, including nation states and even those who issued money, usually the central bank. It was also deliberately aimed to overturn the idea that money must be anchored to a precious metal; still less that gold or silver were themselves money. The extent of the influence of his ideas can be seen in an influential later publication, *A Tract on Monetary Reform*, by Keynes, where he states: 'Money is simply that which the state declares from time to time to be a good legal discharge of money contracts' (Keynes 1923). We are all Knappians now, said Keynes.

With the D-mark after World War II, money became the embodiment of (West) Germany's national identity. For the philosopher Jurgen Habermas, the symbol of 'the new confidence of an economically successful nation' was the Federal Republic's currency—a phenomenon he called 'Deutsche mark nationalism'. Habermas wrote that essay in 1990. Soon after, what he saw as the new symbol of German identity was removed by the decision to replace the Deutsche mark with the euro. For a decade, Germany also struggled with the costs of reunifying east and west—another challenge, a calling, for which Germans were "called on" to make a monetary sacrifice.

Then there is the special German regard for saving and thrift. Far from being overturned by the Keynesian revolution in economics, savings is still seen as having a 'sacred' value. Money or saving is required not so much to finance investment and growth, as in the Anglo-Saxon (Keynesian) conception, but rather in case the nation should be called on to make further sacrifices. It must have reserves to carry it through hard times—both those inflicted from without and those accepted stoically by the people. By learning to save, to respect money, children are taught prudence, sacrifice and readiness to face adversity. Austerity is to be embraced as a modern equivalent of purification and justification through faith. Savings is an ethical duty, a version of the Protestant Ethic. The key point is that, all in all, Germany is still a very different country from even close neighbours. To the bafflement and dismay of Anglo-Saxon economists, it has never accepted Keynesianism. On the other hand, it has not remained true to its commitment to sound money and price stability either.

Of course, it did not have much choice but to ditch its anti-money culture. True, World War I was not sufficient by itself to bring this about; only after being defeated in two world wars did Germany give up its distinctive ideals. Only when it signed up to the Anglo-American *Weltanschauung* in the Occupation following World War II did it rejoin the concert of nations and flourish under US military and ideological tutelage. It had to sacrifice its money, import Anglo-American values and suppress its own. Having done that, as a model student of the competitive market economy, it then, like Japan, duly beat many former foes at their own game.

Lessons Not Learnt?

One lesson Germany did not learn from its experience in the 1920s was the need for creditors to compromise if faced by the reality that, in some circumstances, their claims for payments cannot be met in full, at least in the timescale demanded by debtors—and that insistence on creditors' rights can do more harm than good (quite aside from the often-neglected point that creditors bear moral responsibility for the debtors' plight in irresponsibly lending them too much money). In the eurozone crises of 2012–15 Germany led the hard-line opposition to claims by Greece for debt alleviation thus poisoning the relations between 'northern' and 'southern' (so-called Club Med) countries. This is discussed in Chap. 15. Countries do not always learn the right lessons from their experience; Germans did learn from experience of hyperinflation; many other countries, including for example Venezuela, have not, even though the cause is obvious and always monetary (Hanke and Krus 2013). On the other hand, whereas the international community learnt the need to reschedule sovereign debts, and indeed to write them down, in certain circumstances, Germany did not.

Origins of Germany's Commitment to Sound Money

The experience of hyperinflation inoculated Germans against such a virus because they were able to learn its lessons. And that was not the only lesson they learnt from the 1920s. They learnt also that institutions had to be established that would place an anti-inflationary policy in the context of a democratic state that would respect civil liberties—that includes, an independent central bank committed to price stability.

This strand developed into 'ordoliberalism'—one of the most important of twentieth-century contributions to economic philosophy. Typically, it is scorned by most Anglo-American Keynesians. This school upholds the ideal of a social market economy, but sees a strong role for the state in setting the rules of capitalism at the national level. It developed as a distinct political philosophy in the 1930s but had its early origins in the experience of the 1920s. As discussed further in Chap. 6, it was pioneered by economists such as Walter Eucken and Franz Böhm as a reaction to both unregulated liberalism and fascist fiscal and monetary interventionism. Ordoliberals believe in government regulation but not intervention in the day-to-day operation of the economy. Moreover, regulations should aim to ensure that results are close to those produced by a competitive market (in which none of the actors are able to influence the price of goods and services). It rejects the use of expansionary policies to stabilise the business cycle in a recession. But this does not imply they were insensitive to the evils of unemployment. On the contrary, as his biographer John Zmirak says, 'Röpke realised that the appeal of totalitarianism in Germany…lay in the protracted uncertainty, poverty and injustice which had dominated life in the Weimar Republic.' He identified protectionism as the great evil. International freedom of trade was an essential condition of regaining prosperity. Both Nazi and Communist parties founded their appeal on promises of increased prosperity more fairly distributed. Fully aware that the 1920s had been disastrous for the image of capitalism, men like Röpke decided to rescue the essence of capitalism from its abuses, and rebrand it as 'the market economy' (Zmirak 2001, 51). His humane, Christian approach enabled him to work alongside other leaders of the German liberal movement. Their time would come, though only after yet another war.

The key aspects of their legacy to Germany and then the European Union, apart from the case for an independent central bank, was the emphasis on strong anti-monopoly policies, the free international movement of capital, the rule of law and the independence of the judiciary. They also opposed exchange rate manipulation to bring the balance of payments into equilibrium

(Willgerodt and Peacock 1988). However, the analysis of the ordoliberals and other schools of the new liberalism did not cut deep enough. They did not fully grasp that the problem was monetary and that a return to gold was not the solution. The moral of this chapter is that, sometimes, it is necessary to re-imagine money entirely.

Germany's failure to establish a sound basis for a new society and political constitution after World War I had its own national features but was part of a broader international failure. It reflected a lack of capacity to see the situation they faced clearly enough, to bring it into focus. People were unable to grasp the scale of the destruction wrought by World War I. Accordingly they could not meet the challenge, which required them to re-imagine money. The scale of the task was beyond their imaginative or spiritual powers. The fatal grip of the reparations controversy reflected a similar lack of understanding. Keynes came close, but ultimately his intervention may have done more harm than good by ratcheting up the bitterness of the debate. Lessons were learnt but not in time to avert the descent to Hell.

Tragic Collapse of Democracy

Weimar's collapse was brought about in large part by mistakes in monetary affairs. The slide to dictatorship was not inevitable. It was the result of resentment building up in the people from hyper-inflation, the demands of the victorious powers for German acceptance of full responsibility and guilt for the war, initially excessive demands for reparations and at the end of the 1920s the shock withdrawal of private American loans which cut off money for German industry. The failure was also in part due to its economic policies of state intervention and fiscal over-expansion. Its demise showed how easily a people with weak democratic roots and unused to thinking for themselves politically can fall for the seductive appeal of protectionist barriers to trade, foreign aggression, economic self-sufficiency and promises of salvation through state intervention—especially when linked to pledges to bring the power of money under state control.

Note

1. A friend whose family then lived in Berlin tells me his mother remembered piles of banknotes in her father's shop.

Bibliography

Doerr, S., Peydró, J., and Voth, H. (2019). 'How failing banks paved Hitler's path to power: Financial crisis and right-wing extremism in Germany, 1931–33,' VoxEU, 15 March.

Fergusson, Adam (2010/1975). *When Money Dies: The Nightmare of the Weimar Hyper-inflation.* 2nd edition. London: Old Street Publishing.

Graham, Frank (1930) 'Exchange, Prices, and Production in Hyperinflation: Germany, 1920–1923,' available as a free download from the Mises Institute.

Hanke, S., and Krus, N. (2013). 'World Inflations'. In *Routledge Handbook of Major Events in Economic History* (Ed Parker, R.E. and Whaples, R.).

Keynes, J.M. (1923). *A Tract on Monetary Reform.*

———. (1919). *The Economic Consequences of the Peace.*

Spengler, Oswald (1918–1922). *Decline of the West.*

Roselli, A. (2014). *Money and Trade Wars in Interwar Europe.* Basingstoke: Palgrave Macmillan.

Willgerodt, H., and Peacock, A. (1988). 'German Liberalism and Economic Revival', In Peacock, A. and Willgerodt, H. (eds, 1989) *Germany's Social Market Economy: Origins and Evolution.* The Trade Policy Research Centre.

Zmirak, John (2001). *Wilhelm Röpke: Swiss Localist, Global Economist.*

4

The Jazz Age: America in the 1920s

As war had destroyed the monetary order, people improvised. One messy experience was examined in the previous chapter. The following chapters look at three longer-lived experiments. They are the American (this chapter), the Soviet (Chap. 5) and the European (Chap. 6).

As we shall have occasion to observe at several points in this story, Americans treat money as a means of realising their ideals and way of life. From the start of the century, they broke with tradition. They would take a new path. This would diverge from the old European routes. Money was a tool like other materials and techniques used to produce and distribute goods. Like other tools, money too could be improved. It too needed innovation and know-how. Not only had the war made the United States the most powerful country in the world but it was a world badly in need of confidence and leadership. So, with some hesitation, Americans stepped onto the world stage. The emergence of a distinctive American brand of idealism, articulated by Woodrow Wilson (President 1913–21) with his vision of world cooperation, played a part too. This new idealism joined with commercial and financial interests in persuading Americans that the international order needed to be reorganised—and that they were the people to do it. How the United States would do this was not fully developed until World War II but its distinctive brand of internationalism, a blend of big money, big ideals and optimism, was formed much earlier. Thus, the United States launched itself as the twentieth-century model society. It would create not only a new economic model but also a new type of individual—the powerful, predominantly female, shopper. Americans would show the world that money, imaginatively used, could fuel capitalism.

© The Author(s) 2019
R. Pringle, *The Power of Money*, https://doi.org/10.1007/978-3-030-25894-8_4

Although it ended in a great crash, America in the 1920s would make a key contribution to the development of modern mercantile culture. Its legacy remained visible 100 years later.

None of this was planned. New attitudes, policies and ideas about money emerged through experimentation, trial and chance. Innovation marked modernism as surely in monetary and financial affairs as in art, music and literature. For the individual, money became a symbol of consumer sovereignty and a means of exercising it: money had always been a unit of account, but now its function in facilitating price formation became the means of comparing the relative attractions of an unprecedented range—a veritable cornucopia—of goods and services, including vast new markets in housing and automobiles. Consumers discovered that by demanding credit they could, in effect, make banks create money on a scale never witnessed before. Money thereby offered a means of self-expression, of self-development and social advancement. Money became the high road to a new way of life for millions. However, it required paying continual attention to matters that had not bothered many people before, such as one's credit status. Lifestyle choice, career and family planning, themselves new concepts, were available for those with sufficient money income or credit and also entailed tailoring plans to budgetary resources, including prospective borrowing power. To be sure, it was an age of 'conspicuous consumption', a term already coined by the Norwegian-American sociologist Thorstein Veblen (1857–1929), yet it was also the first time that prudent budgetary calculations and careful long-term financial planning became routine for millions of people in the rising middle classes. Financial markets and institutions expanded rapidly to cater for a huge rise in the number of people with bank accounts. Financial services proliferated. There was no blueprint.

The Birth of Popular Culture…

While the economy was growing rapidly—at an annual average rate of 4.2%, with real per capita output rising by 2.7% per year, rapid rates by both nineteenth- and twentieth-century standards—young people threw off the tight constraints of their parents' generation, creating new styles in fashion, music, architecture and new norms of behaviour. They created many new ideas about and attitudes towards money, also. The booming economy and the rise of advertising led to a shift in consumer attitudes. Spending on credit soared. Many ordinary Americans, once known for 'prudent and thrifty' habits, were now happy to purchase cars and other luxury goods on easy consumer credit.

Instead of saving up money to buy a consumer durable good, a consumer could make a down payment and take immediate possession of it. A new monetary philosophy for shoppers—'Buy now, Pay later'—was born, a means of manipulating time by bringing purchasing power forward that would spread to many other parts of the world over the next half century.

The age signalled the dawn of America's pre-eminence in popular culture. Ever since then, whatever has been fashionable and popular in the United States—whether a movie star, food fad, dance, songs, art or design—was soon to be found on the streets of Paris, London and Berlin. National brands were promoted through mass advertising. Business had become America's secular religion, thanks to advertising. Bruce Barton's 1925 book comparing religion and business, *The Man Nobody Knows*, declared Jesus Christ's parables to be "the most powerful advertisements of all time....He would be a national advertiser today" (eyewitness to history 2002). Demand for the vastly expanded range of new products led to the general acceptance of buying on credit. Output of refrigerators rose from 5000 to more than 1 million a year over the decade to 1930, whereas such items did not become commonplace in Europe until the 1960s. From small beginnings—the first commercial radio station started broadcasting in 1920—by 1930, 40% of Americans owned radios and 70% of them were purchased on credit. Business became a pillar of democracy.

Women Build New Roles

Women, newly empowered by gaining the right to vote in America in 1920, quickly re-defined their role to match that of money. Americans' pioneering spirit moved from the frontier to the shopping mall. While historian FJ Turner announced 'the end of the frontier', as America's westward expansion finally reached the Pacific coast, Hollywood, situated on the very western edge of the continent, started manufacturing new dreams to succeed the old dreams. New frontiers of the mind and imagination were opened just as old physical frontiers were reached. In this, women would often take the lead. They pushed open the doors not only of the great new department stores, but also of the banks and professions previously closed to them. They not only developed and then indulged in the pleasures of what would later be called 'retail therapy'—spending money as a means of relaxation—but also often became, in effect, the family's chief financial officer. Gradually, they were also demanding the chance to make money themselves. Money became a means for millions to express their identities, aspirations and their ideas of their future and that of society.

The American Dream

As Americans became conscious of the unique character of their society—or, as it came to be called, 'American exceptionalism'—some writers tried to define it. One of these books coined the term 'the American dream'. This book was *The Epic of America*, published in 1931, just as the Depression was in reality snatching away the hope of millions of Americans of ever being able to realise their dreams. The author, James Truslow Adams, said the Dream was that 'life should be better and richer and fuller for everyone, with opportunity to each according to ability or achievement'. Interestingly, he added that it was not merely a dream of motor cars and high wages but a dream 'of a social order in which each man and each woman shall be able to attain to the fullest stature of which they are innately capable, and be recognised by others for what they are, regardless of the fortuitous circumstances of their birth'. New art forms matured, such as movies, popular music, musicals—arts that were themselves products of America's uniqueness. An epic film such as *Ben-Hur* alone grossed $5,500,000. By 1929 over 25,000 cinemas had opened, and an average of 100 million Americans went to the movies on a weekly basis. Audiences of such vast size ignited the imagination of manufacturers and merchants with products to sell. The movies became one of the most important advertising mediums of the 1920s.

Social Critics of the Jazz Age

With *Main Street*, Sinclair Lewis exposed the social and cultural attitudes typical of the 1920s, notably the way people chased after money and celebrity. Small-town business owners were often the butt of his wit. *The Magnificent Ambersons*, by Booth Tarkington (1918), contrasted the decline of the old-wealth Amberson family with the *nouveaux riches* of his day who derived power not from family names but by 'doing things'. The great family vanished overnight, submerged by the new city that grew up around them. Many of the writers of this period hated the new business culture. So did some crusading journalists and social critics. Journalist H. L. Mencken viewed his fellow Americans as stupid and violent fools. As for politicians, all they did was buy votes with other people's money (an American version of Spengler's cynical views noted in the previous chapter). Politicians, Mencken asserted, are dedicated wholeheartedly to waste and corruption.

A 'Gigantic Mistake'?

It was also the decade when the ideas of Sigmund Freud, Viennese founder of psycho-analysis, started to spread. His popularity in America was to reach its heights and became a mass movement only after World War II, but his teaching on the role of unconscious motives, of the sex drive and the psychological interpretation of dreams was already the talk of the 'bright young things' in the Roaring Twenties. On money, Freud's idea was that, in the unconscious mind, gold—and perhaps money in general—was a substance akin to excrement. The gold standard established a sense of control and mastery over this valued object, saying in effect, that money must be tied to gold to avoid being 'flushed out' by inflation. Fiscal austerity equals anal retention, and so on. Freud became more influential than Marx in America, but answered to similar anxieties—the isolation (alienation), loneliness (anomie), and despair that many Americans experienced as a result of rapid industrialisation and the growth of mega cities. Where angry Europeans would join Marxist/socialist political movements, for solidarity, anxious Americans would search for an analyst. Like many other European intellectuals, Freud came to dislike America for its money-mad consumerism, which he saw as the sublimation of suppressed sexual desire. 'America is a mistake', he declared, a 'gigantic mistake'.

Mistake or not, Americans were showing what could be done if they took control of money, inventing new ways of making it serve their ends as consumers and producers. In the process they created a culture that would influence the rest of the world for the remainder of the century. This culture would in its turn determine the social and economic setting within which money and monetary policy would operate. The American way of life and the American dream would mould the aspirations, values and attitudes to money of people throughout the world.

Doubt in the Midst of Plenty

To be sure, prosperity was accompanied by doubt. In a time of unprecedented material well-being for many, the greatest novel of the age, *The Great Gatsby*, the people in it, and the whole tone of the novel, are pessimistic. It is deeply critical of the emerging society with its adulation of wealth. America's most influential philosopher of the time, John Dewey, questioned whether contemporary American society offered—or even could offer—a meaningful and satisfying life. If society failed to offer the realistic prospect of such a life, was it not to be condemned? Dewey pointed to the poor conditions of manual and factory workers, who were forced to carry out repetitive tasks devoid of personal interest. For the masses of people, life at work offered little prospect of showing what you could achieve. He was no Marxist, but, like contemporary social critics in Europe, he deplored the alienation of the worker from his work and the distancing of the arts from ordinary life. Meanwhile, the poison of corruption and political scandals that went with the new age of money power horrified many Americans, preparing the public to support the state when, under President Roosevelt, it grabbed power over money in the next decade.

But Who Cared?

Apart from a brief (13 month) and mild recession in 1926–27, for the remainder of the 1920s—right up to the peak of the cycle in mid-1929—business and the stock market flourished under the benign gaze of three Republican presidents—Warren Harding, Calvin Coolidge (1923–29) and Herbert Hoover (1929–33). Harding cut taxes to put more money in the pockets of ordinary Americans but was completely out of his depth (In his own words, 'I am a man of limited talents from a small town.' and 'I am not fit for the office and should never have been here.') Coolidge, a former Republican governor of Massachusetts, provided an aura of stability and respectability in an era of fast-paced modernisation.

Financial markets also took on a wholly new significance for investors, for corporate America and for the public sector. The new borrowing and investment opportunities, faster payments, and corporate financial planning became ingredients in a new American business philosophy, 'scientific management'. And it was the decade when the whole idea of modern monetary policy was first articulated—immediately becoming a central locus of political as well as economic debate. No country had ever used collective control of money deliberately to steer the economy. Now, in the Federal Reserve, the United States had a central bank that could, in principle, do that.

But the Federal Reserve in the period was still 'flying blind'—it did not have any rules for, and only a few years' practice in, operating monetary policy. It was caught between incompatible objectives—helping other countries to return to the gold standard at the old parities (fixed gold price), an objective widely seen as indispensable to restore international monetary order, and promoting stability in the United States. The former required deflation—a fall in the general level of prices and wages—in other countries as prices in most countries were far above their pre-war levels, a deflation that would have bad consequences for the world and for the United States itself. Another problem was that officials held to the 'real bills' doctrine, that is, they thought that it was justifiable to extend bank credit in response to genuine needs of trade but not for speculation. But this doctrine, like so many others that policy-makers have used to support policies over the ages, failed the real-world test. It was too easy to use it to expand the money supply. (Arguably it can be a good means to issue money, assuming that the total supply is under proper control.) Unfortunately, the financial establishment and markets were in the grip of a euphoria typical of asset bubbles; they also believed, like their successors 80 years later in the lead-up to the collapse of 2007–09, that the fallout of a crash, if one were to occur, could be contained.

The Great Crash and the Hangover

Americans of all social classes became imbued with the mindset of monetary calculation—another contribution of the 1920s to contemporary culture. New ideas about money and what we would now call asset management proliferated. Suddenly, many more people had savings to manage—their own monetary assets. As mentioned above, there were many new and tempting ways to use money—to spend in new shops and entertainment, save it in the bank, invest it for the longer term—or speculate in the hope of short-term gains. Speculation became a popular sport—and for some, an addiction. The Dow Jones industrial average index set a record in each of six consecutive years from 1924 to 1929. On January 5, 1928, the Dow Jones industrial average closed just below 200, having risen by 50 points during 1927. Herbert Hoover, who had been Commerce Secretary under Coolidge, became President in 1929 following his promise to 'put a chicken in every cooking pot, and a car in every garage'. Hoover believed in laissez-faire and rugged individualism. As an activist First Lady, his wife Lou embodied the new woman of the post-World War I era: confident, active in good causes, at ease as a guest speaker and regular radio broadcaster, she was aware of the opportunities opening up for women. Many shared Hoover's optimism, and in the next six months the market soared, lifting the industrial average index to its peak of 381 on September 3, 1929 (a level it would not reach again until 1954). But then the stock market crashed, signalling the beginning of a new era.

America was like a teenager feeling his new strength—swaggering but inwardly beset by worries. The period was full of such paradoxes. While it sowed the seeds of a new consumer society and ethos, thoughtful people expressed profound doubts about them. Some people dreamt of a new world order but the time was not ready for it. It saw the beginnings of a new approach to official management of money sidetracked by fruitless attempts to re-establish the old monetary order. Though doomed, these attempts included an institutional development that was to grow into an important feature of twentieth-century monetary history—central bank cooperation. At the time, efforts to coordination may have done more harm than good—Benjamin Strong, Governor of the New York Fed, kept monetary policy loose and extended a line of credit to the Bank of England to facilitate its return to gold in 1925 and then cut its interest rate in July 1927 to protect sterling—a move later blamed for fuelling the Wall Street boom that burst in October 1929 and ushered in the Great Depression. True, the legacy of such cooperation, which found institutional form with the establishment of the Bank for International Settlements in Basel in 1930, did have positive results after World War II. Yet, as in the case of Germany discussed in Chap. 3, policy-makers were unable to escape from their time, their society and its inherited ideas. In that perspective, as in Germany, there was a failure of imagination—a failure to comprehend fully the scale of the changes that had been wrought by World War I.

The question of what caused the Great Depression can never be conclusively answered because the underlying policy questions remain controversial. Two leading scholars sum up a mountain of research as follows:

> Many argue that adherence to the gold standard caused the Great Depression because of 'golden fetters'—due to the gold constraint, countries could not follow lender of last resort policies....Others argue that the Depression was caused by inappropriate Federal Reserve monetary policy. (Bordo and Schenk 2018)

Others argued that a depression of some sort was made inevitable by the loose monetary policies of the mid-to-late 1920s.

Referring to the wide discrepancy in the explanations offered by leading free-market economists of the century, Brown (2018) asks a pertinent question:

> How could Milton Friedman and Anna Schwarz have described the years 1922–1928 as the heyday of the Federal Reserve—doing everything right, apparently—when von Hayek, Rothbard, Robbins and many others viewed the same Federal Reserve during the same period as responsible for a huge credit boom and asset price inflation culminating in bust and the great depression? (Brown 2018)

Such questions show that business and economic history is much more subjective than often thought. It is written often more out of a desire to prove a pre-existing hypothesis (or prejudice) than from a genuine desire to explain what happened; that is why history written by economists, though informed by an understanding of theory, is often less insightful than when written by historians with fewer theoretical axes to grind. In my view, the Federal

Reserve's expansionary policies were a natural (maybe unavoidable) product of the buoyant mood of the times. As I have attempted to portray earlier in this chapter; people wanted to party and the real economy was bowling along. Forget what parents or grandparents had said, forget the hard war years, now it is time to celebrate, America!

In this case, the lesson drawn in the longer run from experience in the Great Depression was that governments/central banks should be ready to ensure adequate monetary demand at all times to avoid a repeat. This is what Ben Bernanke, as a governor of the Fed, told Milton Friedman in 2002 at a conference honouring his 90th birthday:

> Let me end my talk by abusing slightly my status as an official representative of the Federal Reserve. I would like to say to Milton and Anna: Regarding the Great Depression. You're right, we did it. We're very sorry. But thanks to you, we won't do it again.

Bernanke was referring to the argument of 'Milton and Anna' in their classic work *A Monetary History of the United States* that the Fed could have prevented the Great Depression if only it had been *more expansionary* in countering the fall in the money supply (Friedman and Schwartz 1963). That this—rather than the lesson that the Fed caused the Great Depression by an *excessively expansionary* policy before it—was the key lesson drawn by the dominant schools of economists inevitably imparted an inflationary bias to policy.

That this lesson was chosen as a warning to future policy-makers naturally fitted the priorities of a democratic society. Indeed, it largely explains why the twentieth century was to be a period of inflation leading to a large reduction in the real value of all currencies. Clearly, the lessons drawn did not follow from an objective study of history but reflected the choices of policy-makers (and indeed academics) sensitive to the demands of the electorate. Commitment to a consistent, rules-based policy, whether of the gold standard type or any other, turned out to be inconsistent with the pressures on governments to spend money (usually to counter unemployment or respond to other shocks). But these often also had *unintended* longer term effects. We would do well to bear in mind the words that Paul Volcker, among the greatest of central bankers, penned in the introduction to a book published in 1994 that I co-authored with the late Marjorie Deane:

> It is a sobering fact that the prominence of central banks in this century has coincided with a general tendency towards more inflation, not less. By and large, if the overriding objective is price stability, we did better with the nineteenth-century gold standard and passive central banks, with currency

boards, or even with 'free banking.' The truly unique power of a central bank, after all, is the power to create money, and ultimately the power to create is the power to destroy. (Deane and Pringle 1994)

Support for Growth

The most important contributions to the evolution of the modern money society during this decade were made by the private sector. Innovations in personal credit, the spread of banking habits to wider sections of the more affluent middle classes, instalment credit, personal financial planning and budgeting and flexible credit arrangements made critical contributions to the emergence of mass markets in a wide variety of consumer goods. Official policy reflected lack of experience in managing fiat money, and a hankering for a return to gold (understandable but wrong). It will always suffer from association with the Great Crash and the Great Depression that followed—an undue build-up of credit prior to the crash followed by a mistaken unwillingness to use monetary policy aggressively when the panic started. For the most part, monetary policy supported the expansion appropriately. But it was an age when optimism and creativity in commerce, marketing and finance were shadowed by doubt and anxiety about the effect of the new consumer society and its money-centrism on the human psyche and on social well-being. In these ways, too, it would prove to be typical of the modern era.

Bibliography

Adams, James Truslow (1931). *The Epic of America.*

Bordo, M., and Schenk, C. (2018). 'Monetary Policy Cooperation and Coordination: An Historical Perspective on the Importance of Rules', In Bordo, M., Taylor, J.B. (eds) (2017). *Rules for International Monetary Stability.* Stanford: Hoover Institution.

Brown, B. (2018). *The Case Against 2 Per Cent Inflation: From Negative Interest Rates to a 21st Century Gold Standard.* Palgrave Macmillan.

Deane, M., and Pringle, R. (1994). *The Central Banks.* London: Hamish Hamilton.

"Advertising in the 1920s," EyeWitness to History, www.eyewitnesstohistory.com (2000).

Fitzgerald, Scott F. (1931). *The Great Gatsby.*

Friedman, M., and Schwartz, A. (1963). *A Monetary History of the United States.* Princeton: Princeton University Press.

Lewis, Sinclair (1920). *Main Street.*

Mencken, H.L. (1956). Minority Report: H.L. Mencken's Notebooks.

Tarkington, Booth (1918). *The Magnificent Ambersons.*

5

The Money-Haters: Experiments in Socialism

The second great class of experiments with money following World War I involved various attempts to do away with it. They were to cause, directly or indirectly, as many deaths as the war itself. Why did some people hate money (we shall see what they meant by that) so much? We must try to understand such passions if we are to understand the twentieth century—a century that is already retreating into a fog as dense as that which obscures the Middle Ages. But the money-haters too have left a legacy. The ideas that moved them are not dead. They come as part of a philosophy and theory of politics that continues to be drawn on by opponents of capitalism and of what they view as the dominion of money over life—'the cash nexus'. No government today is committed to realising these ideals and in the absence of official endorsement, there cannot be a repeat of the scale of the crimes and murders committed in its name. But individuals and groups still look to these ideals for inspiration. They do, indeed, have merit and some form of such ideas is needed again now. As always, beliefs come first.

A Twentieth-Century Creed

In 1928, just as the crazy, credit-fuelled Wall Street boom was reaching its climax, showing an ugly side of money, on the other side of the world, the world's largest nation was embarking on an even crazier programme to eliminate it. In the USSR private property would be abolished and money made

---

Marx: 'I do not like money. Money is the reason we fight.'

© The Author(s) 2019
R. Pringle, *The Power of Money*, https://doi.org/10.1007/978-3-030-25894-8_5

largely redundant. That was the plan when in 1928 Joseph Stalin launched a policy of comprehensive nationalisation and seizure of grain from farmers—followed, when they resisted, by forcible collectivisation of their land. Ever since the revolution that had swept the Bolsheviks to power ten years early, the true believers in the party had fretted at Lenin's compromise with a market economy, which went under the name of the New Economic Policy, and Lenin himself had declared it only a transitional stage. On his death in 1924, they saw their chance to implement a basic tenet of the communist creed: 'Finally, when all capital, all production, all exchange have been brought together in the hands of the nation, private property will disappear of its own accord, money will become superfluous, and production will so expand and man so change that society will be able to slough off whatever of its old economic habits may remain' (Friedrich Engels, *Principles of Communism*, Section 18).

The campaign to 'slough off old economic habits' such as private property and money would fail, but not before several million people had been killed by governments in their attempts to realise that dream. Stalin's experiment would be followed later in the twentieth century by countries such as Vietnam, Laos, Cambodia and Eastern Europe.[1] At its height in the early 1980s, over a third of the world's people lived under regimes that professed to be communist and included people from a variety of cultures, ethnicities and standards of living. Moreover, communist ideology greatly influenced several countries that had socialist but not communist regimes, notably India. After independence in 1947, with Nehru at the helm, India enthusiastically embraced state planning, on the assumption that bureaucrats with the interests of the community at heart would make better economic decisions than money-grubbing entrepreneurs. State-owned companies controlled 'the commanding heights' of India's economy. In 1955 the ruling Congress Party declared its intent to establish a socialistic pattern of society in India. If India and other countries dominated by extensive state planning are included, for a considerable part of the century up to one-half of the world's peoples lived in countries whose governments were committed to reducing if not fully eliminating the role of money, markets and the profit motive.

How so many governments came to adopt such ideas, and how most kept power for so long, despite the immense suffering their efforts to put them into practice caused, are mysteries as profound as any in the twentieth century. They were not planning or committing genocide; it was not the Holocaust. In some ways, and one hesitates to say this, it was even more terrible. It is not just that more people died, but that many of the killers acted out of apparently idealistic motives....

How It All Started

In the West, the ideas go back to the founding of Christianity and before. Following St Paul's condemnation of the love of money, medieval moralists taught that a market based on greed was inherently sinful; as soon as greed was allowed to run full rein, people involved in market trading and financing had no obligation to anyone or anything.[2] The philosopher Thomas Hobbes (1588–1679) saw this; because of people's greed, markets could only exist under an absolutist state, 'which would force us to keep our promises and respect one another's property' (Graeber 2011). Sir Thomas More (1478–1535) described an imaginary ideal society with no money. The contemporary definition of the English word 'utopia' derives from his work of that name, published in 1516. Thomas More urged communal ownership as a way of controlling the sins of pride, envy and greed. Land and houses would be common property. Everyone would work for at least two years on the communal farms and change houses every ten years so that no one developed pride of possession. With no money, people would take what they need from common storehouses. All the Utopians live simply so that—as in Keynes's later vision—they are able to meet their needs with only a few hours of work a day, leaving the rest for leisure. Then came the founders of modern socialism, Charles Fourier (1772–1837), who wanted society to be based on cooperation rather than competition; Pierre-Joseph Proudhon, who believed passionately in equality; Henri de Saint Simon (1760–1825), who advocated a society in which each person was ranked only according to his or her capacities and rewarded according to his or her work; Robert Owen (1771–1858) a successful Welsh businessman who devoted much of his profits to improving the lives of his employees and set up an Owenite commune called New Harmony in Indiana, the United States, which banned the use of money and other commodities for trade; and William Morris (1834–96), who believed that society should be centred around useful work as opposed to useless toil, and that all work should be artistic, in the sense that the worker should find it both pleasurable and an outlet for creativity.

A feature of these strands of socialist thought is the abolition of private property, which implies the abolition of money as we know it, because money is a token of purchasing power—the potential ability now or in future to acquire an asset/commodity and treat it as one's own.

Marxist Ideals

Marxism relies on a direct and centrally organised distribution of consumers' goods without recourse to a market. This would be morally superior to an economy based on private property and wage labour, where social relations between people were reduced to mere 'exchange relations' between things. It was generally accepted by Soviet Marxists in the 1920s that socialism would see the abolition of money; the capitalist's law of value would be replaced by planning. Only under socialism could social relations be fully human.

Marxism seems to open up routes to a deeper understanding of the social significance of money than does Western economics (which often consigns it to a supporting role as a mere 'veil' over the economy). Those who want to consign liberalism to the dustbin of history know that one of their greatest strengths is the fear and hatred that money arouses in many people, especially those who don't have much of it! Throughout the past 100 years this strand has linked many seemingly disparate situations. Even 100 years after the Russian Revolution, and despite the rise of a global monetary economy, many continue to deplore the reliance of the market system on 'selfish individualism' and pecuniary incentives. They blame it for the periodic financial crises, and for the unfairness of the outcomes of unfettered markets. They also point to the corrosive, anti-social effects of the market's tendency to discount the value of public goods, to place monetary values and objectives on every institution and its tendency to reduce every social relationship to a market transaction.

Communism in Action

The ideas outlined in the previous sections were taken up by many governments of the twentieth century. Those who shared a distaste for the pecuniary motive and market-determined money values more generally may, however, have very different ideas of other aspects of policy and different visions of society. Many who would not call themselves socialists believe that a free market society relying on monetary links and measures of values has an inherent tendency to lead to an excessive financialisation of daily life. Communism is a particular kind of socialism. By communism I mean, here, a society ostensibly dedicated to realising the principle of 'from each according to their abilities, to each according to their needs'. This society would come about as a result of state action after a revolution led by the 'dictatorship of the proletariat'. Here, we focus on the Marxist-Leninist tradition as this was the ideology that, in one form or another, was the official doctrine of all the states involved.

Under this tradition of communism/socialism (we discuss terms later), the role of money would be reduced by establishing an economic system based on shared ownership of the means of production, distribution and exchange. The economy was to be organised by the state, private property to be abolished. Workers would be rewarded in proportion to their contribution to output.

The Russian Revolution of October 1917 and subsequent implementation of Marxist-Leninist doctrine had a far-reaching influence on world politics and economics over the next half century. Even in the mid-1960s, most observers expected socialism to continue to spread. This was because it was widely seen as ethically superior, due to the absence of the profit motive. Business itself was not an occupation for a gentleman. When I was at Cambridge in the 1960s, higher education was basically a preparation for a calling, a vocation, entry to a profession or life as a scholar or a career in the higher levels of the civil service, or the Church—all careers where service, influence, status and perks were the attractions. And many intellectuals still hankered after Marxism. I was taught by one of them: the famous economist Joan Robinson, who used to enthuse about Fidel Castro's land reforms in Cuba. We can turn to literary sources to see how long this support lasted. For example, the writer Hanif Kureshi (born 1954) says in his novel *Intimacy* (1998) about his generation, 'we disdained materialism':

> We were an earnest and moral generation, with severe politics. We were the last generation to defend communism.

As Kureshi says, many went on praising the Soviet Union's ideology even as it invaded Afghanistan in 1979. This all goes to show how new our assumption that money and prices set in markets play a naturally central role in our lives and in society is. Assumptions that are normal in one generation may become anathema or incomprehensible only a few years later.

The Road to Serfdom: USSR Style

Under state planning, which lasted from 1930 to the late 1980s, the Stalinist system in the USSR aimed to suppress the market, severely restrict the role of money and money prices, and organise the production and distribution of goods and services by means of central planning. Successive five-year plans set targets for production of individual industries and sectors in terms of physical quantities—so many cars, so many tonnes of wheat and so on, all in enormous detail. Consumers had no influence on the pattern of production.

Entities called banks existed but they had no power to create credit or money. Just at a time when banks were becoming key agents in the coordination of economic activity under capitalism, the communist authorities would plan economic development without reference to money, market prices or the wishes of consumers.

Although money was a medium of exchange, to avoid forcing people to resort to barter, prices were rigidly controlled. The planners allocated wage funds to industrial organisations that were used to pay workers, who could then choose how to spend the money on the limited range of goods and services available in the shops. But planners could not respond to changes in demand from consumers, resulting in huge shortages of some items and gluts of others. Money became a token representing a certain amount of 'things' available for purchase—with the range and quality of the things on offer in exchange for these tokens decided by the state. Soviet money was not convertible into foreign currencies. The Soviet Union was a closed, command economy. The authorities aimed at self-sufficiency.

In short, money served as an instrument of political power. Banks existed to exercise financial control over enterprises. At the roots of this system was the authorities' fetishism of command planning. They viewed the people as the passive instruments of the state. They claimed not to understand why sections of society opposed their plans, as apparent in mass resistance to collectivisation, worker demoralisation, and high rates of labour turnover, absenteeism and industrial accidents. Many participated in semi-legal and illegal trade and resorted to all kinds of tricks to distance themselves from the plans. Even draconian punishments could not prevent markets from springing up. Such phenomena could only be viewed, officially, as the survival of petit-bourgeois tendencies, the work of class enemies and of foreign agents. In 1932–33 alone between 10 million and 15 million people vanished—deported, shot or died of starvation—mostly in Ukraine (Sebag-Montefiore 2008). The total death toll of the collectivisation programme was much higher.

China and Cambodia

The Chinese copied the system of central planning from the Soviet Union. Then in 1958 came The *Great Leap Forward* which called on spontaneous heroic efforts by the entire population. When farms were organised into communes and the output distributed through planning, food production collapsed. From 1958 to 1961, an estimated 14 million people died of starvation. This was followed by the *Cultural Revolution* between 1966 and 1976 which was supposed to purge the country the last remnants of capitalism, such as money and markets. The Red Guards were allowed to confiscate property, with their motto of the Four Olds: 'old ideas, culture, customs and habit of the exploiting classes'—all needed to be destroyed. In addition, virtually all engineers, managers, scientists, technicians and other professional personnel were 'criticised', demoted, sent down to the countryside and their property confiscated. The Holocaust memorial museum in Washington puts the resulting death toll at between 5 and 10 million.

Cambodia's Maoists were proud to be purer Marxists than those in the USSR and decided to go one better even than Mao in the Cultural Revolution. They declared not only that the communist ideal was incompatible with industrial civilisation but also that a communism that lived up to its principles would have to destroy cities and all industry. When the Khmer Rouge seized power in 1975, they took the shocking step of evacuating the capital Phnom Penh and other Cambodian cities. The entire Cambodian population were enslaved on collective farms. Any dissent would be punished by the offender getting clubbed or starved to death—about 1.7 million between 1975 and 1979, out of a total population of 7.5 million. Fields of corpses became the macabre hallmark of the regime. And so the story, with local variants, carried on in the other 40 or so countries fated to suffer under communist regimes.

Old Order Replaced

The New Deal in America, fascism in Europe and the communist states in Russia, Eastern Europe and elsewhere can all be seen as rejections of the old-world order, including its concept of money. It was not only that this order had been destroyed in war. People abandoned the ideas and ideals that had inspired it. So they easily grabbed hold of any idea or followed any politician promising to restore order without a return to ideas that had underpinned the previous order. In Chap. 2, I argued that the ideas that led to the socialist and fascist experiments of the twentieth century were laid during the apparent heyday of laissez-faire in the nineteenth century, how these were championed by artistic and literary geniuses, and how they made many educated people not only in the West but also in the rapidly industrialising countries turn away from capitalism.

Absurd and ugly though it was, the Soviet experiment had a huge influence on the twentieth century. It showed that a radical alternative to capitalism was possible; as late as the 1960s most observers expected the world would move in that direction and the movement reached its apogee only in the 1980s (in terms of the population living in communist-style states). What accounted for this? First, passionate aversion to the pecuniary motive/hatred of 'money and private property as instruments of the exploitation and domination of one class by another. Secondly, a yearning for a better society on earth after the 'death of God'. Both motives were then used to establish horrific dictatorships. Solzhenitsyn declared towards the end of his life, after spending 50 years working on the history of the Russian revolution, that lack of religious faith was its fundamental cause: 'if I were asked today to formulate as concisely as possible the main cause of the ruinous revolution that swallowed up some 60 million of our people, I could not put it more accurately than to repeat: "Men have forgotten God; that's why all this has happened"' (Ericson 1985).

For the Anglo-Saxon monetary outlook to triumph globally, which is a leading theme of this book, it was essential to crush Marxist socialism and to discredit the ideas behind it. (This applied also to potential challenges from Japanese and German cultures.) The collapse of the USSR and other communist states in the 1990s removed the political threat. Everybody could see that it was not love of money that secured victory but a better system backed by superior political and military power. America would show that money could be a dynamic ingredient in an economy based on competition and the search for profit under a rules-based order. However, it took many years for people to be convinced of the ethical superiority of capitalism. In this, even the wretched Soviet experiment had an ironic upside. There is little doubt that the existence of a powerful rival made capitalism behave itself, put on its best clothes and disguise its undeniably ugly side. As soon as the political threat was removed, capitalism had no need for the disguise. People with a lust for money could pursue it openly and feel fully entitled to their gains, even if their activities brought no benefits to society. Many again found this highly distasteful. It is no surprise, therefore, that the aversion to money as a driving force in society survived the end of Socialism as a practical state project and lives on (see in particular the 'outsiders' discussed in Chap. 18). Marxism in its various guises remains the source of the main intellectual critiques of capitalism.

Notes

1. Communist Countries in 2018 were China, Cuba, Laos, North Korea and Vietnam.

   There were 42 formerly Communist countries (by current name), including 15 that had been formerly part of the Soviet Union and 27 others:

Formerly part of the USSR were Armenia, Azerbaijan, Belarus, Estonia, Georgia, Kazakhstan, Kyrgyzstan, Latvia, Lithuania, Moldova, Russia, Tajikistan, Turkmenistan, Ukraine and Uzbekistan.

Other Asian countries: Afghanistan, Cambodia, Mongolia and Yemen.

Soviet-controlled Eastern bloc countries: Bulgaria, Czech Republic, Germany (East), Hungary, Poland, Romania, Slovakia.

The Balkans: Albania, Bosnia and Herzegovina, Bulgaria, Croatia, Rep. of Macedonia, Montenegro, Serbia and Slovenia.

Africa: Angola, Benin, Dem Rep. of Congo, Ethiopia, Somalia, Eritrea, and Mozambique.

2. The New Testament: 1 Timothy 6: 6–12: 'There is great gain in godliness combined with contentment; for we brought nothing into the world, so that we can take nothing out of it; but if we have food and clothing, we will be content with these. But those who want to be rich fall into temptation and are trapped by many senseless and harmful desires that plunge people into ruin and destruction. For the love of money is a root of all kinds of evil, and in their eagerness to be rich some have wandered away from the faith and pierced themselves with many pains.'

Bibliography

Engels, F. (1847/2013). *The Principles of Communism*. Prism Key Press.

Graeber, D. (2011). *Debt: The First 5,000 years*. New York: Melville House.

Kureshi, Hanif (1998). *Intimacy*.

Ericson, Edward, E. Jr. (1985, October). '*Solzhenitsyn – Voice from the Gulag*,' *Eternity*, pp. 23–24, cited in Wikipedia.

Sebag-Montefiore, S. (2008). 'Holocaust by hunger: The truth behind Stalin's Great Famine', Mailonline 26 July 2008.

6

Europe Between the World Wars: A Ferment of Ideas

The third cluster of monetary innovations that followed the cataclysmic destruction of the 1914–18 war took place, initially, not in the market but in the study and in the imagination of scholars. Only later did they infiltrate the corridors of power and through that route, the real world. These innovative ideas, generated primarily in Europe in the 1930s and 1940s, turned out to be as influential as the practical experiments in America in shaping the longer term evolution of society on both sides of the Atlantic and more enduring than the planned economy of the Communist USSR. This all amounted to another effort—this time, at the intellectual level—to 'put the world to rights' after being shattered by what was called the Great War. By the late 1930s, thoughtful people had concluded that attempts to restore the world's economic system as it had worked before 1914 could not succeed. That world had gone for ever, and so had its idea of money and its role in society. By the outbreak of World War II, the Great Depression had lasted—with intermittent short-lived recoveries—for a full ten years in the United States and had devastated many other economies. A new approach was needed. This applied not only to domestic affairs but also internationally. How would trade, investment and economic relations between states be organised? And if money was not to be gold, what could it be?

The essential contribution was to show that capitalism could survive democracy. One school favoured the use of active policies over money and sustained state action to promote social ends such as full employment and protections for workers. Moreover, these ends could be achieved without resort to a Communist-style (or indeed Fascist-style) takeover of the whole economy. Other schools of thought emphasised the need for constitutional

© The Author(s) 2019
R. Pringle, *The Power of Money*, https://doi.org/10.1007/978-3-030-25894-8_6

limits on the state's powers, including powers over money. These thinkers fashioned economic and political theories that reconciled capitalism with democracy. This reconciliation was on one hand highly successful—so much so that by the early twenty-first century, some commentators were saying that capitalism and democracy naturally supported each other and generally were good friends. On the other hand, one branch of these theories could also be used to provide the intellectual pretext for the state not only to dominate economic management but also to infringe individual liberty and property rights (e.g. by nationalisation of banking and other sectors) if this was deemed necessary. At the same time, another branch would be used to justify extreme so-called 'neo-liberal' policies in the late twentieth century. Both were responses to two challenges: the need for a new idea of money and a swing among opinion-formers towards the political (non-communist) Left.

How New Ideas Germinated

The ideas generated in the intense heat of those ideological clashes would, in time, provide a new framework for thinking about money and economics. The idea of money had to be flexible if it was to adapt to changing needs. Otherwise it would become what the Victorian philosopher J. S. Mill had called a 'monkey wrench' disrupting the economy. To sketch a picture of the ideas of the inter-war years from 1918 to 1939, I focus on those pertaining to the roles to be played by money and business in society including brief discussions of the following topics: literary attitudes in Europe; the socialist alternative; why socialists were in several countries unable to seize the moment; Keynes and the Bloomsbury Group; the various schools of liberalism in Continental Europe; the Chicago School and finally the contributions of Hayek, Polanyi and other economists in the 1940s. I conclude by summing up their legacy.

The great works of literature of the period, the equal of those of any other age, testified to major changes in social and political thought.

The leading writers pondered deeply on the chaotic economic and political conditions of their time. How had Europe pitched the world into such a catastrophe? To explain how it had come about, they re-examined the course of Western history. Many found in it as an unhealthy obsession with money. They pointed their fingers at the bourgeoisie, seen as the main social group guilty of transmitting material values to future generations. Such authors used various means—satire, mocking humour, biting wit—to lampoon traditional bourgeois values and contemporary society. Some (such as T. S. Eliot) while culturally conservative, attacked the materialism of contemporary culture for having betrayed the best in the Western tradition. Some were plunged into despair. Others (such as D. H. Lawrence and Sigmund Freud) showed human beings starved of means of expression, warmth and sincerity in their emotional and sexual lives. Money and the money motive were central forces of a society portrayed as decaying, corrupt, vicious, class-ridden, emotionally stunted—you name it. It had failed to find any noble ideas to replace religious belief.

Their work was not entirely negative; far from it. They retained from their Victorian parents/grandparents visions of progress, of better futures for mankind. However, the kind of progress they envisaged was quite different from that of the eighteenth-century Enlightenment or the optimism of the nineteenth century. Some, such as the novelist and popular science writer H. G. Wells, captured the popular interest in scientific advances. Others, such as George Bernard Shaw, amused audiences by their intellectual fireworks, hoping to arouse their finer instincts and make them go into battle for a better world. Although they were not all duped by the promise of Communism, by the 1930s they were largely socialist. This signalled a major change from the dominant ideas of the world before 1914. As part of this swing to the Left it was natural to see money too as needing to be brought under better collective control and to believe that its influence in daily life and in culture should be reduced. Politically, socialism was promoted by many influential thinkers. A writer such as Richard Tawney, for example, dwelt on the corrupting influence of money:

> A society which reverences the attainment of riches as the supreme felicity will naturally be disposed to regard the poor as damned in the next world, if only to justify itself for making their life a hell in this. (Tawney 1926)

Tawney's vision of a good society was that of an Oxford-educated gent of the late nineteenth century: sweetness and light, the pursuit of high culture, knowledge of the classics and of the best that has been written and said, a society imbued with Christian faith and values. This would have been his wish for the whole world, not just England. His books were extremely popular and his teaching had a lasting influence up to the 1960s, especially in the United States. It accorded with the spirit of the age. As Harold Macmillan, a future Tory Prime Minister of Great Britain, wrote in 1938:

> Throughout the whole of the post-war period, there had been growing an uneasy consciousness of something radically wrong with the economic system....One of the consequences of the crisis was to confirm these suspicions and to liberate men's minds from continued subservience to the economic orthodoxy of the pre-war world (referring to the world before 1914). (Macmillan 1938)

This turn to the Left changed the climate of opinion within which monetary and economic policies were formulated and implemented. People would no longer submit to the idea of money and its rules as being beyond the reach of politics. If governments could use money constructively for social ends, to reduce unemployment, stabilise the economy or finance needed government social spending, then they should. No longer would the stability-oriented assumptions and policy nostrums of the world before World War I be accepted without demur. After all, these were the views of people who had led Europe into a disastrous war. Their views on money should not be seen as sacrosanct any more than their tastes in art, literature, personal relations or morality. But there was no guide available on how to use money as a tool for the improvement of society, and it was obviously very challenging to produce one that would work.[1]

If the mood demanded a change, one man above all responded to it in a way that would change policies by creating a potentially viable theoretical framework to make change practicable—Maynard Keynes.

Money Re-imagined

During the 1920s, people could put down the disorder of the time to the pains of post-war recovery, industrial re-organisation, the reconfiguration of great powers, post-war debts and so on. The Great Depression forced a deeper rethinking—and people came to view active money management as being central in any way forward. It was no longer justifiable to think, like the Victorians had done, that once put on a sound basis, money could be left to itself, to get on with its function of oiling the wheels of trade, as J. S. Mill put it. Victorians could believe money was unimportant in economics—merely a veil—just because they had by accident inherited such a good money—one that fitted their needs. They could take it for granted. The persistence of the Great Depression—only World War II brought real, lasting recovery to America—forced economists and other observers to ask new questions about money, to separate its functions into distinct compartments and look at them squarely and ask: who or what are you? This required a leap of imagination, like looking in the mirror for the first time and asking: 'is that me?' No wonder they were scared to touch it. This is what economist George Shackle called the years of high theory, requiring all the inventiveness the age could muster (Shackle 1967). That is why the Great Depression is a turning point: money could never be the same again.

Keynes re-imagined money as an active but dangerous and mysterious force, like electricity, or as an alive being like a serpent. If the main defect of

capitalism was its failure to stabilise investment, then money—which introduced a wedge between income and spending, between savings and investment—was critical. Keynes was able to see money in a new light. Money, he
said in *The General Theory of Employment, Interest and Money*, 'in its significant
attributes is, above all, a subtle device for linking the present to the future'.
Because the future is uncertain, people may hoard money as what I call a
comfort blanket. As such its behaviour responds to emotion, to fear as well as
greed (see also Chap. 18). Understanding it, seeing it in such a new light,
required the imagination of an artist. And that is how Keynes saw himself:
'Keynes's view of his General Theory was that of an artist who has reached a
point of self-understanding that allowed him to see his creative work in a
longer historical perspective' (Backhouse and Bateman 2011). We need such
'artistic' imagination again—as I shall argue in Chap. 22.

Keynes the 'Bloomsberry'

Roy Harrod, Keynes's first biographer, noted his 'extraordinarily powerful intu-
itive sense of what was important'. It was intuition that told Keynes that the
old economics was 'inadequate'. The new approach 'gives a sense of immense
release' (Harrod 1951).[2] To effect this, Keynes needed inspiration; here I believe
the rebellious spirit of the time and especially of his group of friends—the
Bloomsbury Group—were crucial. Keynes himself blamed 'ingrained beliefs'
as the cause of the economic tragedy and the main impediment to a cure.

Keynes's whole body of work is a prolonged meditation on the nature of
money. It shows throughout the pervasive influence of—and his commitment to—the ideals of the Bloomsbury Group. They would sneer at pomp-
ous Victorians and rejoice in turning Victorian morality upside down. Here
too, as with Adam Smith, we see a utopian spirit at work in seemingly dry
analysis of money and markets. This utopian vision of ideal communities of
civilised men and women was the spur. The greatest pleasures of life were to
be found in refined enjoyment of the arts, personal relations, and progress in
spreading civilisation and cultivation. Keynes despised mass culture, was
sceptical about democracy and shared with Marx an aristocratic aversion to
the pecuniary motive. He believed like Marx in a 'vanguard' to lead a revolution—instead of the proletariat, it would be the Bloomsbury Group. He may
have delighted in overturning Victorian values in his economics, but in life—
how to lead a good life—he remained firmly in the tradition of eminent
Victorians such as Matthew Arnold and of John Ruskin and his mentor, the
philosopher G. E. Moore. You only have to look at the literary output of the

Bloomsberries to see their abhorrence of money and its corrosive effects. For instance, it runs through E. M. Forster's novels. In a future society, Keynes said, the love of money as a possession 'as distinguished from the love of money as a means to the enjoyments and realities of life' will be recognized 'for what it is, a somewhat disgusting morbidity, one of those semi-criminal, semi-pathological propensities which one hands over with a shudder to the specialists in mental disease…' (Keynes 1930).

In the meantime, however, the only way the economic problem could be removed would be through the accumulation of capital. Without the desire to make more money, this would not be possible. Therefore, the money motive was a necessary but temporary evil. 'Avarice and usury and precaution must be our gods for a little longer still', he acknowledged, perhaps unconsciously echoing Marx (see Chap. 2 and Keynes 1930). But—and this is crucial—rather than expecting society to adapt to money, it was rather money that had to adapt to the 'natural tendencies' of society and the *system as it actually is*. The state, as protector of the public good, had a duty to regulate money. Thus was the new idea of money—and hence modern monetary policy—conceived. Greed was assigned a similar role to that of forced labour and collectivisation in the USSR—a necessary if unpleasant means for reaching utopia.

Keynes could distance himself from money sufficiently to re-imagine it because the artistic circles in which he moved were also re-inventing the visual arts, seeing the world in a new way, and the authors he talked with, like Forster, were writing in a new way, discovering and exploring currents in human relationships that nobody had ever noticed. At the same time, Keynes's new ideas—when he got round to formulating his insights in a logical format—could influence events only because the whole political culture of the age had shifted to the Left. They would never have gained a hearing by his parents' generation with the Victorians' proud beliefs in freedom of exchange, free trade, private property rights, small governments and balanced budgets—and an invariant monetary standard. But then Bloomsbury's idea of fun was to mock their forebears.

A Clash of Ideologies in France

Across the English Channel, both Right and Left lamented the dominance of the money motive. Where the Bloomsberries reproached their parents for this, the French blamed the English. After all, as Napoleon was supposed to have said, they were only a nation of shopkeepers. In France, the Right also became anti-capitalist and anti-parliamentary. On the Left, the Russian revolution of 1918 acquired huge prestige—the French communist party was founded in 1920. The left-wing Popular Front came to power in 1936 at the height of the depression.

Yet, France played an important role in the transmission of ideas of liberty that would in time sow the seeds of a resurgence in that country of libertarian thought. Among intellectuals who influenced that development was the economist Jacques Rueff, one of the few French defenders of liberal political economy. In Rueff's view, the coordination of the desires and activities of so many individuals in society should be left to the price mechanism, mediated by money, not to human design (Chivvis 2010). Raymond Aron, another leading intellectual, deplored the American 'reign of credit', complaining that the United States was 'colonising' France and French culture', but later became a champion of Anglo-Saxon liberalism, along with my friend Bertrand de Jouvenel, a co-founder of the Mt Pelerin Society, and member of The Colloque Lippmann.[3]

Liberalism Re-imagined

Economists in the German-speaking parts of Europe who rejected fascism and socialism had to find other kinds of response that measured up to the challenges posed by the turmoil around them. Like Keynes, they reflected on problems such as high unemployment, currency wars and monetary instability (the hyperinflation of 1923 was a recent memory). But they were conscious of other challenges as well. Whereas Keynes lived in a country that maintained its democratic institutions, economists in continental Europe were confronted directly with the rise of totalitarian governments and their fascist rationalisations. They observed dictatorships working closely with cartels of industrialists. Thus, for them the constitutional issue came first: how to create a stable political environment. Without a state able to set the rules of the game, without price stability, without secure property rights and the rule of law and a means to ensure markets were competitive, markets could not deliver their supposed benefits. In particular, it was crucial to come up with a theory that would limit the arbitrary power of the state. For them and their generation, it was already too late. Mussolini made himself dictator of Italy in 1925 and Hitler took power in 1933. But if they could develop ideas to guide future generations and help them avoid the same fate, such ideas would indeed make a crucial contribution to avoiding a repeat of the disaster. Their interest, in academic terms, was as much in the legal framework of an economy as in economics itself.[4]

German-speaking liberal economists came up with a different set of responses to the crises of interwar Europe to those being developed by Keynes.

These were as innovative as Keynes and possibly may prove to be even as influential in the long run. A doctrine of sound money was at the centre of the new approach. They did not regard money as abhorrent but as dangerous. If the gold standard could not be resurrected—members of the group differed on that subject—an adequate replacement would have to be found. Whereas Keynesian thought favoured discretionary monetary policy, Continental liberals wanted to constrain the discretion of state and its bodies over money.

Their ideas, which I outline below, would take two routes to power—first through their input into the re-building of Germany after World War II and from there to the wider European arena, and second via their intellectual influence at American universities and thereby on the world. True, their ideas could gain purchase only when society was ready for them—when the world had done with its orgy of slaughter in World War II. But their time would come; and then their ideas—including notably their ideas on money—would leave a lasting imprint.

The Freiburg School and Ordoliberalism

Freiburg University was home to Walter Eucken and Franz Bohm, founders of the influential brand of liberal thought known as ordoliberalism, as mentioned in Chap. 3. Bohm (1895–1977) was a politician, lawyer and economist (his first work was a critique of Adam Smith). With his collaborator Walter Eucken (1891–1950), he developed the concept of an economic constitution—the idea that the state must provide a legal framework for the economy. Both worked in secret during the war to develop plans for the post-war world. Bohm served as a member of the Bundestag, Germany's post-war Parliament from 1953 to 1965 while Eucken advised Chancellor Ludwig Erhard on the economic reforms and abolition of price controls in 1948. This school was to influence events also through the way the Deutsche Bundesbank was made independent bank from its foundation in 1957 and though the influence of the 'Bundesbank model' on the design of the European Central Bank (ECB). In 2019 the German candidate to succeed Mario Draghi as president of the ECB, Jens Weidmann, was fond of quoting from Eucken's works.

This group was sensitive to the social ills experienced as side-effects of a dynamic market system, including the decay of social order and personal strains of isolation, loneliness and alienation experienced by individuals under capitalism. They rejected laissez-faire, individualism and the ideal of a small state dedicated to defence and law. They emphasised the importance of institutions, and the way in which institutions create space.

The key concern of leaders such as Eucken and Bohm was how a desirable economic order could be created and maintained. As one scholar emphasises this was 'a question that they approached as a problem of constitutional choice, that is, as a question of how a desirable economic order can be generated by creating an appropriate economic constitution' (Vanberg 2004). Their aim was to improve the economy by changing the rules of the game rather than by specific interventions in the economic process. They rejected proposals that would involve the state managing overall demand in the economy as that would be to give too much discretion to government.

In their policy prescriptions, ordoliberals believed there should be a division of labour between the various functions and organs of the state. The central bank, which should be independent, would have the single aim of assuring price stability. A competition authority would be charged with ensuring a level playing field, and that markets were open to new competitors. An independent judiciary would assure the rule of law. These conditions for economic liberty and a flourishing market economy were taken for granted in Britain, where they had evolved gradually and after the civil war in the seventeenth century reached a fruitful compromise in the Glorious Revolution of 1689 and a balance of power between merchants, the City of London, the aristocracy and the Crown. In the United States, also, such an economic constitution was implicit in its political constitution. But the creative work needed to spell out the key ingredients of such a constitution would not only serve Germany well but also over time influence political and economic thought in the Anglo-Saxon countries also.

Whereas ordoliberals' focus was on the national level rather than the world economy, other allied schools of thought were more universalist in their aims.

Neoliberalism

The term *neoliberalism* was coined in 1938 at the Walter Lippmann Colloquium. It was chosen to distinguish the group from classical liberalism which was widely seen as discredited by the Great Depression. Again, as with the Freiburg School, a central aim of this school was to redesign states, laws and constitutional arrangements so as to protect the market and allow it to fulfil its role allocating goods and services and as an arena of free choice. The emphasis on the 'new' element was to recognise the state's role—some talked of the need for a strong state. This group did not hold to utopian beliefs about the virtues of free markets. Markets were not seen as natural but as requiring explicit effort and social agreement; there needed to be a settlement between state and market. How this could be achieved in a lasting way under democracy with all its pressures was a challenge that much exercised them. In contrast to Keynesians, most were of the view that fiscal deficits would have to be severely constrained and many held to the idea of balanced budgets—otherwise the pressure on governments or central banks to finance the debt by creating new money would be irresistible. Inflation was tantamount to theft of private property—and protection of private property rights was a key part of their programme.

The Geneva School

This is a name that has been proposed by a recent scholar, Quinn Slobodian, to present a narrative about a set of thinkers who have been neglected in the English literature and to reframe those like Hayek who have simply been labelled as members of the Austrian School. This group was especially concerned—a concern that became more pronounced after World War II—with the implications of the disintegration of the former European empires for world order. They did not believe that the market could operate independently of human intervention; they were not, in that sense, market fundamentalists: 'the focus of both German ordoliberalism and Austrian economics is not on the economy as such but on the institutions creating a space for the economy' (Slobodian 2018). They looked beyond the nation state to the world order. Modern scholars talk of the neoliberal project as referring to this group's ambitious ideas of forming what I shall call a global money space. They are modern in their claims that such a global monetary order would not require a world government. Although they had no input on the design of the international post-war monetary order known as Bretton Woods (see Chap. 9) and had deep reservations about it, the global money space constructed towards the end of the twentieth century came close to the neoliberal vision of an economy protected from state intervention. At a time when all but a few countries would have free capital movements, what instruments are there for states to intervene in the world economy? Their dream was to bring about a world in which everybody is linked by money, information and flows of goods and services seamlessly and where the world economy has its own space, protected at its frontiers by border police, with national governments operating a quite separate system. For such a dream, democracy is a problem, as it is unpredictable and veers towards interference. Is that not precisely where we are now, in the 2020s—a global space under threat from nation states?

As presented by Slobodian, the school includes thinkers such as Wilhelm Röpke and Ludwig con Mises (1881–1973) (both of whom held academic positions there), F. A. Hayek, Lionel Robbins and Gottfried Haberler and some economists who worked at the GATT trade body (the General Agreement on Tariffs and Trade) in the 1960s. These European intellectuals consistently viewed the world as a whole, whereas their American intellectual descendants, the Chicago School led by Milton Friedman and the Virginia school of public choice led by James Buchanan, saw the outside world through American eyes. As Slobodian puts it, these schools 'exhibited the peculiarly American quality of ignoring the rest of the world while assuming that America was a working model of it' (Slobodian 2018).

Geneva School neoliberals would criticise the post-World War II regime of autonomous, sovereign nation state as inimical to the world economy, undermining its promise of prosperity and freedom. An international order worthy of the name must safeguard capital and protect its right to move freely throughout the world. The world of nations should exist alongside a global money space. The latter was 'a world of property where people owned things, money and land scattered across the earth'. The world of modern capitalism was what they called a *doubled world* of states *and* money space (very close to what we have now). Money should work almost anywhere and be exchangeable freely into national currencies. Röpke, who taught at Geneva for almost 30 years, endorsed a view of the world articulated by a former Nazi jurist, Carl Schmitt, in 1951: 'Over, under and beside the state-political borders of what appeared to be a purely political international law between states', he wrote, 'spread a free, i.e. non-state sphere of economy permeating everything: a global economy' (Schmitt 2003).

Later Influence

In trade, neoliberals were also influential. Gottfried Haberler (1990–95) was born in Austria and, like von Mises and Hayek, emigrated to the United States, where he became a professor of economics at Harvard. He was an influential advocate of free trade and the division of labour internationally, which were essential to achieve maximum productivity and standard of living for all participants. While in Austria in the 1920s and 1930s, Haberler was a member of the Mises Circle of economists, sociologists and philosophers. However, Haberler rejected some aspects of the Austrian theory of the business cycle and in later writings, opposed any idea of a return to the gold standard.

One problem raised but not fully answered by international liberals remained: how to control money? Röpke favoured a return to gold, as did many members of the Austrian School. But those who accepted that this was not practical had no answer; without a world government, or granting a body such as the International Monetary Fund (IMF) discretionary power over world money, liberals were driven to rely on each state and central bank to control the money it issued.

The Chicago School

This was the most influential of the legacies of the neoliberal philosophy pioneered in central Europe between the wars. Its leading economist, Milton Friedman, rejected much about the Austrian School—including its theory of the business cycle—but paid tribute to Hayek in his memoirs. He remarked that his interest in public policy and in political philosophy, which had been 'rather casual' before he joined the faculty of economics at Chicago was reinforced by reading the *Road to Serfdom* (which he called a 'profound book') by his attendance at the first meeting of the Mt Pelerin Society, which included also Wilhelm Röpke and von Mises, and by discussions with Hayek after the latter joined Chicago University in 1950 (three years after Friedman himself). He noted that Hayek also attracted 'an exceptionally able group of students' (Milton and Rose Friedman 1998).

This establishes a clear line of descent from the neoliberalism of Vienna and Freiburg and Geneva to the nascent libertarian movement at Chicago and to probably the most influential economist of the last quarter of the twentieth century. Friedman advised both Ronald Reagan and Margaret Thatcher. True, Friedman had a quite different view from Hayek of the relation of money to the economy. In his magnum opus, A *Monetary History of the United States*, written with Anna Schwartz, Friedman portrayed the period 1922–28 as a good period for the Fed giving reasonable price stability when Hayek saw it as fuelling a huge credit boom leading to an inevitable bust in the Great Depression (Friedman and Schwartz 1963). But here I am concerned with the transmission of ideas about money and liberty.[5]

A Study in Contrasts: Polanyi Versus Hayek

This section discusses two influential and contrasting interpretations of the interwar swing to the political Left with its backlash against markets and money. The first is that offered by Karl Polanyi in *The Great Transformation*

(Polanyi 1944); the second is *The Road to Serfdom*, by F. A. Hayek, with its warnings of the new dangers of putting power over money into the hands of state officials (Hayek 1944). Both books were published in 1944 (for America's very different experience, see Chaps. 8 and 9).

Polanyi's thesis was essentially backward-looking. Nineteenth-century civilisation had rested on four pillars—namely, the 'self-regulating market', 'the balance of power', the gold standard and 'the liberal state'. The self-regulating market (SRM) was an idea that had developed gradually in the decades after publication of Adam Smith's *The Wealth of Nations*, in 1776. The idea of the SRM was, Polanyi claimed, 'utopian'—that is, it was an aspiration of an unlikely future world, not an account of an actual world. In the next 100 years Britain made huge efforts to realise that utopia—that is, to create a society that would fulfil the preconditions for an SRM. That, Polanyi said, would have astonished Adam Smith himself. Britain then tried to make the whole world adopt this model: what effrontery!

This utopian vision required revolutionary upheavals in society; never before had there been a society directed by money prices. Contrary to Adam Smith, people do not possess an innate 'propensity' to barter. Traditional societies had no concept of the individual as maximising his or her personal gain, as society depended always on cooperation. Markets had always been strictly restricted and regulated. And yet, 100 years after Adam Smith, a society had come into existence based on the idea that all factors of production—land, labour and money—must be continuously available on the market at market-determined prices.

Such a seemingly callous theory would have shocked previous generations. Whereas production had in earlier centuries been organised by merchants, drawing on money, skills and networks immediately to hand, now factors of production needed to be continuously available on the market in the huge quantities required by modern industry and trade. To realise this, a new type of human being would be needed, said Polanyi. This human would be 'migratory, nomadic, crude and callous'. A new kind of token money and credit money would also be needed. Land, people and money had to be treated as commodities. By 1900 a new way of life had spread throughout Europe with claims to universal application not seen since the advent of Christianity. In Polanyi's view, it embodied a materialistic creed built round the ideal of the self-regulating market. Polanyi believed that this was the moment when British, Western and world history became all about money. This idea was, he assumed, so contrary to human nature it would inevitably be rejected. Yet by the 1830s the new materialism had become what he called a fanatical creed. Under this regime, money had to be seen to be immutable, part of nature. Bank notes had to be the equivalent of gold. Economics had to be separated from politics. Small countries had to be compelled to adjust to the rigorous rules of the standard, as did poor people everywhere. Private property had to be sacred. This is the background for the attempt, inevitable in Polanyi's view, to restore that self-regulating world after the destruction of World War I. The restoration of the old, pre-war international monetary system also had to be attempted.

But then, he said, 'society' hit back. 'Nineteenth-century civilisation' was finally destroyed by the measures society needed to take to avoid itself being destroyed by the effort to restore the self-regulating market. It was always obvious, he declared, that people would have to be protected from the market—in the 1920s only Ludwig von Mises (an old sparring partner of Polanyi) called for an end to trades unions. World War I inclined people towards protectionism. Modern central banking with its centralisation of credit policy under public control developed precisely in order to protect business. Monetary policy was from the start political. It naturally became interventionist at home, and national currencies came to the fore internationally, instead of gold. The bankers were the last to notice that the old order had ended. Money experienced a sudden, complete rift from its moorings in the social order. It was no accident that, in the United States, the development of a monetary policy by the Federal Reserve coincided with the end of the frontier—the end of an age when the United States had enjoyed 'free' land, labour and money. An age of jealous national sovereignties came along instead.

In future, Polanyi expected politics and society to reclaim powers they had lost during the attempt to bring about the ideal of a self-regulating, monetary economy. A self-regulating market had inherent weaknesses; it ended up destroying society, nature and even mankind, leaving what he called a wilderness. The subordination of society to an unrealistic economic doctrine and to the demands of money could not last. Adam Smith himself would never have approved the idea that society could be controlled by the market.

So Polanyi's implied answer is, essentially, this: unwind history, abandon forever the unrealistic idea that the market can regulate itself, subject money to social constraints, and restore a sense of community and neighbourly solidarity as had existed before the coming of the fully monetised economy. This critique of what would later be called *market fundamentalism* had enduring influence.

Hayek: Beware of the State

In *The Road to Serfdom*, a best-seller, Hayek wanted passionately to show that the trend towards state planning was neither desirable nor inevitable. In marked contrast to Polanyi, Hayek saw the rise of the free market economy as deriving not from a bid by the state to realise the theories of Adam Smith but from an evolutionary social process. Over the centuries, a rigid hierarchic system had evolved into one where men could at least attempt to shape their own lives. This transformation was associated with the spread of commerce during the late Middle Ages, the rise of cities and the development of science. It had overcome obstacles placed by rigid social doctrines and lifted barriers to the exercise of human ingenuity. The theory of economic freedom was the outcome, not the cause, of an entirely undesigned process.

Contrary to a common misconception, Hayek saw the state, dangerous though it could be, as indispensable. He opposed rigid adherence to the principles of laissez-faire. There were many areas, and he specifically singled out money as one of them, where the government possessed and should keep enormous powers. Indeed, there was 'every reason to expect that with a better understanding of the problems we should some day be able to use these powers successfully' (Hayek 1944). What he objected to was the 'entire abandonment of the individualist tradition which has created Western civilisation'. The individualist approach was to ask how we might make best use of 'the spontaneous forces found in a free society'. This had been replaced by the notion that we should direct all social forces to deliberately chosen goals. Hayek claimed that this 'retreat' from English ideas of freedom began about 1860; since then a new set of ideas began to advance 'from the East'. Germany became the fount of ideas—as described in Chap. 2—that would rule the world in the twentieth century. Germany had led above all in socialist thought, backed by the extraordinary reputation that German thinkers and scientists had acquired in every field. Most of the Socialist ideas that the English imagine they developed in fact came from Germany—for example, that free trade pandered to self-interest. Ironically, even the British had been converted to the view that free trade was a doctrine invented to further their selfish interests, and began to be ashamed of the ideals they had given to the world. The British even proudly proclaimed their conversion to socialist ideas that were originally German. Echoing Hamlet, he said that intellectual history since the 1870s was 'a perfect illustration of the truth than in social evolution nothing is inevitable but thinking makes it so'.[6]

Both Polanyi and Hayek grounded their analysis in moral ideals, ideas about the kind of society best suited to man's highest aspirations. For Polanyi, these were nurtured by communities in which market processes and especially money were 'embedded' in a web of social obligations, subject to tight social moral and prudential standards and controls. For Hayek, man's capacity for fine achievements would only flourish in a social climate that allowed him to explore, to experiment, to innovate, to advance scientific knowledge in freedom: 'What is misleadingly called the "economic motive" means merely the desire for general opportunity. If we strive for money, it is because money offers us the widest choice in enjoying the fruits of our efforts—once earned, we are free to spend the money as we wish.'

'Money is one of the greatest instruments of freedom ever invented by man' says Hayek. He continues: 'It is money which in existing society opens an astounding range of choice to the poor man—a range greater than that which not many generations ago was open to the wealthy.' Just imagine, Hayek said, what it would really mean if, as many socialists propose, the pecuniary motive were largely displaced by non-economic incentives. If all rewards, instead of being offered in money, were offered in the form of public distinctions, or privileges, positions of power over other men, better housing or food, opportunities for travel or education, 'this would merely mean that the recipient would no longer be allowed to choose, and that whoever fixed the reward would determine not only its size but the way in which it should be enjoyed'. Government, he pointed out, has no resources of its own:

> The only way government can give one person money is to first take it from another person. Doing so represents the forcible using of one person, through the tax code, to serve the purposes of another.

This, according to Hayek, would be immoral, akin to slavery. Yet neither Hayek nor Polanyi was as extreme ideologically as they have sometimes been made out to be. Polanyi was no Marxist but rather stood in the tradition of the British cooperative movement. He wanted to reconcile what Hayek called 'economic freedom' with a society that rejected a market model grounded in the money motive. Equally, Hayek believed that markets required not only law and order but a competent government. He hated being called a conservative.

Their Legacy

Both these thinkers and their contemporaries—economists such as Irving Fischer (1867–1947), Ludwig von Mises (1881–1973), Joseph Schumpeter (1883–1950) and Dennis Robertson (1890–1963)—remained committed to the values of liberal democracy and believed that economics had great potential contributions to make to society. Although several of them (notably Schumpeter) thought that capitalism was destined to make way for socialism, they all believed that it could in the meantime lead to a better world. They all confronted the challenge of how society should manage paper money. Their varied and contrasting answers to the challenge would define the terms of the debate about money in the second half of the twentieth century. However, they all underestimated the power of naked money—money shorn of its moral and social clothing. In fact, money power, once released, would demolish the barriers that, they had too easily assumed, would prevent it from running amok. These men were refined representatives of early twentieth-century European culture—a culture that was destined to die out. For them it would have been inconceivable that within half a century educated people would regard the making of money as a high calling. They would have been shocked to know that a majority of undergraduates at top universities would see the value of education in monetary terms. They would have been dismayed to observe that the main purpose of leaders in the worlds of the professions, of business and banking would be to enrich themselves. They all assumed that the power of money, its tendency to delude people, would be held in check naturally—as it was in their day. This would be done either by the state, as Polanyi expected, or by individuals in their self-imposed, ethical behaviour and enlightened self-interest (Hayek) or in both ways. Making such assumptions was a flaw in their prognostications and policy proposals. Whereas Keynes's ideas on demand management were victorious, his insight into money as mysterious, unpredictable and potentially dangerous was neglected. They left the door open for money to escape.

Notes

1. Such questions still troubled such economists as Milton Friedman half a century later, after extensive experience of the difficulties of managing paper money. In 1986 Friedman said that while he was not advocating a return to the gold standard, he had come to the belief 'that leaving monetary and banking arrangements to the market would have produced a more satisfactory outcome than was actually achieved through government involvement'.
2. It was an intuition that, it must be said, sometimes led Keynes astray. For example, he admired the Soviet attempt to do without money. Indeed, he shared the objective. Although he saw capitalism as being driven by love of money, he would have liked to eliminate such a motive from it. Bolshevism had a moral edge over capitalism precisely in condemning personal enrichment and for its attempt to build a system that would not need to rely on it (Skidelsky 1992).
3. This conference is now viewed as a seminal turning point in twentieth-century liberal thought. Organised by Louis Rogier, French philosopher editor of Librarie de Medicis, key publisher for Rueff and other liberals, this brought together Raymond Aron, Robert Marjolin, Wilhelm Röpke, von Mises, Hayek and Michel Polanyi (brother of Karl).

4. As Ernst-Ulrich Petersmann, a leading international economic lawyer, wrote in 1983:

> The common starting point of the neoliberal economic theory is the insight that in any well-functioning market economy the "invisible hand" of market competition must by necessity be complemented by the "visible hand" of the law. (Slobodian 2018, 7)

5. Neoliberalism is also sometimes used almost as a term of abuse, to refer to market fundamentalism—the notion that, crudely expressed, 'markets are always right', 'let the market decide'; it is a view attributed to people who believe that the role of the state should be as small as possible.
6. HAMLET: 'there is nothing either good or bad, but thinking makes it so.'

Bibliography

Backhouse, R.E., and Bateman, B.W. (2011). *Capitalist Revolutionary: John Maynard Keynes*. Cambridge, Mass: Harvard University Press.

Chivvis, Christopher S. (2010). The Monetary Conservative: Jacques Rueff and Twentieth-century Free Market Thought.

Friedman, M., and Shwartz, A. (1963). *A Monetary History of the United States*.

Friedman, M., and Rose, D. (1998). *Two Lucky People: Memoirs*. University of Chicago Press.

Keynes, J. (1930). *Economic Possibilities for our Grandchildren*. In J.M. John Maynard Keynes (2015). "The Essential Keynes", p. 534, Penguin, UK; (1931) "The Future", Essays in Persuasion.

Harrod, R.F. (1951). *The Life of John Maynard Keynes*. London: Macmillan.

Hayek, F.A. (1944). *The Road to Serfdom*. London: George Routledge & Sons.

Macmillan, Harold (1938). *The Middle Way*. London: Macmillan and Sons.

Polanyi, K. (1944). *The Great Transformation*. New York: Amareon House.

Schmitt, C. (2003). *The Nomos of the Earth in the International Law of the Jus Publicum Europaeum*. New York: Telos Press, 2003, cited By Slobodian (2018).

Shackle, George (1967). *The Years of High Theory: Invention and Tradition in Economic Thought 1926–1939*. Cambridge University Press.

Skidelsky, R. (1992). *John Maynard Keynes: The Economist as Saviour, 1920–37* London: Macmillan.

Slobodian, Q. (2018). *Globalists: the end of empire and the birth of neoliberalism*. Cambridge: Harvard University Press.

Tawney, R.H. (1926). *Religion and the Rise of Capitalism*.

Vanberg, V. (2004). 'The Freiburg School: Walter Eucken and Ordoliberalism', Freiburger Diskussionspapiere zur Ordnungsökonomik, No. 04/11, Paper is available at: http://hdl.handle.net/10419/4343.

7

How Europe's Culture Kept Money Under Control (1940s and 1950s)

By and large, democracies get the money they deserve. They have particular needs, demands and ideas about the kind of world they want to live in and these are reflected in their money. So, this chapter is about the demand side of the relationship between money and society, with special reference to European culture in the 1940s and 1950s.

Despite pockets of privilege, post-war Europe was an egalitarian society. Western Europe, which is the focus of this chapter, saw the high tide of democratic socialism. The arts of the time reveal a deep engagement with existential problems experienced by individuals in contemporary societies. If one includes Samuel Beckett's *Waiting for Godot* (1952), the creative output of the period compares well with the flowering of modernism after World War I. In the process, it forged a new relationship between society and money—almost a new kind of money. The best authors of the period dwelt on money's insignificance in the grand scheme of things. Anyway, few people had any significant amounts of money and there was in any case not much to buy. Everybody knew how fragile the economy was, how thin the veneer of civilisation. People knew that wealth as well as humans were being (or had recently been) destroyed on a cosmic scale, for the second time in 30 years.

Money's power was curbed by social attitudes; government policy recognised and reflected that. Rigid control over interest rates, credit, international capital flows and nationalisation of banks were possible because people's social and political views favoured them. People had come to believe that money must be controlled at almost any cost, and so it was. They came to such views through watching, reading and absorbing ideas from the society round them. As a result money acquired a new and contested meaning as a tool to achieve social goals.

© The Author(s) 2019
R. Pringle, *The Power of Money*, https://doi.org/10.1007/978-3-030-25894-8_7

Economists whose views accorded with this climate of opinion were influential; others, such as free market liberals, went underground. Ideological seeds need to fall on fertile ground if they are to take root.

Disdain for the money motive and self-interest was pervasive in works with claims to art. Along with this consensus on a low valuation of money and the money motive (people who made a lot of money risked being called 'spivs'), went also a broad egalitarianism. Class distinctions remained very wide, accentuated by manners, dress codes, strict demarcation of occupations in class categories, but actual distribution of wealth and income was less unequal than at any other period of modern history. World War II was a great social leveller.

Not everybody was happy. The old upper middle class felt undervalued, under attack as described in the classic book on *The English Middle Classes* by Lewis and Maude (1950); but all classes shared in a gradual, broad-based return to moderate prosperity during the 1950s. National approaches diverged, in so far as this was permitted by the new international system. In Britain and the United States, economists were deeply involved in planning the post-war order. In Britain the 1941 Budget presented for the first time an accounting framework that made possible measurement of the output gap—the amount by which actual production fell short of potential output. Keynesian economic management became central to official policy-making. Governments learnt how to change the general level of taxation either to increase monetary demand in the economy (if there was forecast to be a large 'output gap') or to reduce the level of monetary demand by raising taxes if necessary to restrain a boom. Other countries used different methods—in France, there was more emphasis on central planning (but falling well short of the total control exercised in communist states), whereas West German governments gave priority to monetary stability and fiscal discipline.

Outside the Monetary Sphere

Large parts of the economy were taken out of the monetary sphere, notably education and health; in others, people continued to use money to pay for goods and services, but allocation of resources to these sectors was decided on political grounds, centrally, as were staffing and investment decisions. In Western Europe, the role of the private sector where market forces operated was confined to about half the economy—an arrangement supported by all political parties that lasted for a long time. Even in the early 1970s, supporters of market did not dare propose privatisation of what were seen as prestige sectors. In Britain free market ideas were kept alive not by economists in universities, occupied by Keynesians but to a large extent by financial journalists, men like Sir Oscar Hobson (1886–1961), City Editor of the *News Chronicle* and author of *How the City Works*, Sir Geoffrey Crowther (1907–72), editor of *The Economist* and author of *An Outline of Money*, and Wilfred King, author of *A History of the London Discount Market* (King, editor of *The Banker*, was my mentor). Whereas most academic economists shared society's disdain for money, these outstanding financial journalists reported and analysed the money markets of the city and the operations of the Bank of England. They and others like them had a deeper understanding of how money worked in markets than all but a few of the economists of the time.

People held a variety of concepts of what money was and how it should be managed. Keynes himself held to several and tried to reconcile them; for example, he thought that money should be actively managed, but, on the other hand, it should also have some contact with a standard such as gold. This is illustrated in the very different concepts and meanings of money that were held by different peoples and countries in the mid-twentieth century. For Germans in 1923, money signalled ruin. For Germans 24 years later, celebrating the currency reform and birth of the D-mark, it suggested hope. For Russians in the 1930s, as Solzhenitsyn's novel *One Day in the Life of Ivan Denisovic* shows, it could have a terrifying significance in that anyone who had any money risked being sent to the gulag. For economists such as Von Mises and Hayek as for the French economist Jacques Rueff, it was still gold (Rueff influenced General de Gaulle's decision to attack the Bretton Woods international system and privileged role of the dollar—a currency he claimed was without real value—in 1965). For Schumpeter and Polanyi it was credit. For Keynes it was gold-plated credit.

In the view of the liberal Wilhelm Röpke, in 1945, money offered salvation (see Chap. 6 for the background to the development of ordoliberalism and the Geneva School). The socialist authorities and the Allies assumed that the command economy inherited from the Nazis had to continue as 'the last bulwark against total chaos'. To end it was 'unthinkable'. But that is just what Röpke wanted to do. He called for the radical reform of the German monetary system. 'This reform must restore the mark as the true measure of values, as the trusted means of exchange' (Röpke 1945). Money prices alone would make the structure of production respond to what people wanted. Only money, by expressing all economic quantities in terms of a common denominator, made it possible again to compare revenues and costs, spending and saving, and facilitate rational economic calculation. He quotes Schopenhauer: 'Money alone is the absolute good' in the sense that it not only satisfies wants '*in concreto*' but also satisfies want as such '*in abstracto*'. As Dostoyevsky once memorably put it, 'Money is coined liberty, and so it is ten times dearer to a man who is deprived of freedom. If money is jingling in his pocket, he is half consoled, even though he cannot spend it' (Dostoyevsky 1861). Certainly, that is true for the millions who in the twentieth century emerged into freedom after having survived a totalitarian regime.

Top-Down Economic Management

For many years after World War II, in the democracies, people were in general content to let governments run the show. This top-down approach was widely shared not only in the industrially advanced nations but also in developing countries, many of which achieved independence during the period. The degree to which the state owned the means of production varied greatly. The broad movement, internationally, was towards the Left. The dangers of money were held in check by people's behaviour and general disdain for the money motive.

People tolerated restrictions on personal liberties that would be regarded as intolerable both by earlier and by later generations because of recent memories that survival had depended on cooperation and solidarity. People felt they had fought the war for noble purposes, to defend freedom. It would be absurd and disgusting to see men and women as if they were driven by pecuniary motives. What mattered was what united people, the general interest not the particular interests of individuals. People had 'needs', not demands; these needs could be met though the expanding welfare state. In Europe, the concept of citizenship was redefined to include the right to basic subsistence for all, health services for all, and protection against the evils of capitalism, especially unemployment. It was not that people hated money or that they tried to drive it out, as happened in the Communist block described in Chap. 5; just that money, the pecuniary motive, merchants and markets generally were treated with wary suspicion.

That helps to explains why money could be controlled even as it also played an important role in that part of the economy—still about half in most European countries, Australia, New Zealand and Canada—that remained in the market sector.

An Inert Substance

The war and immediate post-war period in Western Europe—right up to the 1960s—are often portrayed by economists as eras of financial 'repression'. This term refers to the fact that money and interest rates were controlled, and banks were subject to state direction. In many countries they were nationalised. Eventually, people and businesses would grow impatient with the controls. Crucially, however, the approach to money provided stability during the first years of post-war economic reconstruction. Over time, confidence grew; there would not be a repeat of the chaos following World War I. Confidence, a fragile plant, recovered. Without that period of relative stability and steady expansion, people would not have been willing to move to the next stage of development that saw substantial progress towards the restoration of a world economy.

Society and policy worked in relative harmony. In such a culture, money had to serve a wider social purpose. Yet money, financial institutions and people who dealt in money were viewed with so much suspicion that money's role remained passive. It was inert, like a World War II bomb with its fuse taken out. Society controlled money. For a long time, that general approach suited people's mood. Gradually, however, people became impatient with the controls and started to fret. Control over money came at a high cost; it was unable to perform its proper functions well.

Bibliography

Crowther, G. (1940). *An Outline of Money*. London: Thomas Nelson Sons.
Dostoyevsky, F. (1861). *The House of the Dead* translated by Constance Garnett.
Hesse, H. (1943). *The Glass Bead Game*.
Hobson, O. (1955). *How the City Works*. News Chronicle Books.
King, W.T.C. (1936). *History of the London Discount Market*. London: Routledge.
Lewis, A., and Maude, F. (1950). *The English Middle Classes*.
Lewis, C.S. (1942). *The Screwtape Letters*.
———. (1943). *The Abolition of Man*.
Orwell, George (1945). *Animal Farm*.
——— (1949). *Nineteen Eight-Four*.
Röpke, W. (1945). The Solution to the German Problem.
Solzhenitsyn, A. (1962). *One Day in the Life of Ivan Denisovic*.
Waugh, Evelyn (1945). *Brideshead Revisited*.

8

New Money from the New World

Americans often regard themselves as a 'chosen people' beyond history. Their revolution represents a decisive break from the cycle of rise, corruption and fall of empires. Their breakthrough, as pioneers, would be followed by other nations as their peoples also became free. Americans hold the precious flame of republican freedom, an escape from the old rule of princes and priests. The hopes of the world rest with them. In 1945, they find themselves with supreme power. What will they do?

The answer came swiftly. Even before the war ended, America's determination to avoid a repeat of the chaos following World War I was clear. Their response: craft a new idea of money and a new role for it, together with new institutions. As ever, beliefs and passions came first. Americans would save the world and make money in the process. It worked. The popularity of US culture softened the hard edges of US money power and helped it win global acceptability while loans and grants from US-led international institutions spread US ideals and ways of doing business. Gradually, after being discredited by the Great Depression, capitalism, the profit motive and use of monetary measures of success became more respectable. But their idea of money and the right use of it was still a long way from the twenty-first century's idea. Domestically and internationally, money was placed under supervision—it was gradually let out of its wartime prison of controls but kept on parole. This and the following chapter aim to show how interactions between money, society and culture changed the world after World War II. In time, it would challenge the controlled, repressive regime described in the previous chapter.

© The Author(s) 2019
R. Pringle, *The Power of Money*, https://doi.org/10.1007/978-3-030-25894-8_8

Money for Democracy

Importantly, the new ideas of money came branded with American optimism and democratic spirit, a much-needed antidote to Europe's gloom and failed experiments with despotism.

Money would help America realise its ideals at home and around the world. The land holding such a sacred trust—humanity's hopes for the future—could not rely on traditional weapons of imperial powers such as armies, colonisation and territorial expansion. But Americans were far too practical a people to believe that preaching the virtues of freedom, democracy and representative government would be sufficient to change the bad ways of the Old World. Naturally, they would use tools that had brought relative prosperity to its continent—business enterprise under the rule of law supported by active government. If used wisely, money would sow the precious seeds of liberty and progress.

At home, the state took on a commitment to full employment, a pledge that also called for it to play much bigger role in the management of money, since it was now believed to be lack of money demand that caused unemployment and misery, such as that of the 1930s. That is what the new economics taught. So, money and state action were needed both to achieve full employment at home and to project American power and its ideals around the world. Money became a weapon in the armoury of a global cultural, political and economic superpower. Old attitudes to money would not do the job now required of it; neither the chaotic free-for-all and competitive devaluations of the interwar period nor the 'rigid' old gold standard order of the Victorian age would do what America desired. Political and economic circumstances had changed drastically, and so had economic theory. With American political and military muscle, it was not only desirable but also feasible to develop a new idea of money and to fashion new institutions to manage it. These institutions would use American money to help spread American ideals and culture around the world and, of course, benefit American business. While the American concept of money evolved from the Western tradition, it was new. Indeed, it was revolutionary.

The United States, itself being the result of a rebellion against British domination, would neither occupy nor rule other countries. If it occasionally had to use military force this would only be in defence of what it regarded as its vital interests. America's interests were seen as synonymous with those of humanity. Force might, if necessary, also be used to support money power, but there again all in the service of high ideals. America was the dominant superpower, but that power would not be used to build an empire on the old model—the model that had held sway for thousands of years—of territorial expansion. Rather, its money, its resources, ideals and its example would peacefully spread ideals of freedom and democracy to independent nations, which would adopt them by popular consent. The power of the purse would help spread the ideals of the founding fathers and of Abraham Lincoln round the world. Money power would also help to dismantle the remains of old empires, such as the British and French empires; such imperialists had in the view of Americans plundered and exploited their colonial possessions—that is, they had taken money out of them. America would give or lend money to them, and in the process make sure they dismantle preferential trade and financial links with old imperial powers. Thus would the United States build a new world order on the ruins of the old.

In future, money would be placed at the service of freedom, democracy—and profit. Not only would US money ditch old ideas and empires, it would also be used to measure success. The benefits to receiving countries—the yardsticks of achievement—would be expressed in the language of money. The newly developed concept of gross domestic product, of the national income of a country in a year, would be used to measure political and economic progress. Standards of living, GDP per capita, expressed of course in US dollars, would become objective measures of success. They would be used to measure the progress of nations as they climbed the ladder towards the American ideal and finally 'graduated'. Other measures of progress were also used, such as the extent to which democratic institutions were established and flows of money and trade liberalised. Americans expected to be loved. They would be so popular that voters in other countries would elect regimes favourable to US interests. Each nation would be responsible for its monetary policies, but they could operate only within the constraints of an international system. US business would have the whole world as its market. It would help realise God's design by spreading the gospel of enterprise and the profit motive as a power for good in the world.

Plainly, the tasks given to money in the new American dispensation were much more ambitious than in the old imperial monetary system. Then its job had been to hold the ring—to provide an unyielding, hard money standard to which everybody, governments, capitalists, were supposed to be subject. Now its task was nothing else than to remake the world, set it free of imperialist exploitation, and give its blessings to societies where money and the ballot box had replaced military force, and invisible liquidity had replaced the jackboot. Enterprise would flourish.

Another Frontier

Half a century after the disappearance of the old frontier to the West, America now had a new frontier and ethical ambition—to push forward the boundaries of democracy and liberty. Money would be used as a peaceful weapon in this struggle. Desperate for money, countries willingly signed up to this new deal, as the United States was just about the only place with any money to spare. Its public and private sectors moved into the vacuum. A new world was born in an outburst of high hopes for a better world, transforming the gloomy age of depression and war into relief, recovery and rejuvenation. American power led by American ideals and a seductively modern brand would be a force for good and for profit. It not only claimed that political power everywhere should be grounded in popular consent but also held out the promise of prosperity.

The foundations laid down in the 1950s, extended by US power, would in time build a global economy. But there was nothing like the modern individualist global money culture as developed at least 40 years later (see Chap. 12). Money remained a servant of the state and of the big corporation. Loyalty to the group, the collective, the community, the State, the nation was the virtue that was most highly valued. Economically, the recovery from the world war was mercifully quick—assisted by defence spending for the Korean War of 1950–53 and the Cold War between the West and the Soviet Union. In the United States, expansion continued through the 1950s and into the 1960s, bringing about a remarkable rise in affluence. Politically, in all major powers, conservatism reigned, with Eisenhower in the White House, Macmillan prime minister of the United Kingdom, Adenauer in Germany and de Gaulle in France.

The Age of Keynes, Samuelson and GDP

As governments tried to avoid the mistakes that were made after WWI and the competitive devaluations of the 1930s, reparations were limited, there was no attempt to return to the classic gold standard, and controls over money and banking remained both at the national and international levels. Practice also reflected the new Keynesian teaching—a startlingly new approach that equipped economists to tell politicians what to do. Keynesian policies of demand management reached their peak under President Kennedy, who launched an ambitious and —for a time—largely successful programme of fiscal expansion. The young saw him as a beacon of hope and change in a rather dull, backward-looking world, a world full of petty moral and legal restrictions, a world lacking opportunity and social space. They flocked to his banner in their millions. With low unemployment levels, people felt secure, despite the Cuban missile crisis of 1962, in the world created by the post-war settlements. Gradually, a decade of growth, security and stability bred also increasing impatience and irreverence.

America's creative applications of money resources were supported by several powerful forces. One was US corporations' search for new markets, resulting in a large rise in outward foreign direct investment in Europe, Latin America and Asia. Another was the government's commitment to full employment. As any return to the levels of unemployment of the 1930s was politically unacceptable, in 1946 Congress passed the Employment Act making it responsible for promoting 'maximum employment, production and purchasing power'. Another was the new influence of economists in policy-making—both at national level and in international institutions such as the IMF (on which more below). Samuelson (1915–2009), the first American to be awarded the Nobel prize for economics, wrote the best-selling economics textbook of all time. *Economics: An Introductory Analysis*, first published in 1948, is based on the principles of Keynesian economics. In its 19 editions, it has sold 4 million copies in 40 languages. Samuelson believed that economics had progressed to the point where it could offer clear advice to politicians. Full employment requires that there be sufficient demand in the economy; demand results from consumption, government spending and investment in new capital equipment. He offers tempered support for monetary policy. Through its influence on money and credit, the Federal Reserve can, he says, 'hope' to affect the level of real and money GDP.

The active role of government was supported by the demonstration in 1958 by A. W. Phillips, a British economist, of a relation between inflation and unemployment—low inflation was associated with high unemployment, and high inflation with lower unemployment—known as the 'Phillips Curve'. In 1960 Samuelson and Robert Solow found that the Phillips curve relation applied over a certain period in the United States. Economists seized on these two discoveries which, taken together, allowed estimates of the amount by which the actual output of an economy fell short of its potential output—and what should be done to fill the gap.

Business and Banks Lead International Expansion

Americans instinctively understood this more purposive idea of money and took it to their hearts. It found a place in their visions for their society and for the world. It opened up new frontiers, just when the old frontiers had closed and only frustration seemed to lie ahead. Private business jumped at the chance, rejoicing in the recognition—granted by the new theories—that money allowed, even required, imagination and creativity to play key roles in corporate life. And it would justify profits as well; good businessmen would be those who make money out of their imagination. To sell the American dream along with products and services 'made in the USA'—that is how the United States would tame money.

Huge corporations arose to meet the fast-rising consumer demand from America's vast domestic market. International expansion was led by its major corporations. And they were followed by the big banks. Indeed, the 1960s witnessed a great burst of US banking internationally. Up to then, only JP Morgan, Bank of America and Citibank had extensive overseas operations—and these were centred in London. But during the 1960s such banks vastly increased their overseas branch networks and were also joined by dozens of small banks. At the same time, New York for the first time opened its doors to foreign banks.

Money, capital, investment, call it what you will—it was available. And for many years, it came from one principal source, the United States. Having doubled during the war, US gross national product doubled again between 1947 and 1960, from US$239 billion to about US$500 billion. The growth of 3.5% per annum in real terms was far more rapid than that from the start of the twentieth century to World War II. And the United States also learnt to recycle its external surplus by making outward loans and investments. In other words, it learnt how to be an international banker. After a pause, Wall Street too responded to the brighter prospects. It had gone through many lean years. It had collapsed in the Great Crash of 1929, been blamed for the Great Depression of the 1930s, then managed by the New Deal radicals who wanted to take power from the financial moguls and who broke up the banks. Then came another war. The election of General Eisenhower as president in 1952 sparked a bull market that was destined to roll on for 15 years—one of the longest in history. The investment habit spread to wider sections of the population. Having a stockbroker became a natural adornment to middle-class life, as mutual funds attracted crowds of new shareholders into the market. Nothing like it had been seen since the 1920s. The consumer boom would, with intermissions, run for the rest of the century.

In contrast with the static idea of money typical in Europe, American money was dynamic. Americans would make it work for them, whereas Europeans received it as a gift of the state. Americans used it as a pledge in the service of a new world order. You can call it an empire if you like (Americans obviously did not). But if so, it was an empire powered by money in the service of enterprise, constructed around rules about money, its success measured in terms of monetary categories like gross domestic product—and it was a regime in which trust in money was essential. Luckily, the US dollar and the US power provided that trust.

How and why did this come about? For that we have to turn to the United States itself. How Americans lived at home determined how they would change the world abroad. Money was to be an instrument for spreading freedom, as they understood it. But that did not imply that at home people were expected to pursue their interests by making money, still less making its pursuit the object of their work and lives. Not at all. Money was an instrument of collective, not individual, achievement. It was to be a tool of moral progress. This would mark a determined effort to re-connect money to a broad political and social philosophy.

Bibliography

Samuelson, Paul (1948). *Economics: An Introductory Analysis.*

9

American Culture and the Dollar After World War II

Having immersed myself in the literature, sociology and public debate of the post-war period, the sound that I hear most clearly, from all the noises that reach me, is the busy sound of America's can-do optimism at work. It was a society with many faults, and we shall come to these, but it had its virtues. People led lives infused with an ideal of public service as well as personal ambition. They were part of an America that looked outwards and took the lead. Money-making was not the main purpose of work, nor was it the only measure of success, nor did it define people's ambitions or the ways in which they expressed their dreams and desires; nor did they disdain it, as Europeans did. They used money to promote American (which they regarded as universal) ideals rather than individual ambitions. They were acquisitive, but without avarice. The arrangements they made for dealing with money accorded with such values. They made a money to suit them, their outlook and their aspirations.

Money's Damage

Europeans often view American optimism as naive. Yet the cultural masterpieces in literature and art produced by American novelists and dramatists reveal their strong sense of the tragic side of life. They are optimistic despite fate, despite all the odds stacked against men and women. Life calls for bravery and heroism as well as stoicism, as well as enterprise. Such are the social values that, ultimately, give monetary value to the dollar.

© The Author(s) 2019
R. Pringle, *The Power of Money*, https://doi.org/10.1007/978-3-030-25894-8_9

Some of the greatest novels of the wartime and post-World War II era dwell on human motivations, fate and history as if to underline the insignificance of money and monetary matters in the grand drama of life and death. Hemingway's *For Whom the Bell Tolls* (1940), for example, celebrates moral qualities at the opposite end of the spectrum from those associated with the monetary economy: physical courage, duty, friendship, faith, the supernatural; above all, facing death, it promotes the need to live in the present. There is nothing else than now. 'There is neither yesterday, certainly, nor is there any tomorrow. How old must you be before you know that?' Arthur Miller's *Death of a Salesman*, 1949 and Tennessee Williams's *A Streetcar named Desire* (1947) show the corrupting, humanly damaging effect of money in distinctively American settings. Or turn to *A Long Day's Journey into Night* (1940–41), by Eugene O'Neil. Perhaps the greatest of all American dramas, it covers a single day in August 1912 at the seaside home of the Tyrones, a family of four, James and Mary Tyrone and their two sons, Jamie and Edmund. The work deals with the serious personal issues of four family members as they grapple with their individual failings and collective deterioration. Conflicts in this dystopian family are rooted in money and its power to isolate, to alienate family members from each other, despite their deep love for each other. Fog is everywhere, the fog of separateness, of money. The father laments that if he had not given up his ill-paid theatre career for money, to succour his family, he would have been a great actor. He sent his wife to an inexperienced doctor so as to save money, a decision that led to her addiction to morphine. Jamie the eldest son clearly sees the truth; he sees that the others are dreamers, and that in reality his father is a 'tightwad' spending his money on his own pleasure and not on his family. The mother is permanently drugged. Edmund the younger son faces a stark choice: avoid reality or have a mental breakdown. Such thoughtful masterpieces, created within a few years of each other, should reach out to us today. With the affluence of the 1950s and 1960s, with affordable consumer goods creating new mass markets, a much more upbeat mood emerges. But awareness of the dark side of life is always ready to spring back into American consciousness.

The Great Age of Hollywood…

Hollywood projected American glamour globally, thrilling and charming millions. It showcased America's new take on money, teaching millions of people the spirit required to acquire it, how they should behave when they have it, how to use it, how it is potentially available to everybody, distant, yet here and now if you know how. The movies accustomed audiences worldwide to American attitudes to money, to the chances as well as hazards of a culture where individual effort could bring rewards to individuals, and where glamour, beauty and adventure were all to be had, at a price. Now people around the world saw alternatives were available to their settled way of life. Those interested and attracted could go to the United States, as millions had done, or they could try to import those ideas into their own societies. The 'American dream', already described in Chap. 4, was brought to life in films and the rapidly increasing spread of TV in the developed countries. Hollywood reached out to people around the world, linking mass production, mass marketing and technological improvement to an enlightened democratic spirit. Progress resulted from private enterprise, 'know-how', a legal system to protect property rights, free speech and freedom. For women, especially, all over the world, films and magazine stories about American life offered the allure of an 'American dream'. New York City especially represented a sort of utopia where every dream and desire could become true. At the same time the iconic film *Citizen Kane* (1941), regularly rated the greatest movie ever, shows money and power as isolating the individual; they drive out happiness and fulfilment. Yet the message is not: avoid pursuit of money. The message is that suffering for a belief—even a belief in money—can turn you too into a tragic hero.

Money in Popular Sociology

Best-selling books in popular sociology convey the mood of the time.

Lonely Man

The Lonely Crowd by David Riesman et al. provides a sociological analysis of the changing significance of money—cash—through people's behaviour as consumers. In the nineteenth-century stereotype, a man of great wealth, the crazy millionaire, is someone who, having established his status as a producer, can do as he pleases on the pleasure front. He could hang a 'Do Not Disturb' sign over his play as well as over his work. The consumer at this stage is marked by 'a passionate desire to make things his'. At that time the adornments of wealthy consumption did not rapidly become obsolete but were good for a lifetime. The new consumer of the 1950s, however, 'seeks experiences rather than things and yearns to be guided by others' as to what they should purchase and appreciate. They are always anxious to follow their peer group and hate to outshine others.

The new man also has a different attitude to money at work. If he is an entrepreneur, he must find respected motives for his business. He will tune in to others 'to see what they are saying about what a proper business ought to be'. It will not be mainly about money. What concerns businessmen is whether their company has attitudes and an ethic 'which an up-to-date company is supposed to have'. Profits are just one among many symbols of status. The ambition of young businessmen is to turn their companies into the model they learnt at business school. Riesman and his colleagues do not admire the type of character that they describe so brilliantly. They wish people could achieve greater autonomy. They do not criticise them for chasing after money, not at all, but rather for 'seeking to become like each other' (Riesman et al. 1950/1953).

Organisation Man

William Whyte's famous 1956 book portrays a culture dominated by a collectivist outlook. Men prefer to serve an organisation, live in suburbs, and they fear slipping below the benchmark income that defines the middle class. The younger couples, however, are optimistic; throughout their early adult years they have 'known nothing but consistently rising prosperity, personal as well as general'. Suburbia has further confirmed them in their optimism. They save little. They have little sense of capital—'the benevolent economy has insulated the organization man from having to manipulate large personal sums'. He does not even have to think much about money. The organisation man is acquisitive, but it is stability that really counts: 'Money itself is secondary'. They care about budgets, not money. Regular, unchanging monthly payments are made on all major items. They care about their goods, but are apathetic about money. As regards students in their last year at college, one recruiter went through 300 interviews without one applicant mentioning the salary. An offer from a smaller company will be rejected in favour of a large company at a lower salary:

'For the most part seniors (students) do not like to talk of the future in terms of the dollar—on several occasions I have been politely lectured by someone for so much as bringing the point up'. They talk little about money, but a lot about the good life. Teaching appeals as being associated with a calm life—'a touch of elms and quiet streets'. *It is not the money that counts.*

Affluent Man

In *The Affluent Society* (1958), one of the most influential texts of popular economics of the twentieth century, Galbraith attacked inequality and the fact that public services and public spending on infrastructure had lagged badly behind private consumption: 'Here, in an atmosphere of *private opulence and public squalor*, the private goods have full sway' (italics added). Galbraith's criticisms came at a time when, in historical perspective, measures of inequality were actually at a low point. Equally, the ratio of public spending to private consumption was also in fact relatively high. As for his views on inflation, he accepted the 'conventional wisdom' (a term he coined) that this should be combated by government measures such as prices and incomes policies. But he was no apologist for Marxism: 'Under capitalism, man exploits man. Under communism, it's just the opposite.' Though a caustic social critic, Galbraith shared many of the assumptions of his time. People were not inherently self-seeking, large corporations would continue to dominate the economy, and inequality would be reduced. These expectations were wrong on all counts: it would come to be widely assumed that people did seek their own interests; small firms would become more important as a source of employment; inequalities of wealth and income would grow.

Manipulated Man

The 1950s was the decade when motivational research took over advertising. Vance Packard's book *The Hidden Persuaders* brought their techniques to popular attention. He showed to an innocent audience that corporate advertisers had already learnt how to manipulate their hidden desires, needs and drives to find those points of vulnerability—especially factors such as the wish to conform, need for oral stimulation and the yearning for security. People did not buy on the basis of price. Each major brand of cigarette attracted customers with a 'typical' personality profile. Buick began selling cars that 'make you feel like the man you are'. The buying process came to be viewed as 'an interaction between the personality of the car and the personality of the individual'. Then there are strategies that manipulate our 'secret miseries and desires'—especially guilt. This all seems normal now, but was shocking when new. People gaped when told that if they sleep with closed windows and an air conditioner on, they 'subconsciously yearn for a return to the womb'.

The Loyal Wife

Corporations used such research methods also on their prospective employees (assumed to be male) and their wives. They examined a man's home life and interviewed 'the wife' before hiring him. It is amusing to find out what corporations were looking for in the wife. She should be (1) highly adaptable, (2) highly gregarious and (3) realise her husband belongs to the corporation. A writer in The Harvard Business Review went even further, telling wives that they must not demand too much of her husband's time or interest: 'Because of his single-minded concentration on his job, even his sexual activity is relegated to a secondary place' (cited by Aldous Huxley in *Brave New World Revisited*, 1959).

Indeed, from the perspective of the twenty-first century, it is stunning that all these books, all written by men who saw themselves as progressive thinkers, uniformly accept the roles women occupied and the attitudes of men to them. Business life is for men only. These men have either fought in World War II or have grown up during the war. They won the war through discipline, following orders and teamwork. They have the security of knowing their basic needs will be met by the system, and many contrast it with the insecurity and joblessness of the pre-war years. If the government keeps its side of the bargain, delivering full employment, they would keep their side; and it works. So long as they earn a fair reward for their work, and budget carefully, money will take care of itself. It is not an overriding motive. From this perspective, the United States, land of enterprise and rugged individualism, seems almost a non-monetary economy. The subordinate status of women fits the pattern.

Racial Exclusion

Also, the stability of the era rested to some extent on racial exclusion. Although legally all adults had the right to vote since the Civil War, in practice various laws in southern states, such as literacy and religious tests (known as Jim Crow laws) amounted to de-democratisation. Southern Democrats became a powerful conservative force—their alliance with conservative Republicans facilitated civility and reduced partisanship in politics: 'But it did so at the great cost of keeping civil rights—and America's full democratization—off the political agenda' (Levitsky and Ziblatt 2018).

What was only seen as decent good manners at the time would be viewed by later generations as conservative complacency, coupled with prejudice.

Business life was conventional, conformity gained at the cost of a denial of individuality and of many people's civil rights. Morality followed an equally conventional model. But the age had many virtues as well, including a spirit of optimism and idealism. Above all, people were expected to keep money and the money instinct under control. They would do this naturally, as good citizens. The virtues that mattered were loyalty to the corporation or union, lifelong service, organisational skills, solidarity and a collective spirit; the interests of the group came before one's own. This ethic was reflected in the prevailing monetary arrangements—low, stable interest rates, a dollar tied to gold, conventional bankers serving their community (as portrayed by James Stewart in the movie, *It's A Wonderful Life*, of 1946), financial stability and little innovation whether in money or anything else. Again, society got the money it deserved.

America's semi-monetary society created a universally desired money. The preponderance of the US dollar as a world currency, which has endured from that time to the present, is not the product of the Federal Reserve, or Wall Street, or even of the vast American economy, though these all influence it, but above all of American values. Its ascendancy can be traced back to a society that did not glorify money and to a time when people would not let it play a major role in their lives. When people all over the world acquire dollars, they hold more than a means of payment or store of value. They share in the American dream.

Bibliography

Galbraith, J.K. (1958). *The Affluent Society*.
Hemingway, Ernest (1940). *For Whom the Bell Tolls*.
Huxley, Aldous (1959). *Brave New World Revisited*.
Levitsky, S., and Ziblatt, D. (2018). *How Democracies Die*.
Miller, Arthur (1949). *Death of a Salesman*.
O'Neil, Eugene (1940–1941). *A Long Day's Journey into Night*.
Packard, Vance (1957). *The Hidden Persuaders*.
Riesman, David with Nathan Glazer and Reuel Denney (1950/1953). *The Lonely Crowd: A Study of the Changing American Character*.
Whyte, W.H. (1956). *The Organization Man*.
Williams, Tennessee (1947). *A Streetcar named Desire*.

10

The Century's Hinge
(Mid-1960s to Late 1970s)

The American-led order brought international stability and material progress and, in the process, fostered new appetites for choice and economic freedom. This chapter looks at the period between the late 1960s and the late 1970s, a period that broke the mould of the post-war consensus. During the period, seeds were sown that would in time germinate a new *Weltanschauung*—outlook and way of life (to be described in Chap. 12). The century creaked on its hinges.

What were the factors that aroused demands for greater economic freedoms? Economically, it was a period of further growth and rising optimism—until shattered by the quadrupling of oil prices by a cartel of oil-producing countries in 1972–73. It was a high tide of Keynesian-inspired fiscal expansion going under the name of 'demand management' which resulted in accelerating inflation. It saw a rapid rise in cross-border lending and international financial growth, focussed on the burgeoning Eurodollar market (a market in US dollars deposited in banks outside the United States). As the generation that had fought the war went into retirement, and as great industries such as coal-mining declined, freedom started to be accorded a higher value than solidarity. As wartime memories faded, rising levels of education and affluence stimulated desires for a freer society. People had more money and could save more. The coordination of activity by government bureaucrats was not working well. Evidently, it would have to be replaced with an alternative: people started to ask, could markets do the job?

© The Author(s) 2019
R. Pringle, *The Power of Money*, https://doi.org/10.1007/978-3-030-25894-8_10

Leading Trends

The period was marked by several trends that eventually facilitated the emergence of a new culture.

First, it witnessed the emergence of a global, cosmopolitan market in literature, art, and music. Such a market had existed for the elite since the eighteenth century, but this had been destroyed by the twentieth century's world wars and revolutions. Now new international markets sprung up. There was an 'avant garde' market for intellectuals and a mass market through which new ideas—including new ideas about money—would later spread quickly round the world. And this was long before the advent of the Internet; innovations in the arts, literature, movies and the sciences were still disseminated by radio, TV, books and films.

Second, it showed a growing concern with securing faster economic growth and a search for new ways of stimulating such growth. This led in some countries to agonised debates about the merits of economic planning. In Europe, France led the way. Germany upheld its version of a social market economy and showed the way to the future of central banking with its commitment to central bank independence, sound monetary policies and price stability. Perhaps, asked people in other countries, we should let markets play a bigger role in the economy, as they do in America and Germany. Or could we stimulate long-term growth simply by adding to monetary demand? This was indeed the course advocated by some leading British economists.

Thirdly, successful people grew impatient with the egalitarian ideology and high marginal tax rates of the time. By comparison with the distribution of income and wealth either at the start of the twentieth century or at its end, inequality in developed economies remained low throughout the period.

Fourthly, in a world still dominated by big government and big corporations, some people began to ask questions like these: is not small sometimes beautiful? (The book by Kurt Schumacher, *Small is Beautiful*, was published in 1973, to immediate acclaim.) Should my wife be subject to a corporate scrutiny and pass a litmus test before I can be offered a position? Are rules against, for example, employing divorced people just? Do I have to wear the same 'grey flannel suit' as my neighbours? Oh and by the way, my wife/daughter/sister also wants to work, not just as a typist but as a professional. Looking back on it from the perspective of 2020, it is difficult to grasp how heavy and pervasive was the blanket of conservatism against which the new ideas had to struggle.

During this period such ideas—ideas that would change the world—barely broke the surface. They were like seeds ready to poke their heads up into the air when they were strong enough and the air warmer.

The American Challenge

Not everybody 'on the receiving end' of the new order imposed by the United States loved it. Many feared their traditions would soon be overwhelmed by American money, power and by its cultural allure. As Harold James, a historian, has put it: 'For every country other than the United States, the post-war settlement was in fact *sugar coating on the bitter pill of dollar hegemony*, which favoured American companies and workers' (italics added, James 2018). This feeling strengthened the Left and gave the Communist states led by the USSR the chance to expand their influence. The West was still on the defensive ideologically. Most developing countries had left-of centre governments led by people often educated at leading universities in Europe where they picked up a Marxist analysis of capitalism.

Anti-Americanism in Europe

By the late 1970s the Marxist attack on capitalism had been successfully resisted politically but, as an ideology, Marxism still pervaded cultural studies and the attitudes of Western intellectuals. Right-wing polemicists also attacked what they saw as US money centrism. From the conservative Right, it was viewed as vulgar and as a threat. For the Marxist Left, it was as an instrument of the US capitalist takeover of the world. Nationalists resented the humbling of European power. Britain suffered multiple humiliations at the hands of its 'great ally', including being forced to abandon its attempt (in alliance with France) to take back the Suez Canal in 1956 from its seizure by President Nasser of Egypt. The British looked resentfully at the balmy friendship America seemed to have struck up with erstwhile enemies, Germany (the bit of it remaining in the West) and Japan. The surge of investment in Europe by large American multinational corporations aroused a demand for a European response. This was articulated by the best-selling book, *Le Defi Americain (1967)*, by Jean-Jacques Servan-Schreiber. The book dramatically underscored the growth of the multinationals and the economic power of American business in Europe. American managers knew better than Europeans how to exploit Europe's resources and markets, so that Europeans might soon become mere subcontractors. Servan-Schreiber betrayed Europeans' anxiety that their economies were being outclassed. However, most people rejoiced in the economic recovery with low unemployment and understood that US leadership was benign as well as essential. The contrast with the chaotic and disastrous years after World War I was obvious, at least to the older generation that had experienced both periods.

Globally, a Left-Wing Mood Prevailed...

Intellectual debate was dominated by a struggle over Marxism. This ideology remained the banner under which those who opposed the status quo, who disliked the 'Americanisation' of society and economics, and argued against liberalisation, gathered. Intellectual life in France and Italy was dominated by dull debates among Marxists. Even in West Germany, where sound money policies and market capitalism took root soon after the war, leading intellectuals such as Jurgen Habermas used a Marxist framework of thought for their explorations of history, society and culture. Despite the accumulating evidence of the horrors perpetrated by the Soviet authorities in the interwar years, many intellectuals continued to support the Soviet Union, as dramatised by the notorious Cambridge spy scandal. (Five spies are known to have been recruited to be Soviet agents during their education at Cambridge University in the 1930s, among them Kim Philby, who defected to the USSR in 1963; the last one, John Cairncross, was only publicly unmasked in 1990. There may have been others who have never been identified. They pursued successful careers in UK government service and passed large amounts of secret intelligence to Moscow. Several were originally motivated by a conviction not only that communism was a superior ideology to capitalism but also that the Soviet Union was the best political and military defence against fascism. The Soviet Union was a key ally in World War II.) But the brutal suppression of the Prague Spring in 1968 shamed many people into giving up their support. And by then a new kind of rage against 'the West' was ready to take its place—as shown in the student revolt of that year. And as we have seen, a strand running through all varieties of Marxism—and indeed Left-wing thought generally—was a hatred of money and the profit motive as organising principles in society. It was money, the cash nexus, above all else that was seen as the force making for alienation, spiritual and cultural death, and a wasteland of isolated egos.

Deep into the 1970s, long after the revival of free market economics, many intellectuals expected socialism in its various guises eventually to triumph just about everywhere outside North America.

...Along with a State-Led Development Model

In Asia, Africa and Latin America similar debates were taking place, and there too generally the left made the running intellectually. In India, the governments that took over when the country became independent in 1947 adopted a state-led, socialist model of development—marked by a large public sector, high levels of protection against imports, encouragement of domestic production that competed with imports, and five-year plans reminiscent of the Soviet model. This model left more room than in the USSR for capitalist enterprise and markets but placed most of the economy in the hands of state-owned enterprises; Steel, mining, machine tools, water, telecommunications, insurance and electrical plants, among other industries, were nationalised. Elaborate licences, regulations and the accompanying red tape, commonly referred to as Licence Raj, were required to set up business in India between 1947 and 1990. In other words, money and the profit motive were deeply suspect and potentially anti-social. Senior civil servants, often educated at Oxbridge, received high status—after all, they didn't work for money. On the monetary front, successive Indian governments waged an endless and fruitless campaign against India's gold culture; India had long been the world's largest gold market as gold was assumed to be the best store of value.

British Society and Culture

Using a contemporary account of British society by Anthony Sampson, a perceptive observer, I pick out a few 'vignettes' related to the social life of/ attitudes to money to illustrate the changing mood (Sampson 1962, 1971). There was talk of the big money to be made in commercial TV, then in its infancy. Advertisers were slow to realise the immense power of the medium— and then, suddenly, says Sampson, 'a whole new breed of millionaires emerged in the course of a few months'. They enjoyed huge influence in changing British lifestyles: 'they were able to project a whole way of life, a whole background of education and values, onto millions of screens'—and it was a world in which money played a much more important role than it did at that time in real life. The basic idea was to make people dissatisfied with their possessions and so go out and buy more. Patronage fell into the hands of what Sampson calls a 'wild bunch' of agents, financiers, radio pedlars and cinema owners. In cultural terms, said Sampson, the first years of commercial TV left very little behind—'only a great heap of money'.

Next, the money in banking: 'Over the past ten years', he reports, 'bankers have slowly emerged into the public eye, like snails coming out of their shells'. Look at the exclusive 'merchant banks', still mostly run by old families like the Rothschilds, Barings, Hambros and Lazards. While British industry lurches from one crisis to another, merchant banks have done better and better. They are the international men, always on the move. 'They appear as prophets not only of the new Britain, but of the new Europe—a Europe united not by a common idealism, but by a common interest in money' (see Chap. 15). Then there are the commercial banks—High Street banks or what used to be called 'clearing banks' like Barclays and Natwest. They live 'in a strange limbo between nationalization and free enterprise'. There is little competition between banks, all of which offer the same services, charge almost identical rates of interest on loans and severely restrict the kinds of loans they can make (no mortgages, for example). They charge the same fees. However, they are 'safe' and 'placid': 'In their dedication, their *lack of greed and their sense of quiet service*, the joint-stock bankers provide a placid, safe core to financial Britain' (italics added).

But they are stuck in a Victorian pattern, catering for the property-owning middle classes, while ignoring everybody else; only 30% of the adult population has a bank account. The banks do not even try to attract the majority of adults without a bank account—as shown by the fact that the banks open when everybody is at work and close before they come home. But could anybody expect them to be in touch with ordinary people when the board directors are public school men and 25% of their board directors have been at to one school—Eton?

Then there's monetary policy: Who is responsible for it? Nobody knows. Sampson encounters 'a maze of mystification', with the trail ending 'somewhere in the confused regions between the Treasury and the Bank of England', both highly secretive institutions: 'What is especially depressing to the outside inquirer is how little either the Bank or the Treasury accepts any need to enlighten Parliament or the public.'

Markets Feared as 'a Kind of Hell'

Even a good public school education is not enough to enter the City; you also need connections: 'The justification is that the city of London is based on *trust.*' The idea of employing an outsider, let alone a man of colour, or a woman in a senior role, is unthinkable. Sampson does discuss 'the new plutocracy' of business, though the sums of money are trivial in comparison with 2018 sums (no chairman of even Britain's biggest companies at the time was paid more than £400,000 in 2018 money, a sum that top executives these days would sniff at). No wonder younger people are looking for an alternative, he says. Sampson sniffs a mood, just gaining strength in the early 1970s, in favour of giving more scope to individual freedom and to money prices set in markets. He doesn't like it: 'A commercial system, without any alternative values, whether academic, aristocratic, Christian or socialist, can yet provide a *kind of hell* for future generations' (italics added).

Seeds of Change

A few advance social indicators stand out, in retrospect, as harbingers of things to come:

1 *The perspective of the individual*: Milton Friedman among others taught us to understand the point of view of the individual and how he/she would respond to monetary circumstances. We should imagine individuals as being capable of making rational plans about how to spend their wealth over their lifetimes. This perspective caught the changing mood of educated people and would potentially have huge implications for policy. If individuals learn from experience to anticipate the future and if they as a result anticipate a rise in prices, this would mean that in the long run monetary policy stimulus would not affect real output, but only prices. Thus, economists should take into account the rate of inflation anticipated by the public. An important think tank championing market economics, the Institute of Economic Affairs, had been founded in 1955 in the United Kingdom by Anthony Fisher, a businessman, on a suggestion by F. A. Hayek. It was very much a fringe group until the mid-1970s when commentators such as Samuel Brittan of the *FT* and Peter Jay in *The Times* challenged conventional wisdom, as did *The Banker* (of which I was the editor).

2 *The student uprising of 1968*: By the mid-1960s young people were growing restive with the world about them, or what they saw in the new TV media. They had lived through the Cuban missile crisis of 1961, Kennedy's assassination and the constant fear of a nuclear exchange between the USSR and the United States. Although this desire for change was articulated best by the New Left, and firebrands such as student leaders Daniel Cohn-Bendit and Tariq Ali, the dissatisfaction with the status quo was shared by others. 'Les évènements' of May 1968 in Paris were exciting in challenging the status quo. The demand for change was irresistible. Intellectuals held centre stage, and got away with it. When Jean-Paul Sartre was arrested for civil disobedience during the riots of May 1968, he was such an important figure that President Charles de Gaulle pardoned him, saying: 'You don't arrest Voltaire.' Ironically, the protests precipitated the resignation of de Gaulle himself in the following year.

3 *New entrepreneurship*: In Britain, Richard Branson, who went on to become the most renowned entrepreneur in the country, set up his first business, Student, in 1966. Trading under the name 'Virgin', he sold records cheaply, undercutting established outlets. He thus started on a career of challenging big groups, cartels, price agreements and suchlike fixes that would be his hallmark. Branson became a role model as an admired business leader and helped make the idea of entrepreneurship appealing to the younger generation. But it would take many years for the seeds planted then, in the 1960s, to germinate.

4 *America chooses inflation to finance a war*: The inflationary financing of the Vietnam War undermined the global monetary system, as it made the United States unable to maintain the dollar at its gold content of $35 an ounce. Devaluation of the dollar cut the anchor holding all currencies together, inviting others to follow suit and float their currencies against the dollar. It became a 'permissive society' in personal morality and increasingly in money and banking.

5 *Technological innovation*: The 1970s saw the first floppy disc, video game, VCR (video cassette recorder), digital watch, Apple computer, mobile phone, word processor, the founding of Microsoft—technologies that put more power in the hands of individuals.

6 *The birth of environmentalism*: The 1972 report from the Club of Rome, *Limits to Growth*, warned that civilisation would collapse in the twenty-first century. This thesis was gaining acceptance despite its dubious intellectual case. The outcome turned on whether humanity took serious action on environmental and resource issues. If that didn't happen, the model predicted 'overshoot and collapse'; the quest for unlimited growth in popula-

tion, material goods and so on would lead to a crash. Man can create a society in which he can live indefinitely on earth only if he imposes limits on himself and his production of material goods to achieve a state of global equilibrium.

Money to Kickstart Growth

This period saw a new twist in the state theory of money. That was the basic idea underlying the attempt by the state to stimulate economic growth by increasing money demand. Thus, we have a paradox: in this quite rigid society where money prices set in markets played only a limited role in allocating economic resources, by contrast there was a naive faith that miracles could be achieved by the correct management of monetary demand by the government. In Britain this experiment with money was taken to extremes. The floating of the pound by the Tory government in 1971 was greeted with wild applause—at last, commentators said, we have broken free of the constraint imposed by the fixed exchange rate to the dollar. At last we can end 'stop-go' policies—whereby for decades Britain had had to rein back growth when it caused a 'sterling crisis'. Thus, economic institutes, the media led by The Economist and even the Bank of England supported an experiment in letting demand rip, pumping up the money supply in the hope that such demand would spur not merely a temporary blip in growth but a fundamental long-term shift to a faster growth rate. British policy-makers had long looked across the Channel with envy at France's apparently successful experiment in what was called 'indicative planning' under its *Commissariat Général du Plan* while Germany had its own successful 'social market economy', which emphasised competition and markets as outlined by economists such as Walter Eucken (see Chap. 6). With Britain cast as the sick man of Europe, they tried gambling on money—fire up the money engine! So monetary and fiscal policy was loosened. It all ended in tears as inflation took off both in the United States and the United Kingdom (Pringle 1976).

The Hinge

Change, political and ideological, was in the air. A world in which the future was expected to be much like the present was replaced by a world where it would be different—possibly radically new. And money was to be a key agent and indicator of this change. Ayn Rand's teaching that 'Money … will take you wherever you wish, but it will not replace you as the driver' was a strange idea to most people outside the United States, and to many Americans too, when first published but proved to be prophetic (Rand 1957). The doctrine of 'rational selfishness' and fierce attacks on the State together with a ruthless application of reason to all mankind's problems was hailed by some as liberating (these included future Fed chairman Alan Greenspan). It was a time when the public sector absorbed half or more of GDP in many European countries. With rising affluence, people were breaking free of the old restraints. They wanted suppliers of services, including services provided by the state, to be more responsive to their consumer demands. They also wanted lower income taxes. In polite circles, in the 1970s it was still outrageous to suggest that market forces could be morally superior to state provision. But within a few years, society would place an astonishing degree of trust in money—at least on the ability of money prices of goods and services set in competitive markets to coordinate human activity. Perceptions of money, even the definition of it, changed out of all recognition. Soon it would be viewed as a means of self-expression, an instrument to prove free will existed, a source of capital for private business—something endowed with almost magical properties. Starting a business would move from being regarded as exceptional—for the petit-bourgeois shopkeeper only—to being quite normal, even admirable. More journalists, for example, went 'freelance'. Instead of lording their power over markets, governments would become the supplicants of bankers. In such a changing climate of opinion, it became natural to urge the case for relying on private initiative rather than state planning. Soon the British would hear a prime minister (Margaret Thatcher) declare 'there is no alternative' to the market. The ideas had germinated long enough; now they would bear fruit. It was time to unleash the power of money.

Bibliography

Club of Rome (1972). *Limits to Growth*.

James, Harold (2018, March 2). *Europe's Bretton Woods Moment*. Project Syndicate.

Pringle, R. (1976). *The Growth Merchants: Economic Consequences of Wishful Thinking*. London: Centre for Policy Studies.

Rand, A. (1957). *Atlas Shrugged*. New York: Random House.

Sampson, Anthony (1962). *Anatomy of Britain*. London: Hodder and Stoughton.

——— (1971). *The New Anatomy of Britain*. London: Hodder and Stoughton.

Schumacher, Kurt (1973). *Small is Beautiful: Economics as if People Mattered*. Blond and Briggs.

Servan-Schreiber, Jean-Jacques (1967). *Le Défi Americain*.

11

1980–2000: Creation of a Global Money Space

The renaissance of a global money space, a milestone in world history, was, like the Italian Renaissance of the fourteenth and fifteenth centuries, unplanned, unforeseen and startling. Everything would appear in a new light and perspective. It would make people feel the flow of events, the future as newly uncertain. At the same time, it would redefine the conditions of survival for all societies and individuals. They would be made or unmade by their capacities to meet its challenges. Within this space a new outlook would form and flourish. Like explorers discovering a new continent, we are just starting to explore its geography. After all, it only arrived towards the end of the twentieth century and has continued to evolve.[1]

A few definitions may be helpful. As used here, a *money space* has geographical, economic, competitive and financial dimensions. It is a *geographical* area within whose boundaries money moves among individuals, firms and states with little friction and at low cost. When it extends to virtually the whole world, it is called a *global money space*. It is an *economic space* in which individuals and enterprises can buy goods, services and assets from any other individuals or enterprises in the space at low (transactions) cost. It is a *competitive space* within which all firms compete with all other firms; and it is a *financial space* to the extent to which individuals have accounts at banks or other financial institutions with access to a range of financial services. It is formed by a *decentralised network* in which the working elements—institutions in the public and private sectors—are interconnected but are not organised or controlled by a central authority. The global money space is probably resilient to isolationist policies by small countries, such as North Korea, but it would be shattered by the departure

© The Author(s) 2019
R. Pringle, *The Power of Money*, https://doi.org/10.1007/978-3-030-25894-8_11

of (or extreme isolationist policies by) a large country such as the United States or China or an area such as the EU.

Within this global money space are a number of *currency domains*. Like large planets or celestial bodies, the major currencies, notably the US dollar exert a gravitational 'pull' on surrounding areas. The global money space is an aspect of *globalisation,* focussing on monetary aspects of the process. However, some features often associated with terms such as 'financial globalisation', or the 'international monetary system' need not apply in a global monetary space. For instance, it is *not necessary* for there to be one dominant currency, or one form of money, even though in practice the US dollar remains dominant. Nor is it necessary to have a common structure of financial regulation, or any particular exchange rate arrangement, still less a world government.

Historic Significance

For the first time, in a few years human beings the world over came to be interconnected by multiple financial ties. This changed their conditions of life, their life chances, the ways they made plans, and the objects in which they invested. They started to think of themselves, of their families, friends, networks, societies in new ways. They could transact business as well as exchange news, ideas and messages of all sorts to anyone and receive such messages from anyone. Indeed, it prepared the ground for a global culture to take root. This contained a new set of beliefs, attitudes and values to do with money and its role. Societies everywhere became imbued with this culture. The global money space was boosted by the development of the World Wide Web and email but was not created by them. On a personal note, when I started Central Banking Publications in 1990, we still sent out publicity material and sales letters by post. Bulky items such as book catalogues were shipped by sea mail. By the time we launched our series of training courses a few years later, most central banks had websites and emails, so we could send publicity material online—an enormous advantage for a small company establishing a global brand. Soon we had subscribers in over 120 countries. Luckily for us, central banks were often pioneers in the use of new communications technology. Without planning it, I ran one of the first generation of companies to build a global franchise based on the Internet and email.

Formation of the global money space was driven by interests rather than beliefs or ideals, but it facilitated the spread of a neoliberal outlook, the origins and importance of which are discussed in Chap. 6. It gave politicians an excuse for cutting back on the welfare state and for doing nothing about widening income inequality—they could explain that their hands were tied by the demands of all-powerful markets. To some, it seemed to offer protection against the 'demos', the claims of democratic leaders with their demands for redistribution and constant meddling with markets. Neoliberals could view it as a space within which the market could fulfil its key role of price-setting with minimal 'noise' from meddling politicians, and even as a route back to the lost world of nineteenth-century 'small state liberalism' and private property rights.

Innovators and people of all kinds of enterprise—not just bankers—scoured the world for new opportunities, continually adding to its new function as the connective tissue of a new society, forging links between far-flung centres, and between individuals. But with this exciting and revolutionary transformation of the world came risks, often at the time only dimly perceived, and the temptations and sin of *hubris*. The fall of the Communist bloc, the opening up of China and liberalisation in India and other emerging economies brought Western monetary practices to a giddying, global ascendancy.

Finance Set Free

This is how it happened. As noted in Chap. 10, the very success of the US-led post-war economic and monetary order led, gradually, to demands for a loosening of its constraints, including rules on money. These were felt at all levels: personal, family/social, at the national government level and internationally. People had more money and wanted more freedom about what to do with it. Governments wanted more flexibility to borrow and spend money without being tied to rigid exchange rates. Money again was an ingredient in demands for change. In particular, more money in people's pockets or at banks—and easier availability of borrowed money—tugged at the constraints imposed by the public money system. It went on tugging until that order collapsed. Everything started to be privatised. Including, to an extent, money itself.

The same generation that had created the subversive cultural innovations of the 1960s, under the guise of left-wing radicalism, went on to reject statist solutions to economic problems, to embrace markets and free finance. They helped to create the global money economy. In time, the birth of the global money space also saw the educated middle classes—children of the radicals of the 1960s—occupy senior positions in business, banking, the professions and state administration. This time, the middle classes made sure they were well paid as well. They knew their value and had fewer inhibitions about using their clout. More freedom to save and spend meant more incentive to earn more, and the income gap between rich and poor widened.

As noted above, the global money space was a joint venture in which the public sector played a key role. However, it was the private sector that administered the *coup de grace* to the old system of regulated finance, often called 'financial repression'. The final blow came in the late 1970s with an unprecedented burst of cross-border lending and bond issuance. The foundations had been laid as far back as the late 1950s with the gradual evolution of the Eurodollar market—a market in dollars deposited with banks in London—which was, to begin with, a private sector initiative—but often fed by public sector money. Bankers followed up their geographical expansion in the late 1960s by aggressively seeking new lending opportunities. Then came the era of 'consortium banking' (groups of banks getting together in an effort to compete with industry leaders, notably Citicorp), of vast Eurodollar 'syndicated credits' and bond offerings, by bankers who saw themselves as heroes, pioneers of a new world. Almost every month, it seemed, a new group was formed in London, complete with its obligatory launching party at Claridges Hotel. I recall one friend coming up to me at one of these:

> Hi Robert, how are you, I am setting up a new consortium bank that will be the first in the world to specialise in West Africa; we have got backing from Citibank and many other major banks, we are doing our first bond issue for (X country) next week—I'll see you at the signing!

The money came from every corner of the world. More currencies were floating, commodity prices were rising fast, and real interest rates were low, so borrowers rushed to tap the money available on the international markets. This surge in borrowing and lending was encouraged by the official sector. Governments needed markets to 'recycle' the vast sums flowing to oil-producing countries after a huge rise in the world price of oil. This came in two great leaps—in 1973, when the OPEC (Organization of the Petroleum Exporting Countries) cartel of oil-producing countries raised the price by 400% and then in 1979 with the Iranian revolution and Iran-Iraq War. Many oil-importing countries were threatened with bankruptcy unless they could borrow vast amounts. Banks were 'intermediaries'. It all ended in tears when one country after another, starting with Mexico and Brazil in 1983, defaulted (said they had to suspend payments of interest). When Western governments rushed to their rescue, in the first international operation of its kind, it was not out of sympathy for the countries affected but to save the Western banking system. That suited the markets fine, as it turned the public sector into their ally—as a player rather than merely a spectator.

The currency at the centre of this, the US dollar, was not anchored to any real asset as President Nixon had cut the dollar's link to gold, which had been the foundation of the world's currency structure, in 1971. International banking remained unregulated. Countries no longer needed to get permission to change their exchange rates, or to borrow money on private markets. They could borrow up to the limit of their creditworthiness. There was no control over the volume and flow of international capital movements. The IMF lost its influence over developed countries and over any others which did not need its money. Governments found they could borrow large sums on global money markets if they could persuade creditors that they had the income and the political will to service the loans—at least to pay interest on it. That led many countries to open their doors to foreign investment, privatise state-owned sectors, encourage exports, modernise their monetary policies and make their central banks more independent.

The Decade of Reagan and Thatcher

The global money space would not have arrived in the form and at the time it did without the personal imprint made by Margaret Thatcher, UK prime minister from 1979 to 1990, and Ronald Reagan, US president from 1981 to 1989. Nor would the global money culture that came to occupy the global space over the following 10–15 years to the early twenty-first century have taken on its distinctive characteristics. These two leaders reshaped the terms of the political debate for the whole world. Their impact was profound and recognised as such by friends and foes alike; their friends welcomed them, rightly, as liberating; their adversaries pointed (equally correctly) to their divisiveness. Although their spells in office were completed before the advent of the Internet (the public World Wide Web arrived in 1993), their legacy endured. Thus, when the world became interconnected, the ideology that would occupy the new space in the 1990s would be coloured by their ideas of individualism, self-reliance, widening opportunity and monetary freedom.

Seen from 2020, their ideology and aggressive championship of free markets now seems to have been going with the grain of history, but they shocked the conventional wisdom of their day. I recall that policy-makers and the economic establishment of the time tried to ignore Reagan and Thatcher, as if they were a kind of bad joke. The Democrat establishment in the United States and prevailing liberal-left leaders in Europe heartily detested them and all they represented. Of course, Keynesian economists believed, markets would always need to be guided by wise governments and economists, people like themselves. How dare such ignorant politicians suggest markets could manage quite well on their own! Most members of the *Group of 30* top bankers, economists and central bankers hated Reagan's economic policies (I was director of the group). I also remember the dismissive way that senior European statesmen regarded Reagan—a 'cowboy' was how Helmut Schmidt described him to me in an interview shortly after Schmidt stepped down as Chancellor of West Germany in 1982.

Mrs Thatcher's signature policies included abolition of controls on capital flows and privatisation of state-owned industries. Both were key ingredients in the huge new scope being opened up for money prices and market forces. True, Thatcher's crusade against socialism was partly rhetorical—she never challenged the basic institutions of the welfare state—but the market rhetoric allied to policies like privatisation and free movement of money was influential. She made it respectable to celebrate markets and oppose anything that interfered with them. Reagan and Thatcher put new venom in the struggle against international socialism culminating in Reagan's call to Mikhail Gorbachev, leader of the Soviet Union, made in Berlin in June 1987: 'Mr Gorbachev, tear down this wall'. Little more than two years later, it came down.

Many countries followed Thatcher's privatisation drive to sell off state assets—bringing money into the government's coffers: nobody had ever told them they could do that. Was this the climax of the neoliberal 'project' that German-language economists had imagined in the 1930s and 1940s and that had filtered through West Germany, US universities, the Chicago School and think tanks? (As discussed in Chap. 6) In some ways it was. It was a stunning example of the power of ideas working with the power of money. On the other hand, both leaders were passionate nationalists/patriots. By contrast, the neoliberal project, at least in its original form, was internationalist, upholding the concept of a world economy. It built institutions that would protect world money from the nation state. This was not in line with the Reagan-Thatcher view of the world. However, both were advised by Milton Friedman and other members of the monetarist counter-revolution. Both admired Hayek. Patriotic as both were, their actions paved the way for the creation of a global money space.

With the fall of the Berlin Wall in 1989 and the dissolution of the former USSR, former socialist states joined the IMF and over the space of a few years the IMF achieved truly global membership. This was followed by the creation of many central banks and new currencies—more money for the markets to invest and speculate with—and huge new opportunities to offer governments market finance. Millions of people enjoyed monetary freedom for the first time. Without the leadership of Reagan and Thatcher, this would never have happened so quickly—and maybe not at all.

What would replace the lost disciplines previously imposed by the former rigid international monetary system with fixed exchange rates and the fixed dollar gold price? As long as these rules had been in place, no country could inflate without risking breaking international rules and commitments. These in effect had imposed limits on government deficit finance and in turn on government's ability to promise benefits to their electors. Would the markets be able to impose an adequate form of discipline? For a few years, it seemed as if they might. If governments borrowed excessively, investors would surely demand higher returns, interest rates would rise on such governments' debt: would the bond markets impose sufficient discipline? President Clinton's political adviser thought so: 'I used to think that if there was reincarnation, I wanted to come back as the president or the pope… But now I would like to come back as the bond market. You can intimidate everybody.' These 'bond vigilantes' would make it difficult and expensive for countries that had borrowed excessively (in the market's judgement) would find the markets closed to them. Or so the theory had it. That was another theory waiting to be disproved.

Money Opens up the World

The new power of money and markets contributed to several mighty geopolitical shifts: the transformation of China under Deng Xiaoping (1978 on), the fall of Berlin Wall, the reunification of Germany followed by the dissolution of the former USSR in the early 1990s and market reforms in India after 1991 under Manmohan Singh as finance minister (he was later prime minister for ten years, to 2014). Huge parts of the world, including its most populous countries, joined the world economy not merely in terms of opening up to trade but especially by connecting themselves to global money markets and all the connections that they offered. Of course, many countries retained controls over capital movements; nevertheless, the dominant trend was overwhelmingly towards progressive liberalisation. By 2000, billions of people around the world were connected by monetary ties to regional, local, national and international networks of money and of communications. A whole new world of services opened up to them. This was the new 'space'. In this way, the severe crisis of developing countries' debt of the early 1980s paradoxically served to strengthen and cement the new order. It did so by forcing official institutions and leading governments to be deeply involved in saving it. They served as the midwives of global money. In my judgement, it was the ready availability of vast sums of money on international money markets to countries willing to make themselves creditworthy that finished off socialism. States that had tried for decades to eliminate money (see Chap. 5) collapsed when money was offered to them. The high walls they had built round their horrid empires were washed away by an ocean of liquid cash. This was another example of the power of money to change the world.

The monetary system was still backed by US military power. One top banker (Sir Dennis Weatherstone, head of JP Morgan) told me in 1982 that he took great comfort from knowing that whatever the risks the banks ran individually, the system was still enforced by the United States—it would uphold the rules of the game with its monetary and military power, if it had to. That meant, he said, that the United States would support the claims of creditors if borrowers defaulted. 'Default by a sovereign country would be theft of property—a foreign policy matter for the US', he said. As the biggest shareholder in the system, the United States saw the institutional infrastructure of international trade and finance as vital to the prosperity of the 'free world'. The creation of the global money space was a joint venture between the public and private sectors. Governments were largely responsible for the physical infrastructure of roads, railways, civil aircraft, airports and telecoms facilities; and public services key to public acceptance of privatisation (education, health services social security, pensions).

Stepping Stones to Nowhere?

Intellectual leaders of free market ideas came mainly from the United States, notably Milton Friedman, though many of the ideas had originated in Europe, with economists such as von Mises and Hayek (see Chap. 6). In Britain, the free market school of economics had few advocates and had little support in the British economics profession. The gradual acceptance of free market ideas was mainly due to the fact that statist and Keynesian remedies, which had seemed to work in the 1960s, lost credibility in the inflation of the 1970s.

Though still backed indirectly by US power, money was no longer the instrument that America had deployed at the end of World War II to project its power and ideals around the world; it was no longer subordinate to political, social or even moral rules. Indeed, in some ways it worked *against* the ideals that the United States had originally upheld. Money began to be used to project various forms of *private power,* beginning to rival state power.

Looking back, it is obvious that only business enterprise, not the state, could have driven the continuous technical and organisational innovation needed to achieve such rapid advances. Governments showered honours on bankers and merchants in money.

People forgot why their societies had treated money with great care and imposed rules on it. They forgot why philosophers and religious leaders from time immemorial had warned against money's corrupting power. They forgot why most societies historically had regarded money men and merchants as low-status occupations. The emergence of the global money space made this a dangerous moment to forget those lessons.

There was more than a note of triumphalism in the way this new world was welcomed by Western thinkers:

> What is emerging victorious, in other words, is not so much liberal practice, as the liberal *idea*. That is to say, for a very large part of the world, there is now no ideology with pretensions to universality that is in a position to challenge liberal democracy, and no universal principle of legitimacy other than the sovereignty of the people. (Fukuyama 1992)

Fukuyama caught the mood of the moment. The global money space was completed in the 1990s, when membership of the IMF became universal. More than 40 countries joined the organisation between 1980 and 1993, promising to abide by rules of good conduct—basically amounting to monetary freedom—that were originally formulated back in the 1940s. It was a magical moment. Most set up their own central banks and began issuing their own monies.

However, the Asian financial crisis at the end of the 1990s made it apparent that the global money space would facilitate the spread of monetary diseases along with new opportunities. Were these to be the twenty-first-century counterpart of the diseases spread by European settlers in earlier centuries? Instead of decimating people, would these money diseases decimate their cultures? Would they prove stepping stones to Oblivion for any way of life incompatible with the new money culture?

Such questions were not asked. As the quotation from Fukuyama shows, people assumed the monetary Renaissance would promote progress in general and democracy in particular. The power of money was harnessed to optimistic ideas. It was that precious link between money and 'Progress'—the assumption that more freedom for individuals to move and invest money would benefit society as a whole—that would come under great strain in the twenty-first century. Money was tugging at its moral foundations.

Note

1. For parallels between money and fine art since the Renaissance, see Chap. 22.

Bibliography

Fukuyama, F. (1992). *The End of History and the Last Man*. London: Hamish Hamilton.

Time Past: How Ideas Drove Actions

Conclusion to Part I: Ideas Drive Actions

In Part I, I illustrated the powerful effects of beliefs about money by taking a new look at some episodes—World War I, the Weimar republic in Germany, the Wall Street boom and crash of 1929, the Great Depression, mass starvation in the USSR under Stalin, America's projection of power after World War II, the rise and fall of socialism, the birth of new states, the era of Reagan and Thatcher, the opening up of China and India and the creation of a global money space. I argued that none of them can be understood without taking into account the influence of beliefs (including mistaken beliefs) about money. Equally, the way people at any time and place thought about money was itself shaped by their society. Sometimes, society would help people keep the power of money under adequate control. At other times, it would encourage money's inherent tendency to excess.

The central question I posed at the outset was this: how did our amazing, unique modern culture come about? We are now in a position to trace its evolution. In brief, World War I shook civilisation to its foundations and destroyed its money, the gold standard. The 100 years since the end of that war saw many attempts to build societies on various (often widely varying) principles. Nations also had to rebuild an international framework ordering their relations with one another. In that search, questions about money, markets and monetary values were often central. I showed how each generation played its part. The diverse experiences of many countries, the general climate of opinion as well as the writing of economists and other social scientists all left their mark. For the modern money culture to triumph various conditions were necessary. Potential rival ideas about the good life and what would make a good society had to be defeated and discredited. Dreams of doing without money prices had to be abandoned. Societies had to become willing to risk wide income and wealth inequality for the sake of monetary freedom. Among the capitalist nations, a consumer culture suitable for democracy had to be created, along with its marketing and financial supports. Money had also to be adapted so as to serve the financing needs of big government and the big state. Only a very specific set of beliefs and attitudes would fulfil all such requirements—there could be no simple application of a pure market, neoliberal or monetarist ideology. We observed the steps leading up to the 'hinge of the century', and we watched as the power of money eroded social constraints. Money dragged its anchor. The tie to gold was cut; we were free!

The evolution of the money culture had reached the stage when a politician of the Left could proudly say he was 'intensely relaxed' about other people becoming 'filthy rich' so long as they paid their taxes.[1] However, the power of money was clearly confirmed when governments abolished remaining capital controls and began acting as market participants and supplicants. A structure of regulation built round the nation state gave way to a global money space, as described in Chap. 11. For the first time in history, the majority of the world's inhabitants became linked by monetary ties (evidenced, e.g. by the rise in the proportion of world population with bank accounts). There have been previous periods of globalisation—notably at the end of the nineteenth century. But the scope and inclusiveness of the global money space was new. So was the fact that it was based on paper monies.

The picture may come into focus if we see the process in retrospect, from the other end of the telescope (so to speak).

From the Standpoint of the Year 2000

We can visualise the process by looking back at the twentieth century from the standpoint of the year 2000. By then the key features of the modern culture had been formed. These included the following: a money space in which virtually all nations participated; a worldwide consumer culture marked by pervasive advertising and other forms of marketing; active monetary policies operated by independent central banks; a belief in market prices as indicators of true value; widespread adoption of the aim of maximising shareholder value as a corporate philosophy; widespread use of monetary targets and bonuses as incentives in the public and private sectors; and an acceptance of the need to achieve equal rights for women and ethnic minorities in the workplace. Many of these were, by the year 2000, regarded as natural, obvious or even taken for granted. But in reality, each of them was the result of ideas that were once new and often opposed by the establishment. It needed an effort to find them a place in modern culture.

Each of the features or distinguishing marks of this *Weltanschauung* can be dated back to specific times and often places. The concept of a global money space goes back to the late nineteenth century. Modern consumer culture and credit were first developed primarily in the United States in the 1920s. The contemporary practices of competitive devaluations and currency wars were first employed in the late 1920s. The practice of large state spending as a means to counteract depression was pioneered by President Roosevelt in the New Deal in the 1930s—the theory used to justify it came later. The current marketing-driven and celebrity culture has its origins in the great movies of Hollywood, magnified by the genius of musicians such as Elvis Presley and Frank Sinatra. The global influence of the World Bank and IMF was based on America's decision in the late 1940s to use money to project its power, along with a drive to instal capitalism, market-based economies and democracy everywhere.

If we take it for granted that the government and public sector is part of the national economy this is only due to pioneering economists—originally, even Keynes saw such activities as subtracting from national output. If we also take active monetary and fiscal policies for granted, it is only because Keynes and others proposed such policies, and the political climate was ready to apply them. If we assume that nations measure their success by GDP, that is only because people such as economist Simon Kuznets thought up the concept.[2] If we assume policy interest rates should be set by central banks, that is only because some of them, starting with the Bundesbank and the Fed, pioneered the idea. The modern policy framework owes its existence to ideas, technical expertise and innovations that were often quite shocking when first introduced.

If the Anglo-American version of a trading, commercial, mercantile capitalism has become the global norm, it is only because ideas that could have posed a challenge to it were defeated. This was the most important result of two world wars. Both Germany and Japan had radically different traditions, held two contrasting ideals of civilisation—and both demoted money to a subordinate role in social life. German intellectuals before World War I defined their culture in opposition to the materialism of the British, while Japan's entire trajectory as a modern nation was a long effort to resist cultural as well as political colonisation. These efforts came to an end in the dust of Hiroshima and Berlin.

Notes

1. The reference is to British Labour party strategist Peter Mandelson, who in 1998 said: 'We are intensely relaxed about people getting filthy rich as long as they pay their taxes.' He later revised his views. Speaking in 2012 on BBC Radio 4's Today programme, Mandelson said: 'I don't think I would say that now. Why? Because amongst other things we've seen that globalisation has not generated the rising incomes for all.'
2. See accounts by Diana Coyle (2014) and David Pilling (2018). Pilling reports that Kuznets had reservations about the concept as a measure of well-being, asking: 'What are we growing? And why?'

Bibliography

Coyle, D. (2014). *GDP: A Brief but Affectionate History*. Princeton: Princeton University Press.

Pilling, D. (2018). *The Growth Delusion: The Wealth and Well-Being of Nations*. London: Bloomsbury Publishing.

Part II

Time Present: Actions Have Consequences

12

The Global Money Culture: An Outline

The fact that, for the first time, we all inhabit a common monetary space does not mean we all have the same attitudes towards, or views about, money. On the contrary, there are few subjects that occasion more disagreement than the part that money plays, and should play, in society and in a person's life. However, there are certain assumptions, rules and norms that members are under social pressures to follow—these form the framework of the culture described in this chapter. It has many positive aspects. Members take it for granted that they can communicate, make online acquaintances with, do business with and transfer money to and from people anywhere on the planet. Such people are 'at home' in this global space; know its customs, techniques and procedures; and became entangled with it. Rules of behaviour in this global business community share certain common features to ensure transactions take place smoothly. They also express certain shared values, which emerge from the intense interaction of billions of human beings in the global money space.

The following brief account illustrates some beliefs and values that a 'pure' or 'extreme' form of the culture exhibits (what Weber called an 'ideal type'[1]). I do not claim that they are found together anywhere or in any individual, country or among people of any faith or none. They refer to social norms/beliefs/values/expectation, not to the attitudes of any individual. Because monetary connections and networks and money prices have become the main ways in which economic activity is coordinated and are thus necessary for an economy to function at all, people and businesses sense a moral compulsion to follow these norms.

© The Author(s) 2019
R. Pringle, *The Power of Money*, https://doi.org/10.1007/978-3-030-25894-8_12

Some Cultural Norms

People are assumed to share certain expectations and assumptions. Norms are established that mould expectations around value and typical behaviour. It is normal to assume, for example, that the best guide to something's value is its price; that people work to make money; that both partners in a relationship work; that many people will work from home; that children are often cared for by the state or a private service; that adults are financially literate; and that they have Internet connections and are digitally literate.

In this culture, achievement exceeding expectations deserve a monetary reward; when it falls short, loss of potential earnings is to be expected. Each adult competes with every other adult in the global money space (of course, this does not exclude—indeed success often requires—cooperation among individuals). Individuals gain monetary value in a variety of ways; they may create their individual brands (what used to be called 'reputation'). Individuals build their narratives and claims to qualifications for the work they perform, along with their credit histories and supply chains and seek a place in the supply chains of others; the more rationally organised the supply chain, the lower the cost of finance. The aim of a businessperson is to maximise his or her monetary returns. Every business competes with every other business. The larger the business, the larger the potential gains to managers who can exploit shareholders by painting a rosy picture of future juicy returns, or who can exploit society by establishing monopolies. Nobody is surprised when managers of a large company enrich themselves from its proceeds before handing any money to shareholders.

The Work Ethic

Work should be enjoyed, especially if you are seen as a member of a team. Long hours of work are normal. A person's hold on a job is fragile, often informal and short term. When interacting with co-workers, people are gender blind. People and businesses are judged by their potential rather than their record.[2] The main purpose of working is to make money.

Communal Aims

International institutions and leading banks aim to connect each adult to the digital economy; communal goals are expressed in monetary terms, such as GDP; programmes are developed aiming to ensure that any stragglers—those still outside the global digital economy—are brought in.

Cultural Symptoms of Stress

It is normal for members of the new global society to live with chronic anxiety. Typically, people struggle to make ends meet. Business duties and an individual's contribution to teamwork trumps other loyalties, putting families under strain. Norms of behaviour can change without warning. Individuals are expected to update their language, manners and modes of communication as required by new norms, so that these have to be constantly monitored. Cyber hacking, malware, spyware and surveillance are constant dangers. Jobs and whole occupational classes emerge and vanish quickly. Uncertainty and fear spread rapidly.[3]

Individuals must be aware at all times of the risks of unintentionally committing an offence, ranging from libel, to harming a person's professional reputation, ethnic, gender or religious hate speech; hacking; extortion; downloading illegal images; sending multiple emails; resending multiple commercial email messages with the intent to deceive; engaging in the business of betting or wagering on any sporting event or contest online; accessing a facility through which an electronic communication service is provided; threatening to cause damage with the intent to extort money; making false promises; and using the Internet to annoy, abuse, threaten or harass. Direct access to the money machine is available only to people with proofs of identity in officially approved forms. Losers have no appeal against exclusion. Regulators may close a person's bank account without warning or explanation.

The New Culture and the Official Sector

The culture is essentially individualist. At the same time, participants often work with—and are advised to cooperate with—the public sector. The culture emerged in a world where nation states and the international institutions they controlled played major roles in financial activities, as rate setters and regulators, and where the general populace still looked to their nation state to offer them social protection and insurance. It was a world where the public sector (the sector financed by taxation rather than by profit-seeking enterprises) accounted for 30–50% of GDP. As we shall see in Chap. 16, in many countries, the links between these sectors have become corrupt.

The Emotional Issue of Motive

The culture privileges monetary measures of merit and reward. It demotes alternative ways of measuring and rewarding achievement, such as status, honour and peer esteem. In principle, it widens the choices open to individuals, but subject to the qualification that these are often, in practice, choices between increasingly similar lifestyles and types of goods and services. It erodes cultures, social classes and systems of belief that uphold alternative lifestyles and have different moral priorities (such as those traditionally linked to the nobility, or to warriors, or the clergy, or the professions). Modern money has been co-opted by the great forces of our age—notably technology. Interestingly, the motives ascribed to people by this outlook do not reflect their subjective experience. The maximisation of monetary returns is a model of behaviour. It is the ethic of post-capitalism and a hard taskmaster: Marx, following Hegel, said that only the State gives the individual the right to exist; now, only a proven ability to make money give the individual that right. But the money motive is one *ascribed to, even imposed* on, people—which is why they resent and will eventually reject it. It is not that people are greedier than before. Rather, they are more dependent on the money stream and monetary/high-tech networks. Threats to the networks giving access to money and technology are scary. People quickly feel vulnerable. That makes it easy to ascribe motives to them that they do not, in reality, subscribe to.

Self-Governance Preferred

Although the global money space has no central authority, participants have evolved rules and conventions necessary for the transaction of business. This also is a partnership between public and private sectors. To anticipate for a moment, there is evidence of this spirit of self-governance being alive and well in the digital age. The idea is to build on the supervisory framework developed under the auspices of official bodies such as the Financial Stability Board. In the words of two advocates: 'In the digital order we envisage, representatives of governments, businesses, and civil society would form peer-to-peer, self-governing horizontal networks' (Slaughter and Chedade 2019).

The idea is that participants in these networks would co-design digital norms, or actionable rules and implementation guidelines that give companies and citizens clear incentives to cooperate responsibly in the digital world. These co-designers would produce the best possible solutions at Internet speed and make them available for anyone to adopt voluntarily. Such arrangements suggest that economic governance adapts to changing circumstances.

Implications of the Global Money Culture

A focus on the global money culture throws new light on some key contemporary issues, such as the global financial crisis, asset price inflation, the rise of populism and crony capitalism. Critical is to understand how the system is policed; governments around the world are determined to retain a grip on the monetary system. Inevitably, this culture creates groups of Outsiders, some of whom remain very angry, while others are simply outcasts or inadequate. The process of rationalisation and the invasion of the money culture into every corner of the world continues to disrupt communities everywhere (Weber 1918).

As the essays in Part Two show, money works best when it serves a social idea or philosophy beyond its own perpetuation. Its guardians, the central bankers, now say their aim is to promote 'financial and monetary stability'. But this is to define the purposes of money in monetary terms, whereas previous generations have seen money as serving a wider effort at social improvement. Examples might include the idea of a society founded on principles of classical liberalism, with clearly defined rights to property and privacy or, at the other extreme of the political spectrum, directed credit to support socialism.

A World Takeover

The money culture and its accompanying measure of value tend to elevate the contribution of the individual to society. They devalue the contribution made by the larger society. Within the firm individual achievement and the fulfilment of targets are emphasised, even though everybody knows that the individual can do little without the group. This ideology may arouse feelings of resentment, phobias, fears, dependencies and addictions. Yet the money culture is global and inclusive. Being global means that humanity is at risk of overspecialisation. Being inclusive, it has imperative demands: *everyone* should be enrolled in this society and fulfil its obligations, or be an *unperson* at risk of *vaporisation* (Orwell 1949). In evolutionary terms, we are staking a great deal on this bet.

Against all the odds, the ideas discussed in Chap. 6 triumphed. To recall, these were ideas for the neoliberal 'project' that originated in Vienna after World War I and hung on by a thread through the age of collectivism. The mantra is familiar: when in doubt, let the markets decide. Market forces, supply and demand, can be trusted more than officials. Motives may be selfish but that is acceptable. If the market is contestable, with new sellers and buyers able to enter, then it can be left to the market to find out if there is a demand for a product or service and to supply it. The price set in free markets may not represent its true value, but it is preferable to a price set by a bureaucrat. We all got to learn it by heart.

A system under strain

After the triumph came the nemesis. The financial crisis severely damaged not only many leading economies but also the credibility of the underlying ideology. The global money space came under great strain. The volatility of cross-border capital flows increased. The ten years after the crisis also witnessed further rapid structural changes. While the weight of the US economy in the world economy declined relatively, as that of China, India and other emerging markets grew rapidly, the US dollar became even more dominant in global finance. One implication was that emerging market and some advanced economies became subject to large, destabilising inflows and outflows of money whenever the United States changed its monetary or fiscal policies. This increased the instability of the system.

Due to interdependence, a tightening of financial conditions in the United States leads to a significant fall in the GDP of the average emerging market economy—and that fall in turn has a boomerang effect on the US economy itself. There is therefore a basic asymmetry between the *dollar-dominated* international monetary system and the increasingly *multi-polar* world economy (Carney 2019). This is making more countries resort to old-fashioned tools of capital flow management, in an effort to reduce or at least cushion the impact of such flows. But there are limits to the effectiveness of such measures, which can easily provoke retaliation, and the forces making for integration still outweigh those tending to disintegration of the global money space.

A culture without a soul

In short, I expect the global money space to survive intact, but I doubt whether the ideology that attended its birth and that in an important sense legitimated it will. Indeed, it has already had the life drained out of it. The modern variant of Neoliberalism no longer commands wide support. I shall argue in Part Three for a restoration of the values and ideals of classical liberalism, while recognising not only that this will be a long haul but also that will need updating if it is to serve as a basis for a new monetary order. No world leader upholds any recognisable form of liberalism. Money is no longer connected to a generally accepted idea of its social function. The global culture that took shape at the end of the twentieth century was originally linked to some notion of the broader purpose of money and the monetary system, that is, how they contribute to social welfare. However, this was fatally undermined by the financial crash. This had another important effect. It induced central banks to turn on the money taps. Therefore while the global money *space* survived, the global money *culture* has mutated under the influences of two big forces: a surplus of state-created money and a deficit of legitimacy.

Naked money has become a pawn in the power game. The loss of a philosophical justification is much more significant than generally thought. In terms of traditional political philosophy, we have gone back to a state of nature pictured by Thomas Hobbes (1588–1679), It is a war of all against all, as it was before the formation of society through the social contract:

> So that in the first place, I put for a general inclination of all mankind a perpetual and restless desire of Power after power, that ceaseth only in Death. And the cause of this is not always that a man hopes for a more intensive delight than he has already attained to, or that he cannot be content with a moderate power: but because he cannot assure the power and means to live well, which he hath present, without the acquisition of more. (Thomas Hobbes 1651)

The international currency war may be just the start. What Hobbes said in 1651 is again true in 2020. People can secure their present power and means to live well only if they acquire more power, with the rider that, now, any form of power is now indissolubly tied to money. It is as true as ever that competition for riches, honour and power inclines people to fight, to 'kill, subdue, supplant or repel the other'.

Notes

1. An ideal type is formed from characteristics and elements that are in some way typical or representative of the phenomenon being described; it is not meant to include all of its characteristics. It has nothing to do with 'ideal' in a moral sense or to a concept of perfection but is used to refer to certain elements common to most cases of the given phenomenon: 'the much-discussed "ideal type", a key term in Weber's methodology, refers to the construction of certain elements of reality into a logically precise conception' (Gerth and Mills 1948).

2. As Sennett points out, this search for potential to grow rather than past achievement suits the peculiar conditions of flexible organisations but is also used to eliminate people; those judged without inner resources are left in limbo: 'They can be judged no longer useful or valuable, despite what they have accomplished' (Sennett 2006).

3. An excellent illustration of the way the money virus can spread diseases—in this case fatal diseases—is provided by the drama *The King of Hell's Palace* by Frances Ya-Chu Cowhig. Based on evidence of Dr Shuping Wang, a virologist, about her work at a blood plasma collection station in the Zhoukou region, Henan province, in the 1990s, the play shows how poor villagers were seduced by the lure of easy money to join a local blood collection centre, unwittingly exposing themselves to—and helping to spread—the Hepatitis C and HIV/AIDS viruses. Profit-oriented business specialising in this work increased rapidly under official encouragement in the 1990s and Dr Shuping's warnings about the risks were obstructed by the Chinese officials and she was dismissed. At the time there were 20,000 donors selling blood in one country alone, 45% of whom tested positive in Hepatitis C antibody testing. Later at least 500 people a day were being infected with Hepatitis C and HIV. In the drama the villages who donate blood die. An estimated 1 million destitute farmers sold their blood plasma at collection sites and were infected with the deadly disease. Shuping had to contend with continuous intimidation by the Chinese authorities even after moving to the United States and becoming a US citizen. She died on September 21, 2019 of an apparent heart attack. She was 59.

Bibliography

Carney, M. (2019). 'Pull, Push, Pipes: Sustainable Capital Flows for a New World Order'. Speech at Institute of International Finance Spring Membership Meeting, Tokyo 6th June.

Gerth, H.H., and Mills, C.W. (1948). 'Intellectual Orientations' in Gerth, H.H. and Mills, C.E. (eds): *From Max Weber Essays in Sociology*. London: Routledge & Kegan Paul.

Hobbes, T. (1651/1968). Leviathan, The First Part, Chapter 11, p. 161 (ed. C.B. Macpherson, 1968). Middlesex: Penguin Books.

Orwell, George (1949). *Nineteen Eighty-Four*.

Sennett, R. (2006). *The Culture of the New Capitalism*. New Haven: Yale University Press.

Slaughter, A., and Chedade, F. (2019). How to Govern a Digitally Networked World. *Project Syndicate*, March 25.

Weber, M. (1918). 'Science as a Vocation' in Gerth, H.H. and Mills, C.E.: *From Max Weber Essays in Sociology*. London: Routledge & Kegan Paul, 1948.

13

Money Delusion and the Crash, 2000–2010

In 2006, a book was published that mocked religion as an 'infection' and as the 'great unmentionable evil at the centre of our culture'. The book was *The God Delusion*; the author, Richard Dawkins. The book was an immediate sensation and became a global best-seller. I say the real problem for society of that time, and ours, is not God but the Money Delusion.

Belief in God, Dawkins said, is like believing that a teapot is circling the earth; it makes no sense at all (Dawkins 2006). But by the early twentieth century religion had lost its hold on society. Few people, at least in Western Europe, believe in the traditional Christian concept of God, least of all the caricature that Dawkins presented in a deliberate attempt to insult the few who hold such beliefs. He failed equally to notice that a form of magical thinking, an *ersatz* religion (or 'belief system') had taken its place. According to this idea, people find adequate satisfaction in a pursuit of happiness/fulfilment on a day-to-day basis. After all, if there is no other existence, if Death puts an end to all the strivings and choices on which the modern liberals set such store, then the present, the world of our senses, is all there is or will ever be. At the core of this outlook is a distinctive approach to truth—the scientific, evidence-based, rationalist method favoured by Dawkins. He was blind to the fact that this approach to truth had already become the established view—and blind to its dangers when applied to social affairs.

When Dawkins published his book, society was, indeed, facing an imminent threat—not from God but from Money. Appearing just a year before the great financial crash, a book alerting the public and policy-makers to the economic risks they were running might have done some good. Almost

© The Author(s) 2019

R. Pringle, *The Power of Money*, https://doi.org/10.1007/978-3-030-25894-8_13

everything Dawkins had to say about the 'foolishness' of belief in God applied more pertinently to popular illusions about money and credit. Dawkins cursed people for their blind trust in God. But it was blind trust in money and its guardians that was to drown the hopes of a generation. Within a few months of publication of The God Delusion, the money delusion had brought great financial institutions to their knees, causing a collapse in world trade and risking a return to the Great Depression. In attacking conventional religions, Dawkins was playing to the gallery; far from being genuinely controversial, far from challenging common assumptions, Dawkins was merely putting in evangelical language the common prejudices of the typical Western man and woman of his time (and ours). People were coming under social and psychological pressure to find in money and 'brilliant technology' the hopes previously found in religion—and to borrow more to fulfil them. Under the influence of the new culture, people were led to believe that the market is superior to other mechanisms for coordinating social life. Obstacles that stood in the way of efforts to apply such an outlook should be cleared. Against such a powerful ideology traditional norms of solidarity and community could only offer feeble resistance. The outlook has much to be said for it, given the right legal and constitutional framework and proper provision of public goods etc., but these conditions are easily forgotten. Yet far from warning against the dangers of a simplistic acceptance of such a worldview, Dawkins championed a technological, materialist worldview that encouraged it.

People Under Pressure...

Let us move from the big picture to the grassroots, where people live out their daily lives. What each individual does with his or her money matters, not just to them but for the rest of us. So do the values they hold and teach, as well as the skills they feel it necessary or desirable to acquire in order to flourish in an unknowable future. If, looking back, we can say that people borrowed 'too much', (or banks lent 'too much') at a certain time the data are only an aggregate of multitudes of individual decisions. The people who borrowed and spent 'too much' can easily be portrayed as reckless, greedy or incompetent, but they took their decisions in the light of information available to them and the beliefs they held. To understand how excess debt came about, it is not enough just to look at the behaviour and policies of bankers and central bankers but at the world of individual level decision-making. If the crash was inevitable, its seeds were germinating in the minds of individuals. What were the pressures that induced them to borrow more?

...In the United States

Wind the clock back to the turn of the millennium. How did people see the world? How did they treat money? In 2000, Robert Putnam published *Bowling Alone*, a study of contemporary American society. He reported that there had been a decline in Americans' membership in social organisations. He cited the sport of bowling as an example. Although the number of people who bowl had increased, more people were bowling alone, rather than in teams. In many other ways, also, people did not interact socially nor participate in political or other civic discussions as much as previously. This was seen in reduced political involvement including falls in voter turnout, public meeting attendance, serving on committees, and working with political parties. This had led to a decline also in relationships based on reciprocity, trust and cooperation, when individuals produce public goods and services for the common good. Social participation and what economists call 'social capital' had declined while Americans pursued more individualist paths to fulfilment. This was in accord with a growing distrust of government. It is generally seen as a form of capital that produces public goods for a common good. Putnam's conclusion was clear: 'Without at first noticing, we have been pulled apart from one another and from our communities over the last third of the century' (Putnam 2000).

What had happened? People said that 'pressures of time and money' limited their ability to participate in social activities. Millions of workers left full-time work for large corporations and became self-employed. This meant they had to pay more attention to budgeting, planning of major expenses, and allowance for possible gaps in their income stream—in other words, money worries. This was a very different world from that depicted in the Organisation Man described in Chap. 9 where large corporations offering long-term job security dominated the business scene.

Richard Sennett points to another source of strain. The kind of person demanded by employers had changed. Increasingly, they wanted people oriented to the short term, focusing on their *potential* ability, somebody willing to abandon past experience. This is an unusual sort of human being. Most people are not like this, they need to sustain a life narrative: 'Only a certain kind of human being can prosper in unstable, fragmentary social conditions.' Sennett sees this as a result of companies' need to look good in the eyes of venture capitalists and other potential investors:

'Enormous pressure was put on companies to look beautiful in the eyes of the passing voyeur; institutional beauty consisted in demonstrating signs of internal change and flexibility, appearing to be a dynamic company even if the once-stable company had worked perfectly well.' (Sennett 2006)

Then, there was the stock market. In what was often a desperate gamble, many ordinary people plunged for the first time into the equity markets. In 1950, only 4% of Americans was in the stock market; by the early 2000s, the proportion had increased to more than 50%, some indirectly through pension plans but, many with direct investments in stocks. Trading in US equity markets soared. Few of those people invested their money in companies whose products they knew and believed in. Many borrowed money in order to invest more with its attendant risks. In the four years to 2008, US household debt rose by 50% to US$12 trillion. When the crash came, many had to default on their mortgages. Any society in which people lack a supportive community—and are thus dependent on money for their survival—will tend to create a money-centric culture. Of course, many people continued to behave in a public-spirited way, as shown by gifts to food banks, the rise in charitable donations, and many selfless acts carried out on a daily basis. More people felt, however, compelled to focus on money at the expense of other things. It was not just a matter of survival but of finding some sort of satisfaction, spending money as evidence of achievement. Behaviour that in most cultures would be condemned as greedy came to be regarded as normal—and by the same token, failure, the great American taboo, also became normal, as the greedy individual is never satisfied. That is how culture prepared ground for the crash and disillusionment—or dis-delusionment, that is, the death of the Money Delusion, which had been the spirit of late twentieth-century capitalism.

...and in Britain

Now let us look at the Money Delusion at work. In October 2000, The Guardian's Maureen Rice asked six mainly British middle-class people from different walks of life the million-dollar question: where does all the money go? The answers showed that while average incomes per head in the United Kingdom had risen in real terms in the previous 10 or 20 years, people did not feel richer (Rice 2000). All the people she interviewed had difficulty saving. The article draws a picture of a high-pressure, middle-class life, and even fat pay-packets weren't always enough to sustain it. They 'spent money like water'. Rice commented that money had become the way people express themselves and demonstrate love, and that money offered a way of *compensating themselves for their efforts*. No wonder they felt as if they could never have enough of it. That is why, by the turn of the millennium, it had become 'more socially acceptable to be greedy and increasingly commonplace to be financially insecure'. In other words, people did not want to be greedy but felt that, in a society which ascribed such motives to people, even against their best intentions they were under pressure to behave accordingly. This is why, as I later argue, people will eventually rebel, to show 'we are not like that at all'.

Hopes That Led to the Debacle

A large God-shaped hole had opened up in the psyche and something would fill it—whether it be spirituality, a resurgence of nationalism, populism or simply money. Each of these philosophies would claim followers. The psychology of dependence and need was much the same in each case. This chapter focuses on one aspect—the cycle of human psychology around risk perceptions. Officials as well as investors and the general population were caught up in this. When times are good, perceptions of risk diminish. People convince themselves that the good times will go on forever. When perceptions of lower risk coincide with a period of low interest rates, as happened in the early 2000s, people see the world through rose-tinted glasses. Then, when the cycle turns, risk aversion increases again, often far beyond normal levels. This approach implicates all of us, notably members of the public who borrowed too much.

Could Maths Manage Risk?

You sometimes hear people say that before the global financial crisis investors and bankers were not aware of risks. On the contrary, never had so much high-powered thought been given to the subject. It was Number One topic at every banking and central banking seminar of the 1990s; I know because I organised many such meetings. The message was: risk management had become professionalised. Risks, while unavoidable, could be managed with appropriate mathematical techniques. Peter Bernstein, in a best-selling book of the time, said that what distinguished the thousands of years of history from modern times was 'the mastery of risk' (Bernstein 1996). This was the 'revolutionary idea' that defined the boundary between modern times and the past. Human beings have 'discovered a way across that boundary'. Until this 'discovery', 'the future was a mirror of the past or the murky domain of oracles and soothsayers'. He compared the thinkers who 'put the future at the service of the present' with the Greek hero Prometheus. Like him, 'they defied the gods and probed the darkness in search of the light that converted the future from an enemy into an opportunity'. To be fair, Bernstein duly warned of the risks of hubris: 'The mathematically-driven apparatus of modern risk management contains the seeds of a dehumanising and self-destructive technology.' But what the markets seized on was the promise, not the warning. Investors were reassured by marketing 'professionals' (who had replaced old-style bankers) that new derivative instruments had spread risks so that only those with strong shoulders would be asked to bear high-risk investments. In other financial markets also, such as foreign exchange and exchange rates, officials found comfort in theories claiming to prove that free markets would settle at correct (equilibrium) levels. They too held an 'irrational' set of beliefs.

The Money Virus

What's in a name? It is ironic that more and more people, from entertainers to airline stewards, started calling themselves 'professionals' even as the traditional professional classes succumbed to commercialisation, becoming merchants. Take accountancy, for example. A friend writes:

When I started training as an accountant in 1963 the profession of Chartered Accountancy was genuinely a 'service industry' because it offered a genuine service, both to the State in that it provided some kind of check on business activities through the audit function, but also by giving genuine, objective and educated advice to the owners and managers of businesses. The drive to maximise profits was not there, although there was a clear expectation that you would achieve a comfortable lifestyle when you qualified. Then in 1979 Margaret Thatcher swept onto the scene in a cloud of reforming zeal, amid general rejoicing from the right, and she forced the professions amongst other entities to compete with each other. The shock and horror this produced in the accounting profession, certainly from where I was, was enormous. Accountancy firms advertising? What an unimaginable and appalling idea! But, over a relatively short period of years the drive for money in the form of higher and higher profits led to some of the larger firms of accountants setting out on an aggressive takeover trail, those in power at the major firms accumulating more power and profit to themselves at the expense of shedding a large number of partners and staff on the way, working standards being put under pressure in the name of efficiency and competition.

The conclusion is that accountancy has in most respects ceased to be a profession in the pre-Thatcherite sense, and become a money driven, profit-orientated business. Similar comments can be made about most of the old professions. As a result much of the professional ethos has disappeared. Many people found the continual drive for bigger and bigger profits, the continuous effort to meet targets for the number of hours charged to clients—the constant feeling that someone was standing behind you with a knife waiting to stab you in the back—was an environment that they couldn't wait to leave.

Another symptom of the increased money centrism of society was the growth of a compensation culture. In the 1950s and 1960s, it was virtually unheard-of—at least in Britain and other European countries—to sue professional people or a public body, such as a local authority. Now, the NHS is setting aside more than £1 billion a year to meet negligence claims and the annual cost has doubled since 2010/11. Estimated total liabilities, which is the cost if all current claims are successful, stands at £65 billion, up from £29 billion in 2014–15. Clearly, the rising cost of clinical negligence is already having an impact on what the NHS can provide. Every business has to budget for possible claims.

Novelists Have Their Say

As Saul Bellow puts it, money has an amazing ability 'to survive identification' as a great evil and 'go on forever'. Novelists track the financialisation of everyday life. 'Without money he was hardly a man', Jonathan Franzen writes in 'The Corrections' (Franzen 2001). Authors such as Aravind Adiga dramatise the corrupting influence of the money virus in poor countries. In Martin Amis's novel *Money*, the maximisation of individual choice through personal consumption is embodied in the figure of John Self, '200 pounds of yob genes, booze, snout and fast food.' 'I really don't want to join it, the whole money conspiracy', he declares as he accepts a large cheque for rewriting a trashy screenplay (see Mishra 2014). Bob Dylan's disdain for money was well known, as was his willingness to advertise anything from underwear to computers in return for lots of it. In 1998, Dylan and his son Jakob were paid US$1 million (quite a lot at the time) to play for 15,000 employees of a Silicon Valley company.

...Higher Education...

Broader culture and educational institutions were influenced. Take higher education. In 1963, the Robbins inquiry in Britain, urging a huge expansion of universities, argued that learning was a good in itself. 'The search for truth is an essential function of the institutions of higher education', it observed (Robbins 1963). Yet in 2010 another inquiry used a quite different metric: 'Higher education matters', it argued, 'because it ... helps produce economic growth, which in turn contributes to national prosperity' (Browne 2010). What a student-as-a-consumer is assumed not to want are all the things that truly define a good education—difficult questions, deep reflection or challenging lecturers. In the early twenty-first century, these came to be viewed as obstacles to attaining a good degree leading to a well-paid job. Many schools defined their task as showing children how to pass exams. Education should have benefits measured as a return on an investment. Universities UK, the representative body of British universities, said university education was valued because it was 'essential' to the modern economy (Universities UK 2015). Academics queued up along with all the other special interests pleading for money: 'in the absence of sufficient and sustained investment, the United Kingdom's research base and university sector will fall behind key competitors.'

.... Good Businesses

Society was permeated by what with the benefit of hindsight was a dangerous set of beliefs, attitudes and values. Yet, at the time they seemed to hold vital clues to the solution of many puzzles and challenges. Take, for example, the 'shareholder value' fashion that swept the corporate world globally—the idea that the managers of a business should aim to maximise monetary returns to shareholders. The challenge was to make companies, especially large corporations, more competitive. People observed that for many decades after the end of World War II, many of them were run more like civil service departments than competitive businesses. A few large companies that exercised considerable market power dominated many industries. Management saw its role as that of balancing the interests of different stakeholders, including workforce, the environment, the local community as well as customers. This was very difficult to implement in practice and was often accompanied by a loss of focus on innovation in the products and services they were supposed to specialise in. Their top-heavy, costly management structure made them vulnerable to hostile takeovers financed by debt. Management seemed a law unto itself, and often to have lost sight of the interests of shareholders. Many large corporations needed a thorough shake-up. The doctrine of shareholder value seemed to offer a way to cut through all such complexities and provide a new focus for corporate objectives; many were restructured in an attempt to achieve greater efficiency and growth in returns to shareholders. A seminal 1990 article in Harvard Business Review suggested that many CEOs were still being paid like bureaucrats, and that this caused them to act like bureaucrats. 'Is it any wonder', Jensen and Murphy wrote, 'that so many CEOs act like bureaucrats rather than the value-maximising entrepreneurs companies need to enhance their standing in world markets?' (Jensen and Murphy 1990).

The solution? 'Follow the money!' The lesson many corporate boards took from such criticism was that their company should aim to make money at all costs. This would be reflected in measures such as earnings per share. They should be paid in company shares so that their interests would be aligned with stockholders. As British economist John Kay and others have pointed out, this was a prescription that, once applied, spelt the ruin of thousands of good businesses (Kay 2015). An aim to make money out of customers does not help meet customer needs. In practice, as Steve Denning of *Forbes* magazine has pointed out 'over the decades since its birth, shareholder value theory has not only failed on its own narrow terms of making money for shareholders': 'It has been steadily destroying the productive capacity and dynamism of the entire economy' (Denning 2017). In *The Future of Capitalism*, Oxford economist Paul Collier tells the story of the most admired British company of his (and my) childhood, Imperial Chemical Industries (ICI) when its mission was 'to be the finest chemical company in the world'. But in the 1990s, ICI amended its primary objective by embracing 'shareholder value'. Collier shows that that single change—chasing monetary returns to raise the share price—destroyed the company (Collier 2019). Another symptom of this corruption was the rise of the bonus culture. Andrew Smithers argues persuasively that declining productivity in the United Kingdom and the United States is inextricably linked to low investment induced by the bonus culture (Smithers 2019). This is Money Delusion in operation.

Many such apparent solutions turned out to be traps. In 2019 the US Business Roundtable of top executives dropped the notion that they functioned first and foremost to serve their shareholders and maximise profits: 'Investing in employees', they declared, 'delivering value to customers, dealing ethically with suppliers and supporting outside communities are now at the forefront of American business goals'. What had gone wrong? What had destroyed so many once-great businesses? They all had one thing in common.

They let pursuit of a monetary objective blind them to its dangers (see Chap. 21 for a contrasting culture). The same was true, by the way, of people who should have been most alive to this risk—the central bankers and financial regulators. Never had so much high-powered thought, effort and expense gone into the design of financial regulation. But they were blinded like everyone else. Indeed, 'poor financial regulation' is probably the single most widely-accepted explanation of the financial crash of 2007–09.

Central Bankers 'Distracted' by Their Targets for Prices

The theory of inflation targeting appealed to central bankers for several reasons. It was in practice coupled with a promise of operational independence—protection against day-to-day interference by politicians—which would be necessary if they were to be given the tools to do the job. They approved of that. They would have the power to set the short-term rate of interest—the price of central bank money. It gave them a mandate to pursue a goal that could be readily understood by, and communicated to, the public. It would also enable the public, through elected representatives, to hold central bankers to account. They believed it was justified by the current state of economic theory—that is, that control over short-term interest rates would be sufficient under a regime of flexible exchange rates to steer inflation close to the target over the medium term (the target was usually set by governments, but in some cases by the central bank itself). It would reassure the public that inflation would not get out of control as it had done in the 1970s, while the target of an annual 2% rise in prices (which became the international standard during the 1990s) would also guard against the risk of sliding into deflation. By defining 'price stability' as an annual rise of 2% in a chosen index of prices, this enabled them to claim they were pursuing price stability—and could promise the public to achieve that. This approach was so appealing it gripped the entire central banking profession and its academic advisers. At last, they said, we economists, qualified people, are in charge! As it happened, economists headed several of the world's leading banks, including the Federal Reserve and the Bank of England. The economists looked at how they were doing against their target. For example, the behaviour of the prices in the 2003–08 period showed the Fed was hitting its target: US consumer prices, excluding food and energy, only increased by 12.4% during that period—at a steady annual rate of 2.1%.

They discounted evidence that this behaviour was due to factors such as the flood of cheap goods from China and other low-income countries. In fact, rapid globalisation, flexible supply chains and technological innovation had placed downward pressure on consumer prices ever since the 1990s. Against this background, a monetary policy committed to delivering sustained inflation had to battle against the natural tendency for prices to fall. Money creation then found an outlet in assets, notably housing. This set the scene for a sequence of booms and busts, as in 1997–2001, 2003–07 and the vast asset price bubbles of 2010–onwards. They had shackled themselves to 2% annual inflation. In many countries, broadly speaking, this was achieved when measured by the chosen price indexes. By contrast, items that were not included in official definitions of inflation soared: between 2003 and 2007, for example, in the United States, house prices were up 45%, stock prices 66% and commodities 92%. Asset-price bubbles were experienced in many other countries as well.

Inflation targets offered the elite of the policy-making world an intellectual framework that, ironically, did not require them to pay attention to money itself; previous monetary targets of the Fed, for example, were sidelined, then relegated to a lesser status and finally dropped (see Brown 2018). At a time when monetary ties mattered more than ever, and performed vital functions in holding society together, central bankers focussed their attention elsewhere—on their inflation mandate—shifting it away from what was happening to money and the financial markets. Their economic models—the theoretical framework for their policy decisions—had no money in them (for further discussion of this point, see Chap. 18). Meetings of their decision-making bodies discussed the outlook for inflation and whether they should change short-term interest rates to control spending and demand. They no longer gave priority to understanding what was happening in financial markets, thus missing the full implications of the rise of financial engineering and derivatives. This was their Achilles Heel, their own version of the hubris infecting society at large. Whereas people were increasingly obsessed with money, central bankers would, if not ignore it, relegate it to a subsidiary role. Why? Did they want to show that they were true professionals, dedicated to service? That they did not need to get their hands dirty? They would show they were gentlemen—perhaps the last of a dying breed. They were aware that banking had never been accepted as a true profession in most societies. So they would downplay the role of money. They would show their insouciant attitude by refusing to tighten policies to reduce the money supply even at the height of an asset-price bubble. "Oh, we can clean up any mess from a financial crisis afterwards", was the sanguine message.

This mood affected experts and laymen alike. Having observed monetary policy officials and regulators during these years, I conclude that officialdom was caught up in the same optimistic mindset as the rest of us. They knew there might very well be a crash but believed they could clean it up afterwards. Which is what, in a way, happened. What nobody expected was the mind-boggling cost of the clean-up or the social divisiveness and anger that would also follow.

When the Fed Also Was Blind to the Danger

Official documents released later showed a key moment when we could see this process at work with all its disastrous consequences.

In the run-up to the great crash, the Fed's policy-making body, the Federal Open Market Committee (FOMC), now under the chairmanship of Ben Bernanke, failed to recognise that a serious situation was developing in the interaction between mortgage market, new financial instruments and banks. The way they analysed the economy, focusing on the level of demand in relation to output, made them uninterested—and indeed unable—in focusing on what was happening to money. In September 2008, the main topic of the meeting was inflation. Bernanke said that 'I think our policy is actually looking pretty good'; that was at a time when several European banks had already signalled market turmoil. Their focus on macroeconomic theory made it difficult for them to connect events into a coherent whole. Macroeconomics dominated each meeting. Housing and financial market remained different topics and they were never connected. They did allude to the ongoing turmoil in financial markets but could not 'see' the connection to the wider economy—they had no inkling of the catastrophic effect that such a monetary shock would have. Money was not discussed. There were many meetings about Hurricane Katrina—what worried them was potential effect on inflation.

The FOMC was slow to recognise the impending collapse of the financial system, as the committee interpreted uncomfortable facts in a positive light, marginalising and normalising information that did not fit their view of the world. All frames limit what can be understood, but the content of frames matters for how facts are identified and explained.

'The Federal Reserve's primary frame for making sense of the economy was macroeconomic theory. The content of macroeconomics made it difficult for the FOMC to connect events into a narrative reflecting the links between foreclosures in the housing market, the financial instruments used to package the mortgages into securities, and the threats to the larger economy' (Fligstein et al. 2017). Look at the September 18 meeting the day after Lehmann Bros went down. The FOMC constructed their own perspective on what was going on. They paid little attention to the sub-prime market, and they did not pay due attention to the downside in housing. They did not ignore it completely but tried to make sense of world in their own economic language: 'I think our policy is actually looking pretty good.' They were blindsided.

In other words, the focus of central banks on their consumer price mandates meant that they neglected evidence that low rates might be undermining financial stability. The minutes of the Fed's Federal Open Market Committee reveal little evidence of concern with growing turmoil in financial markets right up to September 2008. As the experienced observer, Anthony Elson, concludes: 'a regime of inflation targeting was inadequate in that it essentially ignored the potential problem of systemic financial risk' (Elson 2015). And more damningly:

> Rarely, if ever, were representatives from the bank regulatory side of the Fed's operations asked to speak or comment on potential financial risks in the economy. (Elson 2015)

'A Dangerous Distraction'

To do them credit, some central bankers—not however any of the main actors of that time—have admitted that central banks' focus on price stability had become dangerous. As Mark Carney, Governor of the Bank of England from 2013–2020, said in 2017: '…the financial crisis exposed how a healthy focus on price stability became a dangerous distraction.' He concluded that following victory in the war against inflation during the Great Moderation, they 'lost the peace' as vulnerabilities built inexorably (Carney 2017).

Central bankers caught in the scientific mindset had mistakenly set aside the old wisdom about money and markets that previous generations of central bankers gained from experience. Just as the rest of society was becoming more money-centric, central bankers, whose job, everybody assumed, was to pay attention to money, decided to have as little to do with it as possible. One reason was the search for higher social status—their aspiration to be seen as full professionals. But the main factor that betrayed society's trust was that they were captured by the Dawkins Delusion—a belief in science as the only basis for true knowledge about the world. Economics had the double advantage of pretending to be a respectable science while (in the version of macro-economics embraced by central bankers) also dispensing with the need to pay attention to grubby money and irrational money markets. It was indeed a fatal attraction.

Thus, from stressed-out housewives, through the upper middle-class high earners, to economists, journalists, novelists, the educational system, government officials, and business leaders, the Money Delusion had us in its grip (and I include myself). It ruined many ancient professions and once-great businesses. Not the God Delusion, but the Money Delusion was the big threat of the early twenty-first century. It was made yet more dangerous by the capture of the monetary guardians, the central banks, by what I term the Dawkins Delusion, an irrational faith in a modern social science.

Bibliography

Amis, M. (1984). *Money*. London: Jonathan Cape.

Bernstein, P.L. (1996) *Against the Gods: The Remarkable story of Risk*. New York: John Wiley.

Brown, B. (2018). *The Case Against 2 Per Cent Inflation: From Negative Interest Rates to a 21st Century Gold Standard*. Palgrave Macmillan.

Browne, J. (2010). Securing a sustainable future for higher education: an independent review of higher education funding and student finance [Browne report].

Carney, M. (2017). 'Opening remarks to the Bank of England Independence – 20 years on'. Conference Remarks, 28 September 2017.

Collier, P. (2019). *The Future of Capitalism: Facing the New Anxieties*. London: Penguin Books

Dawkins, R. (2006). *The God Delusion*. London: Bantam Press.

Denning, S. (2017). 'Making Sense Of Shareholder Value: The World's Dumbest Idea', Forbes magazine, July 17, 2017.

Elson, A. (2015). *The global financial crisis in retrospect*. Palgrave Macmillan

Fligstein, N., Brundage, J.S., and Schultz, M. (2017). 'Seeing Like the Fed: Culture, Cognition, and Framing in the Failure to Anticipate the Financial Crisis of 2008.' American Sociological Review September 7, 2017.

Franzen, J. (2001). *The Corrections*.

Jensen, M.C., and Murphy, K.J. (1990). CEO Incentives—It's Not How Much You Pay, But How. Harvard Business Review, 1990

Kay, J. (2015). *Other People's Money: The Real Business of Finance*. New York: Public Affairs.

Mishra, P. (2014). 'How Has Fiction Handled the Theme of Money?' New York Times, Bookends APRIL 8, 2014.

Putnam, R.D. (2000). *Bowling Alone: The Collapse and Revival of American Community*. New York: Simon and Schuster.

Rice, M. (2000, October 15). 21st century money, *The Guardian*.

Robbins, L. (1963). Report of the Committee on Higher Education

Sennett, R. (2006). *The Culture of the New Capitalism*. New Haven: Yale University Press.

Smithers, Andrew (2019). *Productivity and the Bonus Culture*. Oxford University Press.

SunTrust Bank, Survey reported by Kelley Holland for CNBC, February 4 2015.

14

Money as a Tool of the State

Introduction

The ten years following the financial crash of 2007–09 mark a further crucial stage in the story of money. This is when the contemporary culture takes its most dangerous form. For the first time, money is not linked to any coherent or widely shared political philosophy—there is no shared vision of how societies should function. The last link to any such theory was shattered in the crisis. When Alan Greenspan, former long-serving chairman of the Federal Reserve (chair from 1987 to 2006), confessed that the financial crisis had revealed 'a flaw' in his belief in free, competitive markets, people were shocked. He said:

> I made a mistake in presuming that the self-interest of organizations, specifically banks and others, was best capable of protecting [the banks'] own shareholders and their equity in the firms … So the problem here is that something which looked to be a very solid edifice, and, indeed, a critical pillar to market competition and free markets, did break down. And I think that, as I said, shocked me. I still do not fully understand why it happened. (Greenspan 2008)

This frank acknowledgment by the world's leading central banker damaged confidence in the model that had legitimated not just America's embrace of free market capitalism but also the new and still fragile global money space. Greenspan merely gave expression to a widespread sentiment. Suddenly, the view that the operation of economic forces could safely be left to the market and the guardianship of money to central bankers became much harder to defend.

© The Author(s) 2019
R. Pringle, *The Power of Money*, https://doi.org/10.1007/978-3-030-25894-8_14

Central Banks Try to Offset Contraction

In most of the advanced economies, the crisis destroyed the private sector's contribution to money creation. People wanted to reduce rather than increase their bank borrowing. The public sector stepped in. So from 2008 on the major central banks led by the Fed started up the money pumps. They created money on a huge scale. They did this by buying government bonds and some other assets from private sector firms such as banks, pension funds and other companies. Central banks paid for their purchases with newly created money. Those selling assets to central banks had more money in their bank accounts, which could be lent out. The idea was to stimulate spending on goods and services and new investment, but the money and loans could equally be used to finance purchase of property, fine art or other assets. Although some commentators urged governments to direct banks to channel credit into 'priority' areas, governments did little to channel credit—it would smack too much of wartime controls. In practice, companies and banks only spent a little of it on new capital investment. Management used a lot of money to purchase the shares of their companies on the market, which drove up stock prices and (as their earnings were related to performance as measured by earnings per share) this raised their pay packets.

Money as a State Weapon

At the same time, money became a weapon in the competitive struggle for resources between states. A larger supply of a national currency tends to lower its exchange rate—how much it is worth in the market. Devaluation of one's currency is essentially a protectionist measure, an attempt to grab market share from existing providers by cheapening one's exports and protecting one's internal market by making imports more expensive. Many central bankers agreed that QE led to an era of competitive currency devaluations, though this was not part of their intention. At the 2016 annual central banker's meeting at Jackson Hole, Wyoming, the late Allan Meltzer argued that the Fed's 'quantitative easing' (QE) was in effect a monetary policy of 'competitive devaluation', and added this stark warning:

> Other countries have now followed and been even less circumspect about the fact that they were engaging in competitive devaluation. Competitive devaluation was tried in the 1930s, and unsuccessfully, and the result was that around that time major countries agreed they would not engage in competitive devaluation ever again. (Meltzer 2016)

Central banks had, in effect, become scourges of money itself by cheapening it (recall Paul Volcker's warning that the power to create is also the power to destroy[1]). They appeared to have been forced into this by the operation of the system. Every crisis of finance destroyed money and this had to be replaced so far as possible. So, the response was to implement the same sort of policies as had got us into trouble before. They would aim specifically to raise the inflation rate by printing more money. That took over as the mantra of central banking. Central bankers, guardians of money, were in this way reduced to using weapons that previous generations of central bankers had warned would undermine faith in money. And they resorted to the old tricks of state intervention to guard against risks. That at least is the charge levelled by several well-informed critics (White 2019). Economic commentators worried whether central banks would have enough 'ammunition' to fight the next recession—interest rates on sovereign developed country debt were already low, and even negative for some countries. In September 2019 the European Central Bank cut its deposit rate to a record low of minus 0.5% and Philip Lane, chief economist of the CB, indicated that it would be prepared to lower them further. If it extended to retail customers, a negative rate would mean that instead of paying the holder interest on the balance in his or her account, the bank would regularly subtract an amount from the balance of the deposit holder. They would punish people for holding 'too much' money. Central bankers would deny that this meant they knew what you should be doing with your money better than you did. But that would be an implication drawn by many customers.

The Results of Political Money

The latest stage in state management of money has had several adverse effects. These include the rise of populism, the hostility to elites, and widening inequality. It also helps to explain, in my opinion, why, by the end of the period, changing attitudes to money and beliefs about it were bringing about a convergence between the various kinds of capitalism—state, crony and liberal-democratic (to be discussed in Chap. 16).

Governments failed to ensure that all sections of society paid their fair share of the cost of cleaning up the financial system and recession after the crisis. Preventing a widening of wealth inequality was not one of the aims of these programmes. On the contrary, central banks quantitative easing and other non-conventional monetary policies relied on boosting asset prices for their effectiveness, thus benefitting sections of society that already possessed significant financial or real estate assets. Creation of so much new money encouraged people to bid up asset prices. People who already had assets found their net wealth increasing even as average real incomes stagnated for the majority. This fuelled anger that allowed populism to thrive.

The public came to the view that the elites' priority in the crisis was to look after themselves. They were the first to scramble into the lifeboats. The lifeboats were quite big enough to accommodate government ministers and senior civil servants, the major commercial banks—and any followers who could scramble on board. Central banks not only saved banks—probably necessary—but also bailed out bankers who all got away with their loot. Regulators who had been in office when disaster struck were promoted and honoured rather than dismissed. No wonder it all whipped up hatred of elites.

Moreover, central bank policies have led to a loss of value of money against a wide range of assets. With asset price bubbles pushing up shares and property prices in the world's major cities, the value of money has been drastically lowered in terms of such assets. Even their pledge to stabilise consumer prices has been more honoured in the breach than the observance, as Hamlet would have said. An American needed US$150 to buy the same basket of goods in 2019 as he/she could have bought for US$100 in 2000. That is far from a commonsense understanding of 'price stability'. To be sure, this was a better performance than between 1980 and 2000, when prices doubled, but it continued the inflationary trend. Finally, as mentioned earlier, monetary policies encouraged currency wars. China was singled out for manipulating its currency to gain competitive advantage but the policies of the United States, the euro area and Japan also depended on such a mechanism.

Revenge

The public took revenge. The evidence suggests a clear causal link between the financial crisis of 2007–09, subsequent recession and the rise of populism. People voted in ways that profoundly shocked the 'establishments' of each nation. Donald Trump was preferred to Hillary Clinton, the establishment's choice. The British chose Brexit, in a direct challenge to the liberal, cosmopolitan elite—and contrary to the advice of a large majority of economists. 'We have had enough of experts', declared British minister Michael Gove. In Italy, voters switched in droves to Metteo Salvini's far-right League party. In 2019, this threatened another euro crisis over Italy's public debt, the largest in the eurozone. The Italian government started issuing 'Bills Of Treasury' or

BOTs in small denominations of euros, as if they were money. Member states are not allowed to issue money—that is a right reserved for the European Central Bank (ECB). The question arose: what are these? Mario Draghi, president of the ECB, said: 'They are either money—and then they're illegal—or they're debt, and then that stock (of debt) goes up' adding that he could see no third option. People asked: is Italy still committed to membership of the euro, the single currency? If so it has to pay interest on its huge debt. No Italian political party was publicly threatening to take Italy out of the euro. But would Italy continue to service its debt? Eurosceptic parties opposed to Brussels captured as many as a third of the seats in the European Union (EU) parliament. The far-right parties of Italian Deputy Prime Minister Salvini and France's Le Pen led the populist charge. Anti-EU ranks were supported by the Brexit Party of British populist Nigel Farage. Pseudo-populist Boris Johnson became Prime Minister of Great Britain.

In reality, the rise of right-wing parties reflects the people's verdict on the governing classes. These classes had not managed public money in a fair or efficient way. Ordinary people felt they had been tricked. Huge firms have benefitted from low borrowing costs and almost free capital. Some have become monopolies. This harms society. Cheap money facilitates political corruption. Governments also enjoy very low borrowing costs; clearly, a large amount of the money they borrow is wasted. In short, money has become a weapon in the struggle for power between countries and between social classes. Many people have seen a decline in their real incomes. They feel they can no longer afford to buy what they need to live. Angry people vote for political parties that offer hope. That is how the fascists came to power in the 1930s; people could see no other way out.

Note

1. See end of Chap. 4.

Bibliography

Greenspan, A. (2008). 'The Financial Crisis and the Role of Federal Regulators: At a hearing of the US House of Representatives Committee on Oversight and Government Reform', October 23, 2008.
Meltzer, A. (2016). Remarks at Jackson Hole Symposium, 2016.

White, William (2017). *Federal Reserve Bank of Dallas, Dallas Fed, How False Beliefs About Exchange Rate Systems Threaten Global Growth and the Existence of the Eurozone*. Working Paper No 250 Subsequently published as a Chapter in "The Political Economy of the Eurozone" Edited by A Cardinale, D'Maris Coffman and R Scazzieri. Cambridge: Cambridge University Press.

White, William (2019). 'The Limits of Macroprudential Policy'. *International Economy*, Winter.

15

The Euro: The Biggest Money Project

The Federation of European States, comprising some of the wealthiest nations in the world, will be a monument to money. Such a federal state does not exist, but if it is essential for the euro to survive, it will be created. That is the presumption underlying the euro project. There is no better illustration of the power of money, 'our money'—indeed, of a specific idea of money—to make history. Europeans are apparently ready to endure any pain and offer any sacrifice necessary to make it succeed. It is Wagnerian in scale. Had they forgotten that the Ring of the *Niebelung*, Wagner's opera, is an epic warning against love of money? That the gold, stolen from Father Rhine, is cursed?

The odds have always been stacked against the euro. No monetary union like it has ever survived; several comparable ventures have indeed already failed. Never has a monetary union endured without being supported by a fiscal union involving a sharing of tax receipts and expenditures. Without that, it would be very difficult for countries with quite different economic structures, levels of development and standards of living to share a single money. The contrast to the world's most successful monetary union, the United States, is stark. By comparison with the United States, with its experience of 200 years of federal government, its distinct national character and political philosophy, not to mention its status as a global superpower, with one language and one American dream, Europe is a mess. Furthermore, the basic economics of the scheme, with its irrevocable fixing of national exchange rates, are faulty, in the view of a majority of economists, who favour flexible exchange rates. To place this project—the creation of a completely new currency—at the heart of the construction of the European edifice still seems foolhardy.

© The Author(s) 2019

R. Pringle, *The Power of Money*, https://doi.org/10.1007/978-3-030-25894-8_15

The euro was introduced by decree following a treaty. That was—at least in the British view—a misguided way to start a currency. Although the risks of the venture were obvious to experts from the start, the people were not told about them. This is not to say that the benefits to the people were not potentially large. But they were not consulted *a priori*; the fact that the governments involved were themselves democratically elected was considered enough to give the project legitimacy. It was a prime example of 'top-down' government and lawmaking. At a time when 'elites' came under attack, this vision of the euro as an elite project damaged confidence. Yet, the doom-mongers had underestimated the power of money, or an idea of money, backed by political will, to be an instrument of change and state-building. They had got their economics right but their politics wrong. Nothing illustrates better the power that ideas and hopes about money can have than the story of the euro from 1990 to 2020.

A 'Sort of Cattle Market'

Money had always played a large part in the construction of Europe. In the immediate post-war years, American insistence that European countries should cooperate in integrating their economic planning would not have got far without the massive dollar credits offered under the Marshall Plan. It was aid money that persuaded France to drop its demand for war reparations and to agree to the lifting of restrictions on German production and output. American money and pressure led to the creation of the European Payments Union, which facilitated the recovery of European trade. At the centre of the EU was a pact: a system of protection and subsidies for French farmers, paid for mainly by Germany (then West Germany) and tariff-free access to the French market for German exports (France was the main beneficiary for 40 years, in 2005 passing the bowl to Spain, Portugal and Greece). Not only at its foundation but also in its expansion, money has always greased the wheels of the EU bandwagon.

'It was in these years', says historian Tony Judt 'that the EC acquired its unflattering image as a sort of institutionalised cattle market, in which countries trade political alliances for material reward' (Judt 2005). In the four years from 1986 to 1989 alone Greece received US$7.9 billion from Brussels. Then, to persuade Mikhail Gorbachev, president of the USSR, to allow Germany to be reunited as a member of the EU, from 1990 to 1994, the EU transferred some US$71 billion to USSR (later Russia), in addition to billions ploughed into former Communist states of Eastern Europe and the trillions poured into East Germany.

State-Building

New forms of official money are seldom created by calm deliberation; usually they are forged in the heat of battle. That applies to the innovations following both world wars and the tumult following the collapse of Communism.

At Strasbourg, in December 1989, only a month after the fall of the Berlin Wall, Helmut Kohl, then Chancellor of West Germany, was moving swiftly to unify Germany while President Mitterrand of France was anxious to tie the unified, enlarged Germany to the West. Mitterand persuaded Kohl to enter into 'serious negotiations' on the Economic and Monetary Union (EMU) by threatening him with a potentially hostile 'triple alliance' between France, Britain and the Soviet Union. This would isolate Germany. Kohl agreed to negotiations, despite the objections of the Bundesbank. This was how the fall of the Berlin Wall brought forward the unification of Germany and the establishment of monetary union. Mitterrand had to accept German reunification more quickly than he wanted, and Kohl had to accept monetary union more quickly. A lonely protest from Mrs Thatcher, Prime Minister of Britain, was brushed aside. Her warning 'Twice we beat the Germans. now they are here again' made her a laughing stock. She talked in terms, reminiscent of the language used between the wars, about the need to hold the Germans down: 'It's not by building Europe that one can bind Germany. France and the United Kingdom need to join forces in the face of the German danger' (Marsh 2009, 140). 'If we have a single currency, the Germans will be insufferable.' But Kohl had France and the United States behind him, and it was Britain that ended up isolated and out of step.

In another age, faced with the emergence of a potential superpower, countries might have forged new alliances; they might have developed closer security agreement with new Germany; they might have looked to other countries around Germany to develop a network of international treaties so as to embed Germany in a mesh of cooperation and solidarity. What did the leaders of the then European Economic Community do? They decided to launch a new currency. What's the point? Might such an effort make citizens even more uneasy? Might it not stir up problems rather than solve them? It, indeed, might have such negative effects—as it did.

But this was an Age of Money; money as magic. Cooperate on money and other problems could be overcome. Such was the mindset of the time. That is how the leaders of Europe came to create the euro, a most unusual kind of money—a stateless currency. In December 1995, the European Council agreed to launch it on January 1, 1999. A timetable was laid down for the changeover to the euro. The project acquired unstoppable political momentum. On May 2, 1998, the heads of state or government decided that 11 member states had fulfilled the conditions necessary for adoption of the single currency on January 1, 1999 and on that date their national currencies ceased to exist. The euro became the single currency for 300 million people. Never before had sovereign states given up responsibility for monetary policy to a supranational institution.

Key omission: Germany was forced to drop its insistence that EMU should be quickly followed by moves to political union.

What a Gamble

It was a gamble on several counts: first, the leaders did not know whether people would accept the new currency—they had not been consulted; second, the irrevocable fixing of exchange rates would deprive nations of one of the traditional prerogatives of governments, the power to define their money—what counted as money in their nations and thus to change the exchange rate; third, there were no collective mechanisms for cushioning the effects of recessions; fourth, they had deliberately given the new central bank, the European Central Bank (ECB), only one objective—price stability, in contrast to the mandates of the leading central bank, the US Federal Reserve, which is enjoined to pursue a 'dual mandate' of employment and price stability objectives. The leaders had no reason to presume that a system requiring Germany to sacrifice the greatest achievement of its post-war order, the strong D-mark and its guardian the Bundesbank, to the cause of Europe would be acceptable to Germans. In the end, Germany even agreed to EMU without a commitment to political union. German leaders wanted to stop the exchange rate turbulence which threatened to tear the common market apart; for Germany, it was vital that Europe's markets at least remained open to free movement of goods, services and capital. As the area's greatest exporter and surplus county, Germany had the biggest stake in the project. If the choice in the end was between freely floating national exchange rates and a common currency, the promised stability benefits of a common currency were sufficient to sway the doubters. But the euro had been born prematurely. Crises were guaranteed: indeed, they were part of the design.

Horse Trading, Fudge and Bribery

There were more political compromises and horse trading about which countries would be in the first wave of members. The markets expected these to consist of Germany, France, Austria, the Netherlands, Belgium, Luxembourg and Ireland. But there was enormous political pressure to include others, and, as the decision would be taken by qualified majority voting, considerable scope for haggling. A question mark hung over Italy. Most Italian leaders demanded Italy should be in the first wave—but was it ready to comply with the demands of membership? Antonio Fazio, then governor of the Bank of Italy, said it would be too risky for Italy. Others, such as his predecessor Carlo Ciampi, warned that if Italy was not in the euro club, it would become even more difficult for it to fulfil the criteria laid down under the founding Maastricht Treaty. The smaller countries clamoured to be in. The Portuguese government argued that it was unacceptable to exclude a country that fulfilled all the criteria laid down by Maastricht, as Portugal planned to do. Finland was equally determined. Yet of the inner group expected by the markets to enter EMU, neither Austria nor Belgium, nor even France was likely to pass the government deficit test (3% of GDP was set as the 'reference value'). Italy was planning a deficit of 4.5% in 1997.

Two EU specialities came to the rescue: the art of the fudge and money—again. The Maastricht criteria would have to be fudged if the project was to go ahead (as they were in the cases of Italy and Belgium, whose public debt to GDP ratios were well above the criteria); as Otmar Issing, first chief economist of the ECB, politely put it, 'a major effort at interpretation and ultimately a political decision were required to enable their entry'. This 'interpretation' reached its *reductio ad absurdum* when the Greek government, advised by Goldman Sachs, a US investment bank, fiddled the data about its government debt to gain entry. Vast cash handouts were granted: as Judt puts it, 'Jacques Delors, the Commission President, all but bribed the finance ministers of Greece, Spain, Portugal and Ireland' in return for their signatures on the Maastricht treaty (Judt 2005). (The big difference was in what the recipient countries did with the cash: Ireland generally used the money to good effect, while the Greeks blew it). A Community of rules? Not exactly. Germany was among those quick to break the very rules it had insisted on to safeguard the single currency—as Issing put it, 'taking an axe to one of the pillars of monetary union'.

The Euro 'Will Make You Richer'

The euro was sold on the argument that it offered a route to greater prosperity—faster growth, higher living standards and improved public services. A low inflation rate—stable money—was expected to make a major contribution, especially in countries that had experienced years of currency depreciation and repeated devaluations of their old national currencies. Indeed, there was no doubt that the single currency would also bring massive savings in costs of conducting cross-border transactions, an increase in trade among member states, greater specialisation and division of labour, more choice for consumers and higher investments in new goods and services. The abolition of exchange rates within the EU would reduce transactions costs—and up to 30% of a small firm's foreign currency earnings can be eaten up by transactions costs. Consumers were also led to expect that interest rates would be lower. Meanwhile, a more competitive market for banking services would lead to lower borrowing and mortgage rates for consumers.

Really?

The people were not told that in the view of many economists, adoption of a single currency was incompatible with high welfare entitlements or regulation of markets (Issing 2008). Germans feared that countries favouring a large welfare provision would call on others to share the cost. There were also worries about whether backward regions could ever catch up with richer areas. Thus the euro was sold to the people on different arguments than those motivating those who actually decided on the venture. The people were told that they would enjoy higher living standards, cheaper borrowing costs, more choice and faster growth; in short, they would have more money in their pockets. Business leaders were promised larger markets, the chance to specialise and raise profits. Political leaders were led by the pressure of events. They had differing ambitions and dreams. In France, leaders dreamt of creating a currency that might challenge the dollar, shackle Germany and give them a say in setting monetary policy for the Continent as well as re-invigorate their economy. Political leaders in smaller countries naturally saw the idea of sitting round the policy-making table, one person one vote, with Luxembourg having as much say as Germany or France, as irresistible. For poorer countries, and poor regions in rich countries, there was the glitter of gold. They hoped for large subsidies from the centre, without too many questions being asked. They naturally warmed to the image of an extended family where members trusted each other.

In short, it was a top-down, undemocratic process. Money would be the foundation stone of the European Union (name adopted in 1993) and would offer European citizens the glorious prospect of—guess what?—more money in their pockets. EU's communication strategy focused on one message—'the euro will make you, the citizens, richer'—it virtually ignored the costs for poorer regions and people and the sacrifices involved in giving up alternative options. It gambled on its capacity to realise a utopian idea of money.

Performance 2000–18

What with recessions, financial instability, bank crises and high unemployment the euro turned into an agent of divisiveness. It entrenched the powers of creditors against debtors, of the centre against the periphery, of the North against the South. In fact pretty much all of the warnings and doubts of the sceptics were proved to be justified. Critics from the free market right complained that the ECB was an institution without clear rules, able to set its own criteria for the collateral it would accept, able to bail out insolvent banks and with no proper safeguards to prevent asset price inflation. Right. Indeed, the measures taken by the ECB to counter the recession caused just as much asset price inflation as in the United Kingdom and the United States. Real wages in the eurozone as a whole increased modestly between 2000 and 2017 although this hid large disparities between individual countries. But this was all predictable:

> In 1950, the French economist Jacques Rueff declared '*L'Europe se fera par la monnaie ou ne se fera pas*' ('Europe will be made through money, or not at all'). (Rueff 1950)

And the EU's founding father, Jean Monnet, said:

> Europe will be forged in crises, and will be the sum of the solutions adopted for those crises. (Monnet 1976)

Doubts Remain, the Euro Carries On

What kind of money is the euro? Germans thought it would be a big Deutschmark. Only that promise would have persuaded them to give up their beloved DM. The Benelux countries and Austria had no problem with that— they had been accustomed for many years to linking their currencies to the mark. But France and other Latin countries, especially Italy, had different ideas. For them the point of the ECB was that it gave all member states a seat at the top table where decisions about money would be made. These constituent countries had quite different traditions and attitudes to money. Through its traumatic experience with hyper-inflation (see Chap. 3), Germans had learnt the need for rules, for an independent central bank and for limits on government debt and more broadly for a monetary constitution. France had a different tradition of state intervention and planning going back to Jean Baptiste Colbert, the founder of the economic system of pre-revolutionary France, in the seventeenth century; rules should be subject to political process, governments should be able to respond flexibly to a crisis, industry may need state support and protection, and money should be a tool to serve broad social purposes. Yet despite these sources of tension, and despite policy errors, and stuttering recovery from a deep recession, the euro commands the broad support of the peoples of the countries belonging to it. Independent analysis of public support for the common currency over a quarter of a century, from 1990 to 2016, shows that, contrary to widely expressed views (especially in Britain), a majority of citizens in each member state of the original Eurozone, including in Germany and Italy, have consistently supported the euro even during the peak of the sovereign debt crisis (Roth, Jonung and Nowak-Lehmann and sources referenced therein, 2016). Commitment to the euro will probably continue to hold.

There are three main reasons to expect this. First, the euro is integral to the entire process of European integration—which, in the view of most citizens of the EU, is more than ever essential in the world opened up by the global money space and its domination by great powers such as the United States, China, Russia and India. The euro is Europe's defence against the danger of being vaporized in this global space. To avoid that, it had to make its own arrangements to govern money, and if it was to do that, it needed its own money. Second, more economists are coming around to Robert Mundell's view that the ability to devalue one's currency is not a reliable way to solve payment imbalances, especially among a group of small countries with high levels of trading and financial inter-dependence.[1] Third, the political bargain underlying the euro remains strong. The countries of southern Europe need the European Community to support their democracies; they fear there may be little chance of sustaining stable government outside it. France needs to bind Germany to Europe. Germany's destiny is to serve Europe by helping to unify it. Might it all end in tears again, as previous efforts to unite Europe have done? It's possible.

Many people in the euro countries feel the whole enterprise is going too far, too fast. On the other hand, the costs of leaving the euro would be prohibitive—as Greece realised when it looked into the abyss in 2015. That, also, was part of the design. Equally, the pressure to build more federal institutions continues. In a *Financial Times* interview on September 29, 2019, Mario Draghi, outgoing President of the ECB, said that a long-term commitment to fiscal union was "essential" for the eurozone to compete with other global powers. 'Given the inherent weakness of national states in a globalised world, what matters is to make the union stronger. In some areas, further integration achieves this goal', Mr Draghi said, later adding: 'To have a stronger EMU [Economic and Monetary Union], we need a common eurozone budget. Clearly the political debate on that still has a long way to go. But I am optimistic' (Lionel Barber and Claire Jones, 2019). In short, money is building Europe.

Note

1. Of 28 economists surveyed by the magazine *International Economy* in 2016, only 7 unambiguously favoured devaluation as a policy tool (*Is Devaluation Overrated?* International Economy 2016).

Bibliography

Barber, J., and Jones, C. (2019). 'Draghi Backs Calls for Fiscal Union to Bolster Eurozone'. *Financial Times*, 29 September 2019.

International Economy (2016). 'Is Currency Devaluation Overrated? A Symposium.' International Economy, Winter.

Issing, O. (2008). *The Birth of the Euro*.

Judt, T. (2005). *Postwar: A History of Europe since 1945*.

Marsh, D. (2009). *The Euro: The Politics of the new Global Currency*. New Haven and London: Yale University Press.

Monnet, J. (1976). *Mémoires*. Paris: Fayard.

Roth, F., Jonung, L., and Nowak-Lehmann, F. (2016). Public support for the euro Vox EU 11 November.

Rueff, Jacques (1950). Revue Synthèses, no. 45.

16

Crony and Criminal Capitalism Since 2010

Is there really no alternative to capitalism? Well, there are several—including crony capitalism, state capitalism, and rentier capitalism. Indeed, the most politically successful forms of capitalism currently are its corrupt forms. But these have little in common with capitalism proper.

Crony capitalism denotes a cosy relationship between big business and government politicians, says George Taber, the person credited with coining the term.[1] In particular, when a government rigs the market to favour its allies, that is a clear indicator that crony capitalism has taken over. It is a regime that, once established, is difficult to eliminate. With political power a person can insulate his or her family and descendants from the dangers and risks of the market. A society in which money is an expression of a shared liberal political philosophy naturally supports strong institutions that defend it against such abuses (ethical and institutional safeguards, unbiased administration of justice and so on). Our money culture has weakened such defences, as contemporary money no longer serves a shared social or political purpose. That is why Western capitalism's loss of credibility after the financial crisis is so serious. It leaves money naked; an object to be desired and taken without scruple. This chapter explores the effects of what may be termed a 'lustful' view of money.

That is one link between the financial crisis and the spread of crony capitalism after 2010. However, it would not have corrupted the system as deeply as it has in the absence of two other forces—the sheer amount of money flooding into the system, courtesy of the central banks, over the same period (as described in Chap. 14) and fears of a political backlash. The financial crash gave the wealthy and powerful of the North Atlantic a new incentive to use money to buy power. They anticipated a popular backlash with a hunt for

© The Author(s) 2019
R. Pringle, *The Power of Money*, https://doi.org/10.1007/978-3-030-25894-8_16

people to blame, notably including so-called 'fat cats', investment bankers, hedge fund managers and the wealthy elites in general. The combination of these factors—removal of defences, a gushing money supply, asset-price bubbles and a new incentive to acquire political power—delivered a series of blows to classical capitalism.

There are innumerable ways in which political power may be used to make money. Politicians can help favoured businesses by making life difficult for competitors, providing lucrative contracts, and granting special tax favours, permits or other kinds of state intervention. Profits are then a by-product of political power, no longer a just reward for risk-taking and innovation. Monied classes gain when there is a close nexus between the political and business class; they can then subvert the public sector and make it serve private ends. It is then a natural but vital step up the kleptocratic ladder to manipulate the law courts and system of justice systems. This gives them immunity from prosecution. They can also obtain court orders banning journalists from reporting or investigating their misdeeds. Kleptocrats then control the main channels of mass media communications.

In many countries throughout the world, people know that their money is being used against their interests. They see that the entire finance system needs a shake-up, that debt is too high and the rewards for risk-taking badly distorted. They know they are paying through currency debasement and interest-rate suppression as well as the tax system for state debts, including state liability for the continuing guarantees and subsidies to the finance sector. They know that Brussels, London and Washington are honeypots for corporate lobbyists aiming to win special deals and favourable regulation for the interests they represent. It's a shame that they cannot turn to economists for guidance and warning of danger. That's the lesson of experience and of course there are exceptions. As economist Luigi Zingales says, however, 'the economics profession has remarkably seldom warned the public about the risks at hand' (Zingales 2012, 93).

Capitalisms' Deformations

Of course, finance has always had political power. The relationship between banks, merchants and the sovereign predates capitalism itself. It was consecrated by the remarkable innovation of central banking. Indeed, as we shall see in Chap. 19, some sociologists believe that the value of money derives precisely from that struggle, that tension between Finance and the State, as well as between Creditor and Debtors. Would-be reforms that fail to take into account this social struggle involved in the creation of money will fail. The questions are not, how do we do away with the power of money? Or, can we make sure that State power always dominates private money power? In a society that values freedom, that has learnt the lessons from twentieth-century history, we cannot take those routes. The real questions are rather, can the power both of governments and of bankers, merchants and the private sector be constrained within certain limits? And how should we define those limits, and then enforce them? Answering such questions points to the need for an agreed constitutional framework, a set of rules which we all agree to obey (Buchanan 1975). At present, we have moved a long away from such a rules-based order, even in the heartlands of capitalism. Finance permeates the inner working of government, changing the incentives facing private and public sector actors, and enabling private persons to use their money or their political power for private gain.

It is useful to group the various types of deformations of capitalism into two main types: in addition to 'crony', there is also 'state' capitalism. Under a regime of crony capitalism, private interests use money and power to make the state and/or its major agencies work for them—to benefit their narrow interests, often with the active connivance of politicians; under *state capitalism*, the economy, though nominally based on private enterprise, is dominated by the state, and politicians use its power to enrich themselves. In both, money becomes an instrument of power, whether public or private. In crony capitalism, private interests use money to influence policies and regulations to favour their interests; in state capitalism, organs of the state—typically answerable to the president or his favourites—use control over the supply of money and credit to ensure that businesses follow instructions designed to bolster their power/income. Typically, under crony capitalism, private interests aim to secure a monopoly or near-monopoly position in a given market so as to maximise profits well above what they would be in a competitive market, while in state capitalism the state (typically identified in the person of its leader) suppresses competition in order to reap the benefits of monopolistic pricing to benefit the ruling group and shape economic development according to its priorities (often for personal enrichment). In both, the well-being of consumers and the health of the economy as a whole suffers from suppression/distortion of markets.

Both types of capitalist deformation have become more firmly entrenched in the twenty-first century. In both cases, one of the driving forces is fear. The wealthy elite—especially the top 0.1%—knew that after the financial crash, the bailouts and recession, there would be a political backlash against them, though they did not know precisely what form it would take. There were large incentives for them, therefore, to turn money into other, more directly useable, tools. Of these, power was the most attractive—use money to put 'our' friends in strategic places, to establish strong lines of communication and influence in both the corporate and political worlds. Use money to ensure 'our' interest would be able to block new regulations or turn them to 'our' advantage. And use our money as a means of forming strong social bonds among the ultra-wealthy, a global elite that could survive apart; a unilateral declaration of independence.

Security is sought in many fields using multiple channels. Power, art, charitable giving, new foundations are all fashionable trades. Investment in lobbying is just one tactic to stop the state from striking back against tax havens, money laundering and dodges. Former regulators are assured of rich pickings in the private sector when they leave official office. (I once suggested to a deputy governor of a leading central bank that former senior officials should be banned from taking posts in private equity or finance after leaving office: he looked at me incredulously—'So you want to destroy my second career, Robert?')

Deformations Become Normal

The dominant forms of capitalism are its deformations. Leading state capitalist economies are those of China and Russia. Leading crony capitalist economies are India, Malaysia, Indonesia, Brazil, Philippines, and many countries of Latin America and Central Asia. Crony capitalism is on the rise in the United Kingdom and the United States. The area of the globe and the proportion of the population under traditional or 'straight' capitalism regimes are shrinking. In the Darwinian struggle between ways of organising economies, it is not 'neoliberalism' but state and crony capitalisms that are in the ascendant. The proportion of world economic output produced in countries with corrupt forms of capitalism has increased sharply since the global financial crisis.

Admittedly, capitalism and free markets have never existed in a pure form, where the state merely 'holds the ring', refraining from any intervention in the economy. But there are crucial differences between a basically free market capitalism with strong state presence (as in the United States until recently) or a European-style post-World War II welfare state with policies designed to encourage competitive markets (e.g. as through anti-trust laws) on the one hand, and the fully evolved forms of state or crony capitalism on the other. While there have long been elements of both syndromes in most countries, they both developed strongly in the years following the global financial crash and recession in 2007–09. In developed countries, private financial interests showed their power by securing state bailouts, avoiding personal liability or punishment, and by blocking radical reforms to banking and finance. State capitalism gained prestige and legitimacy from the loss of credibility of the model advocated by the United States, United Kingdom and international agencies prior to the crisis—basically advocating financial liberalisation with some regulation—and the rapid increase in the share of such state-led economies in global output.

Where the United States Leads…

Although it is usual for government officials in the United States to divest themselves of their business holdings on taking office, to forestall any suspicion of wrongdoing, when Donald Trump became president, he merely granted his sons control over his businesses. Critics accuse him of breaking norms that are 'essential to the health of democracy' (Levitsky and Ziblatt 2019). His appointment of his daughter, Ivanka, and son-in-law Jared Kushner, though legal, 'flouted the spirit of the law' in the view of many. He has also encouraged the perception among Americans that the political system is corrupt: 'about half of self-identified Republicans said they believe that American elections are massively rigged' (ibid. p 197). Such perceptions are very damaging. The Trump family and associates have used their proximity to presidential power to accumulate even greater wealth. Ivanka and Jared Kushner were reported to have already made more than US$80 million in personal income in 2017, during the first year of the Trump presidency, while they were official White House special advisors.

The rot did not, however, start with the election of Donald Trump. One reason for his election was the perception that his opponent Hillary Clinton was the candidate of a corrupt Democratic/Wall Street establishment. Also, as in Britain and other countries, the way in which the fallout from the financial crash was managed led many to assume crony capitalism was at work. Two respected economists gave this verdict:

> The bottom line: only eight years after the end of the worst financial crisis since the Great Depression, the US Treasury has shifted from becoming a leading proponent for enhancing the resilience of the global financial system to an advocate for the private interests of a few financial behemoths in the name of boosting growth. (Cecchetti and Schoenholtz 2017)

The largest banks were fined more than US$340 billion for money laundering and other wrongdoings in the ten years following the 2007–09 financial crisis—more than the entire annual output of countries like Ireland or Finland. Not a single top banker was prosecuted. Their impunity encouraged them politically; Trump Administration's top ranks are packed with powerful former bankers. Despite the labyrinth of regulations and vast supervisory apparatus, the United States remains highly attractive to kleptocrats and leaders of organised crime as a place to invest their gains. As Frank Vogl, a co-founder of the anti-corruption watchdog Transparency International, says: 'The stink of corruption pervades much of the top echelon of American finance' (Vogl).

Although market capitalism's defences and moral underpinnings were under siege prior to Trump's election, his first term certainly witnessed a further decline in norms. As the watchdog Freedom House puts it:

> Challenges to American democracy are testing the stability of its constitutional system and threatening to undermine political rights and civil liberties world-wide…. While democracy in America remains robust by global standards, 'it has weakened significantly over the past eight years, and the current president's ongoing attacks on the rule of law, fact-based journalism, and other principles and norms of democracy threaten further decline' (Freedom House 2019). America's constitutional system, while older and more robust than any in history, 'is vulnerable to the same pathologies as have killed democracy elsewhere. (Levitsky and Ziblatt 2019)

....Britain Follows

Another observer with hands-on experience is Avinash Persaud, an economist who has worked with several governments. Persaud claims that it is no accident that London has become the global capital of money laundering. Money launderers and those financing terrorist activities have two main requirements:

> The first is a place crowded with financial transactions, in which their own will be easy to lose. The second is a place where those who enable the setting up of companies and opening of bank accounts are prepared to turn a blind eye to who is the owner of a business. Secrecy over the beneficial ownership of companies is the main conduit of money laundering.

According to the UK Home Affairs Select Committee, the London property market is the primary avenue for the laundering of £100 billion of illicit money a year. Persaud quotes the investigative journalist Roberto Saviano as saying of the international drugs trade: 'Mexico is its heart and London is its head'.

There is little point in relating more horror stories (many more are entertainingly reported by Bullough 2019). The cry goes up for such activities to be banned and regulated out of existence. But the costs of the global anti-money-laundering bureaucracy are massive and growing fast. Many ordinary people merely suspected of involvement are being excluded from the money networks. There are limits to what can be done within the current legal framework while respecting the sovereignty of independent countries. That is why successive inquiries into 'offshore centres' and even startling disclosures by campaigners such as Glenny, Bullough and Vogl have failed to make lasting impact beyond further elaboration of the already top-heavy anti-money laundering 'know-your-customer' rules.

Sad Decline of Banking

Right up to the 1980s, banking was populated by proud names—great institutions with histories to celebrate: Citibank, Chase Manhattan, JP Morgan, Wells Fargo, HSBC, Barclays, Lloyds, Deutsche, Standard Chartered, UBS, Credit Suisse and the rest. The reputation of these institutions—and others—is not what it was. True, many bankers are trying hard to restore public respect for their profession. New bodies have been set up in an effort to raise standards. But the rot spreads. We have also learnt that the practice of imposing fines on banks rather than the individuals responsible has been misguided. Such fines have no effect on incentives (Goodhart 2017). But the practice continues. Meanwhile, the use of money to influence the political process has become shameless.

This is not only a matter of the vast sums spent on political lobbying, there is also the revolving door: as mentioned above, many public policy-makers plan on getting positions in private finance; it is childish to believe that this anticipation has no influence on their judgements while they are holding a public office. It is hardly surprising that the banks have successfully thwarted popular demand for fundamental reform. In a report on a major scandal involving Danske Bank, Vogl wrote that so long as board directors provide major bonuses to senior executives on the basis of short-term profit results, banking cultures that place making money above sound ethics and concern for their public reputation will persist: practices are accepted as normal that would once have shocked so much that they would not have been tried.

A World of Bribery

At the grassroots level, bribery has become a common experience in many countries. About 1.6 billion people a year pay money to access services such as healthcare, education and other services or to escape obligations to pay through official channels. This can involve clearly illegal forms, such as payment to police to avoid prosecution, or payment to bend rules in one's favour, as in queue-jumping for a hospital appointment. Every year, approximately 24% of households worldwide pay at least one bribe to a public official. The lowest ratio is found in Japan at 1%, the highest in countries such as Haiti, Azerbaijan, Cambodia and some parts of Africa, all with ratios above 50%. In the EU, it averages 4%, with the highest frequency being observed in Lithuania (29%). The global corruption barometer of Transparency International showed that in 2013, 51% of people surveyed said corruption, defined as the abuse of trust for private benefit, was a very serious problem in their country (TI 2013). According to the watchdog Freedom House, 2018 was the 13th successive year to see a decline in democracy and democratic institutions worldwide. The share of the 'not free' category of countries in the world economy is growing fast.

Dead Aid

Foreign aid—the billions of dollars that go in grants and cheap loans to emerging markets every year—has long been regarded by insiders as one of the main sources of capitalisms' deformations. The official target is that each donor country should aim to provide a sum equivalent to 0.7% of its GDP—another monument to the delusions fostered by contemporary money. Of course, aid agencies have safeguards designed to ensure aid reaches those it is aimed at and prevent abuse yet they give even higher priority to maintaining their cooperation with all regimes of all kinds, irrespective of their records. They do not insist on press freedom, or an independent judiciary, or human rights. They say that to do so would be interfering in countries' internal affairs. No wonder their work is treated with cynicism. Dembisa Moyo argues in her powerful book, *Dead Aid*, that foreign aid has done more harm than good (Moyo 2010). She pays tribute to Peter Bauer, a pioneering market economist whom I knew quite well. Among the 'kiss-and-tell' exposes by former foreign aid workers, my favourite is *Tropical Gangsters* by Robert Klitgard, a former professor of economics at Harvard—an amusing but savage account of the author's two-and-a-half year stint in Equatorial Guinea (Klitgard 1991). Yet, the aid wagon trundles on.

The spread of the money virus may be compared with the way that in the eighteenth and nineteenth centuries imperialists forced themselves on other societies. Where the tools of imperialism were trade, military aggression and (religious) missionaries, our instruments are money, high-tech and (economic) missionaries. Whatever the prevailing doctrine in the West may be at any one time, international agencies make the rest of the world follow it. If prevailing Western norms demand that countries on the receiving end portray themselves as democracies, adopt the latest ideas about gender relations, the role of women and ethnic equality, so they scramble to catch up. This is monetary aggression: the forceful use of money power to impose alien ideas and norms of moral behaviour on other people.

As insiders testify, the main institutions of international monetary cooperation, the IMF and World Bank, have, until relatively recently, turned a blind eye to corruption. Frank Vogl, who worked at the top of the World Bank for many years, knows this and has had the courage to speak out (consultants hired by these agencies are specifically banned by their contracts from exposing corruption even when they see it at work). But the aid agencies have always one over-riding imperative: to expand the volume of their loans and grants, their money assets and liabilities, as that means bigger budgets and more jobs. They should, as Vogl says, focus on the quality not the quantity of aid, and they have made efforts but…: 'they all want the cash to flow' (Vogl 2012).

The compulsion to keep the foreign aid bandwagon going testifies to the influence of the money culture. Let us imagine what would happen if governments were presented with incontrovertible evidence that foreign aid resulted in slower development, more corruption and more misery than would be experienced in its absence? They would carry on just the same. When David Cameron as Conservative Leader needed to get rid of its image as the 'nasty party', he pledged to raise foreign aid. As a result, Britain is one of the handful of countries that has in recent years met the 0.7% 'target'. Often one hears this reflects the West's 'guilt' for its imperialist history. That may be part of it. But the real reason for keeping aid flowing is that we are clenched in the mindset of the Money Delusion. We pride ourselves on following policies based on evidence, but we do not. We have to believe that aid works.

China, Russia and India: Where Fear Breeds Repression

'The only people you are afraid of in this country and the Party or the Police—nobody else. So you have to keep them onside', explained Paul French, a British businessman and author living in Shanghai. 'Nobody gets rich here by being 100% clean', he continued. 'I'm not 100% clean and nobody else is. If we did everything by the book, nothing would ever get done'. Anybody doing business in China had to take care of the police and the Party as China was in effect run by them—a 'Political Criminal Nexus' (PCN). Powerful provincial leaders were comfortable with PCN as both a system of governance and an economic strategy, and warded off interference from Beijing. The provinces may be as corrupt as they wish in making their money, 'as long as Beijing does not catch them red-handed'. China used fear to keep a tight grip on its people because the Party itself was frightened. The anarchic collapse of the Soviet Union in the 1990s had 'struck terror into the hearts of China's bureaucrats'. It was, on one account, 'the single most important cause of the exponential growth in organized crime that we have seen around the world in the last two decades' (see *McMafia*, by Misha Glenny first published in 2008, for above citations).

Russia eventually wound up under President Putin with a novel system that brought together aspects of capitalism and Soviet socialism. This was a creation of the oligarchy that seized control of Russian assets following the botched reform programmes of President Yeltsin. The economic programme included liberalisation of the prices of bread and rents, while prices of Russia's vast mineral resources were held down. A new class of traders sprang up to buy these commodities at the old Soviet price, which was one-fortieth of the world market price, export them and sell them at the world price, pocketing the difference. This enrichment is said to have been the biggest theft in history.

India is another country with an active PCN. The public sector banks had been abused for decades by politicians and their cronies, and while ordinary citizens struggled to borrow money, those with connections continued to milk the system. Many of the non-performing assets (NPAs) stem from the collusion and influence-peddling involved in sanctioning loans. This leads to extensions, moratoriums and restructuring packages. Entrepreneurs in India range from rent-seekers who prosper either by close relations with the state or by exploiting the weakness of state institutions, to entrepreneurs who have built major businesses without relying or depending on state influence. India contains examples of crony capitalists on the one hand and, on the other, of capitalists who rely only on their own enterprise and available social resources to build large businesses. In other countries, rule by oligarchs is blatant. In Ukraine, for a time, they were the government. A gangster called Leonid Kuchma became president of the country: 'It was a period when the state was converted into a criminal political mafia', said MP Omelchenko, who headed the investigation into political crime and corruption. Very few corners of the world are free of the nexus of criminality, state corruption, bribery and extortion.

The Changing Meaning of Money

When money becomes power, the ways in which money works in society change and the 'meaning' of money in that society alters. When money develops such alternative uses, it modifies the incentives of everybody in the society. Increasingly, they trade favours, rights, permits, exemptions, information and privileges in place of goods and services with prices set in competitive markets. At the extreme, only a fool spends money to purchase anything at the going rate. Everything is negotiable. When people receive money, their first thought is not what should I spend it on, but, rather, how much is this worth in other uses? Surveys have shown that in many countries more than half the population uses bribery on a regular basis.

Money power changes the way states fight. In an age when monetary networks hold the global economy together, what could be a worse punishment than being deprived of access to them? When your value, or the value of your enterprise, is determined in global money markets, to be cut off from the money network is a death sentence. This gives new power to the people who control payment networks such as Swift, the vast messaging system used by banks. The collapse of the Iranian economy in 2019 was a result of sanctions.

Common strands link these change. Money is needed as a tool of political as well as of purchasing power. Anybody with power searches for ways of turning it easily into money and anybody with money to convert it to power. At the extreme, everybody would need power to get anything. And people who controlled things that people wanted could choose whether to accept money or power in exchange. An active trade linking money and power skirts the fringes of the law. The chances of getting caught and convicted are negligible.

Corrupt capitalism undermines public support and raises business costs. An increasing share of overall income comes from corrupt sources. The temptation to manipulate politicians is overwhelming. Once the right connections are established and the right incentives are in place, crony capitalism is a licence to print money. Public support for market capitalism has declined. As I write the presidents of five of the seven most powerful nations in the world are widely believed to be using their political power to amass incredible fortunes. It is scarcely surprising that public trust in government is near an all-time low—having sunk to only 17% in the United States (Pew Research Centre, April 2019).

Note

1. Taber, a former business editor of Time magazine, tells the story in the Wharton School website: 'The Night I Invented Crony Capitalism'.

Bibliography

Obama, B. (2010, February 9). Interview. Bloomberg Business Week.

Buchanan, James (1975). *The Limits of Liberty: Between Anarchy and Leviathan.*

Bullough, O. (2019). *Moneyland: Why Thieves and Crooks Now Rule the World and How to Take It Back.* London: Profile.

Cecchetti, S., and Schoenholtz, K. (2017). 'The US Treasury's missed opportunity'. Vox EU 14 July 2017. An earlier version of this column appeared on www.moneyandbanking.com.

Freedom House (2019). Freedom in the World.

Glenny, Misha (2008). *McMafia: Seriously Organised Crime.* London: Vantage

Goodhart, Charles (2017). 'Why regulators should focus on bankers' incentives'. Bank Underground blog post, April 5.

Hart, Keith (ed) (2017). *Money in a Human Economy.* New York: Berghahn.

Klitgard, R. (1991). *Tropical Gangsters: One Man's Experience of Decadence and Development in Deepest Africa.* New York and London: Bloomsbury.

Levitsky, S., and Ziblatt, D. (2019). *How Democracies Die: What History Reveals about our Future.* London: Penguin Books.

Moyo, Dembisa (2010). *Dead Aid: Why aid is not working and how there is another way for Africa.* London: Penguin Books.

Persaud, A. (2017). *London: The money laundering capital of the world. Prospect,* April 27, 2017.

Pew Research Centre (2019, April). 'Public Trust in Government: 1958–2019'.

Transparency International (2013 and 2019). Global Corruption Barometer. https://www.transparency.org/gcb2013.

Vogl, F. (2012). *Waging War on Corruption.* Lanham, Maryfield: Rowman and Littlefield.

———. (2019, January 4). 'The Danske Bank Money Laundering Trail'. *The American Interest.*

Zingales, Luigi (2012). *A Capitalism for the People.* New York: Basic Books.

17

Global Money: Insiders and Outsiders

Most people find their own way of living with modern money in the global money space; however, some do not. These are the Outsiders; they include sub-groups that I call the Opponents, the Outcasts and the Others. Taken together, they form what I call The Resistance. Insiders usually assume that Resisters will gradually be absorbed into the mainstream, possibly leaving a remnant that can be safely ignored. Such sentiments echo the attitudes of pre-industrial Christian Europe to infidels. Against this, I argue that the Resistance will remain a significant force. Resisters come in all shapes and sizes. Their diversity gives them strength. They experience the dominant money culture society as aggressive and intolerant. It may arouse not just impotent anger, but also a determination to resist that can effect change, as it often arises from deep wells of tradition, culture and beliefs. Much of the Resistance takes place underground. It would be a mistake for the guardians of the global money space to dismiss alternative traditions and ideas. There are radical alternative visions of human destiny. The Resisters will have a say in shaping our future.

Plainly, the evolution of a global money society has made it difficult to escape money's reach. With the possible exception of members of remote, isolated communities, few can now be unaware of modern money's power and reach or untouched by its troubling allure. We are trained to want it, while at the same time fearing that the connection carries risks—not least the threat of the connection being cut. Each of the six billion adults on the planet may choose what attitudes to take towards money and, to some degree, the terms of their engagement with it: they can accept it, fight it, manipulate it, hate it, love it, but nobody can easily disengage from it. Not only is everybody obliged to train how to get money and what to do with it, but they are also intimately

© The Author(s) 2019
R. Pringle, *The Power of Money*, https://doi.org/10.1007/978-3-030-25894-8_17

affected by other people's monetary behaviour and habits. The money that people have, or have access to, determines their life chances. Money our governments spend changes society.

Membership of the global money society has distinguishing obligations and entails acceptance of the rules of the game. As outlined in Chap. 12, members have one or more bank accounts or other means of making and receiving payments—a condition for participating in the formal monetary system. They reside in a country that permits cross-border payments with few, if any, restrictions or (in cases such as China which has a non-convertible currency) can access ways of making and receiving such payments without too great difficulty. The written and unwritten rules of behaviour include, for example, a determination to observe contracts, fulfil promises and pay one's dues to society, including taxes raised by a legitimate state or other duly constituted authority. The law-abiding citizen may seem to have no alternative: there are few wild spaces left. Over time, each of us develops a lifestyle that includes as one of its basic parameters the terms in which we engage with the world of money. It reflects our beliefs, values and attitudes. We adopt an approach that suits us. Within these limits, we carve out a personal monetary space—our own little blob in the multitude of blobs that populate the global money society. We jostle with other blobs for a good position, a place from which to view the passing scene and a place from which we reach out to other blobs. We connect our sensory organs to the pipelines. Our fingers, eyes and nostrils quiver as they pick up waves of sound and light and send them to the cerebral cortex for processing and tremble as it decides to send answering waves back. One way or another, we find our place and get on with our lives.

This chapter is mainly about people who do not follow this normal model. This may be either because they will not or because they cannot. For whatever reason—and the reasons, as we shall see, are many and diverse—such people are not at home in the global money space. However, we also have to look at ways in which this space is maintained and defended. As I said at the end of Chap. 11, in describing the Monetary Renaissance and the birth of a global space, the latter may splinter as a result of macroeconomic forces, notably volatile capital flows and protectionist barriers. It is certainly under pressure from such macro forces, although I believe that forces making for integration are too strong for it to crumble as a result. However, it may, and I believe will, also come under pressure from micro-economic and sociological forces and from a perceived lack of legitimacy. To defend the space over the longer term requires that the powers of its guardians be justified and legitimated. Force will always be an element in upholding a monetary order (payment of taxes is not voluntary), and in a state of nature, it is the only power that matters. But unless the order regains legitimacy, and we return to a society governed by contract rather than naked power, it will eventually founder.

Accordingly, while this chapter focusses on the Outsiders, I start with a look at the Insiders, and, in particular, at those who control and regulate the global money space.

Insiders

It is in the nature of present-day money to divide society into Insiders and Outsiders. People who patrol the perimeter of the global money space are its guardians. They include, for example, those with authority to grant or withhold qualifications in education, the professions, business and other fields. It is possible to be a member without qualifications of any sort, but, as we shall see, it can be challenging. Then, there are the public servants who determine standards and qualifications required on issues such as criteria for establishing identity, such as the right to a passport of a particular nation state, those who give or withhold vital ID forms such as national insurance numbers, green cards and all the other certificates and records of the modern state. There are the police, immigration authorities who determine whether a particular individual can legally move across a national border and find a new identity in another state. In 2018, there were an estimated 60 million refugees in the world; in the United States 1.3 million were homeless, in the United Kingdom 250,000. Not having a fixed address and/or ability to prove one's identity in the approved form make it impossible to be a member of the global money society.

Hierarchy of Power

The ladder of money power ascends from that bottom level of the 'ordinary member', through the middle ranks of businesses, the public sector, the media, the professions right up to the levels of partners/CEOs and then to the central bankers and regulators. Economists who are also public intellectuals mingle with these senior circles, reflecting and, in turn, influencing the climate of opinion, guiding norms of behaviour and official policy. Just as attitudes, values and beliefs about money undergo quite rapid changes, we should examine how ideas about, and defence of, the global money society develop. This is far from a matter of pure economic theory, as it depends on power relationships. There are various channels through which ideas and power structures interact to change dominant currents of opinion (on matters ranging from capital flow management to inflation control and policies on reserve management). One is the annual get-together of central bankers and economists at Jackson Hole, Wyoming, USA, an event awaited with great anticipation by markets as well as policy-makers. There are a number of other fora and institutions which insiders use to test their ideas and opinions.

The Super-Elite

From 1979 to 1986, I was chief executive of an elite institution, the Group of Thirty. Indeed, I helped set it up. Membership was, and is, by invitation. There are no explicit or formal definitions of the qualifications needed. They are selected by a steering committee from among those individuals who they consider combine great institutional power (e.g. as head of a major bank, central bank or business) with a capacity to contribute to high-level debates about current issues of money, banking and international economics. Members usually include former or current central bank governors of leading countries and the European Central Bank; two or three heads of major banks and business corporation; a few economists. The annual Davos conference organised by the World Economic Forum, which sells itself as the international organisation for public-private cooperation, is another binge for the super-elite. It includes politicians as well as opinion leaders in culture and many fields other than money and finance. But it is used by the top financiers and policy-makers more as a way of testing and disseminating their policies than to test ideas against peers during the period of policy formulation and to trade in the currency of influence and patronage.[1]

Members of the super-elite share a way of seeing the world. It is their oyster. The tone is set by the private sector, media, entertainment, finance and business moguls. Although, as individuals, they have been promoted on meritocratic grounds, and some come from modest family backgrounds, the ethos at the very top is one of considered, controlled entitlement. They have massive egos painfully brought under control, at least in public. The super-powerful guys—including top officials and regulators—are distinct sociologically from the super-rich. Members of both groups share the conviction that they have earned the right to their positions, whether they be ones of wealth or of power. It is too obvious to need any assertiveness. But power trumps wealth. So, the wealthy aim to have power as well. Being merely a billionaire does not get you to have dinner with the Queen of England or the Emperor of Japan. Being president of the United States does.

These insiders are the core operators and supporters of the global money space. They run not only its finances but its other networks—personal, media, business, entertainment, high art, healthcare and sport. In finance, they have migrated largely from the over-regulated formal banking sector to asset management, hedge funds, fin-tech, unregulated real estate and alternative finance. They lead the world. Economists are on hand to provide a theoretical legitimation in terms of the benefits that the system has brought or will bring to ordinary members of the global money society. Their confidence has not been destroyed by the disasters, but public trust in the Insiders and guardians has been eroded.

Outsiders

I identify three groups of Outsiders: Opponents, Outcasts and a category that I call Other Outsiders. *Opponents* reject the global money society. They challenge the legitimacy of the emerging order and wish to replace it or radically reform it by the light of other ideals. They resent the tendency of the culture to ascribe monetary motives to them when their motives are in fact always mixed. They may more radically hold out visions of ways of life and a future for humankind quite different from that peddled by Insiders and in the media. The *Outcasts* are groups who do not fit in not because they do not wish to but because they cannot. Many do not have the right qualifications, with officially approved ID; others have had criminal convictions (a third or more of young men in some countries). In all, this group probably represents a significant fraction of global output and income. *Other Outsiders* are a large and heterogenous group. They include people who, while able to cope with money's rules and demands, prefer to live as far as possible in an environment sheltered from the harsh disciplines of the market and money—protected communities, professions or callings where basic needs of life are provided collectively.

I now examine the make-up and attitudes of these groups in a little more detail.

Opponents

Economic Aspects

Many people and social groups feel the system is not working for them economically. Globalisation is hurting rather than helping them; the creation of a global monetary economy has not given them more opportunities but rather generated new fears and threats. The groups include not only members of the working classes in developed economies undercut by lower wages in China and the emerging markets but also increasingly professional people worldwide who feel newly uncertain about their job prospects given that many services can be (or soon may be) delivered at a distance, obviating or greatly reducing the need for face-to-face contact; diagnoses, routine legal work, education, are among hundreds of professional occupations being transformed. But this group also includes many underprivileged people in developing and emerging economies who have neither the skills nor the interest to migrate to the big cities where work is available or are too old or ill-educated to attempt to adapt. Thus people who reject the global money space on economic grounds have little in common except that they believe they are economically losers by modernisation.

Opponents also include the people who joined anti-globalisation movements in the latter part of the twentieth century. They regularly protested against world trade rules, the international economic institutions and multinational corporations. They were recruited mainly from people in developed countries who often had high-status positions, such as university lecturers, but who opposed economic globalisation often on the grounds of the stresses it set up in many communities in the developed countries where people found their jobs under threat from imports and the exploitation of workers in low-wage economies. These critics targeted in particular the neoliberal agendas of many Western governments in the 1980s and 1990s, and were given another cause by the invasion of Iraq by the United States, Britain and their allies in 2004. There were both nationalist and internationalist versions of this opposition, which, after fading away in the early 2000s, gained new vigour after the financial crisis. Among the intellectual leaders of the movement were prominent economists such as Nobel Laureates Amartya Sen and Joseph Stiglitz.

Social

Close-knit communities may not suit everybody but often do make for healthy, happy societies. Thus, many people mourn the erosion of community bonds that follows inexorably from the geographical, economic and social mobility that comes with rapid economic change. Such people are often seen as backward-looking and stuck in their ways, obstinately resistant to change. Certainly this group includes such people, people who treasure the old days, who say 'things aren't what they used to be', the people who regret the loss of social support that personal ties in villages and small towns worldwide used to give them and have vanished as young people move out to find fame and fortune in the big cities. But it also embraces that not insignificant number of young people who wish to retain close ties to their parents and grandparents but are seduced away by the attractions of paid employment, pressures of work and professional life, people who would like to return home but find 'home' has vanished.

Ethical/Religious

This group includes people who feel that the attitudes that typically accompany the money-centric society are ethically offensive, anti-human, selfish and anti-social. They see this as a descent into a worse kind of free-for-all society—the kind of free for all that they and people like them have spent many years trying to avoid, a state of society from which we need to move out of. Religious rebels include people who frame life on earth in a spiritual light, who view the meaning of life as fulfilment of God's will, who place service to God in quite a different category from the economic, and who feel threatened by the money-centric culture; they may believe it is impossible to lead the life that God has called them to. Those who regret mechanisation, modernisation and money centrism on ethical and/or religious/spiritual grounds come from a variety of distinct ethical and religious standpoints.

Cultural/Intellectual

Some people see the contemporary culture as undermining everything that humans have learnt from the great thinkers, composers and writers about how to live together. A good society celebrates those who contribute to its music, art, literature and philosophy. This group is also diverse. It would include the old cultured elite of Europe, horrified by modern materialism and vulgarity (but would be the first to man the defences of what they view as civilisation against the attack by leftist extremists). Many mourn the passing of the old European bourgeois high culture. Then there's the existentialist school in the tradition of Dostoyevsky and the novel that epitomises in its title—*L'Etranger*, by Albert Camus—its whole stance on the world. This book tops many lists of the twentieth century's greatest novels; man is alone in an 'absurd' world, and all he can do is to make a gesture, to act to prove he exists and that he or she is free to create his or her own life, to paint it like an artist, even to the extent of suppressing normal feelings of humanity just as the servants of the totalitarian dictators of the previous 20 years had done to execute their masters' terrible crimes. We live under the shadow of such creative stars. Another was George Orwell, whose book, *Nineteen Eighty-Four*, published in 1949, uncannily anticipates conditions in a world of perpetual warfare. Orwell's nightmare vision of a totalitarian, bureaucratic world foresaw the ubiquity of gadgets such as TV as surveillance devices, the distortion of the language, and how all this would lead to a hell on earth. He perceived that in such a global economy the labour force and industry would be centred around war so as to keep the people in a constant state of dependence. People would live a miserable existence with no hope of improving their standard of living. By far the most influential critics of the corrupting effect of money and the profit motive are on the left—writers such as George Bernard Shaw, DH Lawrence and members of the Bloomsbury set described in Chap. 6 such as EM Forster.[2] No wonder British universities hated Mrs Thatcher. The enterprise culture she championed was considered odious. To be interested in money was seen as vulgar. Such an attitude to money-making was insufferably snobbish. But was it any worse than a model of *Homo sapiens* as nothing but a rational, maximising, evaluating, calculating creature of unsatisfied wants? Surely such a self-portrait, widely dispersed as it came to be throughout society, is abusive. The interests it serves are those of people who have something to sell.

Heroes Who Walked

One intriguing group of opponents are those traders/financiers/hedge fund managers who were once seduced by the glitter of money, like Alberich in the *Ring of the Niebelung*, but later rebelled against their cultures and occupations. Some of them had the guts and the skill to tell their stories—these also make a contribution. Let me highlight Geraint Anderson of *City Boy: Beer and Loathing in the Square Mile* (2009), Greg Smith, author of *Why I Left Goldman Sachs* (2014) and Sam Polk, author of *For the Love of Money: A Memoir* (2016), I like in particular the account by Geraint Anderson, who draws on his experience as a young analyst in the City to expose its corrupt culture, its monstrous egos, and the everyday verbal and substance abuse that fuels the world's money markets and how it almost cost him his sanity. They all testify to the seductive grip that finance comes to acquire over the men and women who surrender to it. The witness statements by the few who saw through it and had the guts to break out and to speak out deserve recognition. Many others quit their jobs voluntarily to enter a profession they regarded as more worthwhile, such as teaching and nursing, without seeking publicity. Some may have turned anti-money after some life-changing experience, or, as one put it online, merely from watching many sequences of *Star Trek* on TV where money doesn't exist and the crew's basic needs are provided collectively.

Finance needs more whistle blowers—when a worker reports suspected wrongdoing at work; in the UK and US firms are now banned from attempting to stop whistle blowers. A worker can, by law, report things that aren't right, are illegal or if anyone at work is neglecting their duties, including if someone's health and safety are in danger; damage to the environment; a criminal offence; the company isn't obeying the law (like not having the right insurance); and covering up wrongdoing. Yet doubtless many still prefer to keep quiet.

Outcasts

The Outcasts are those who have been rejected by the global money society. Reasons vary widely. They may have fallen foul of official regulations or for any other reason have been denied access the banking system. An important group of outcasts are criminals, especially criminal gangs, whose work directly undermines the rules and operations of the global money society. But anybody who has been in prison may struggle to open an account (2.2 million Americans have served prison terms). Highly corrupt rulers are also classed as outcasts, even though they use the services of the official money society. The number of outcasts is likely to grow substantially. There are several reasons for this.

For example, governments and financial regulators are tightening up rules under which banks may reject applications to open bank accounts; these include lack of the proper, officially approved ID, a record of fraud, undischarged bankrupts and poor credit rating. With intrusive financial surveillance (Know Your Customer rules, etc.) being a principal weapon against crime and money laundering, the number of potential Outcasts will grow rapidly. At a time when financial sanctions have become a principal weapon of foreign policy by the United States and some other powers, greater reliance on them is another trend likely to swell the ranks of the Outcasts (to include, e.g. Iran). So would a move to abolish cash. The massive flows of money from the proceeds of corruption point to another source of recruits as the people involved are unmasked and denied access to financial services.

Anybody who has been rejected by a bank will find it extremely difficult to open an account with any other institution in the formal economy. There are a growing number of people whose bank accounts have been closed without any reason being given—something banks are quite entitled to do on certain grounds. Some governments are encouraging banks to act as spies on their customers, reporting any suspicious activity. All these people can end up as outcasts. This group also includes the criminals and members of gangs whose survival strategy calls for theft, plunder, extortion, people trafficking and terror.

Others

The Other Outsiders do not belong in the global money society, as they do not follow its rules and do not participate in the monetary system and institutions. However, unlike the Opponents, they have not rejected it, and unlike the Outcasts, they have not been rejected by it. They include, among other groups, people without bank accounts or other means of making and receiving payments other than by cash. There are also people who cannot cope with the complexities of modern money, whether for reasons of mental capacity, age, inability to handle technology or other reasons. There are also still social groups outside the global monetary space. This category also includes citizens of nations that adopt a policy of isolation, such as North Korea. Until the 1970s, the category included most working-class people in industrial economies. Most women even in advanced economies, were Outsiders until 50 or so years ago. Most did not have money or a bank account. They were connected to the formal financial system, if at all, through a male relative or guardian. In other words, the majority of the population even in developed countries were outside the system.

Many people are still excluded from access to core financial services and advice. In the United Kingdom almost two million people do not have a bank account. In the most deprived parts of the country, over a third of people do not have access to a bank account. Globally, the World Bank estimates about two billion out of six billion adults have no access to financial services. This is changing, but not that quickly. We often forget the billions of people struggling on the margins of society, including those who do not have the money to buy shelter nor food and drink to keep body and soul together. Despite the drive for Inclusion, I expect the divide between Insiders and Outsiders, between the Watchers and the Watched, to widen further. Qualifications and conditions of membership will become even more demanding. Much will depend on the fate of nation states, often seen as the natural protectors of the weak and vulnerable. Yet nation states are swimming in the same monetary ocean as everybody else. In sum, inclusion is not enough: inclusion for what? Unless insiders recognize the need to restore legitimacy, the new order will rely increasingly on force.

Notes

1. I once organised a private meeting there. It was between heads of major gold-mining companies and presidents/governors of major central banks. This was in 1999 when central banks were selling gold on the market, depressing its price. Commentators were urging them on, saying that gold was an outdated reserve asset and would continue to fall in value against the US dollar. This fall in the gold price was damaging gold-producing economies around the world. Thabo Mbeki, then deputy president of South Africa and designated successor to Nelson Mandela, chaired the meeting. It was an invitation that no central banker could decline however much they wanted to. So, people like Wim Duisenberg, who had just been appointed to be the first head of the European Central Bank, came along. There were only about 12 round the table. Mbeki introduced the meeting by laying out the damage that the falling gold price was doing to South Africa at the worst possible time only a few years after the end of apartheid. The central bankers had no answer. It worked. On September 26, 1999, Duisenberg himself announced the first central bank gold agreement. Participants promised not to sell more than a certain pre-defined amount of gold over a certain time period. The Guardian reported the decision: 'In announcing the decision, the president of the European Central Bank, Wim Duisenberg, said the central banks were responding to the pleas of the World Gold Council, South African mining groups and the cause of stability'. The agreement transformed the gold market. The gold price rose from US$290 an ounce to US$1000 an ounce in the following ten years.

2. When I was at Cambridge university in the 1960s, the idea of a graduate going into business, banking or trade would send a collective shiver of horror through my group of friends, many of whom read English Literature in the spirit of the critic, FR Leavis (and nearly all of whom came from State schools). As Noel Annan, who was provost (head) of my college, later remarked of that generation: 'most of them still found it difficult to understand that making yet more money could also be enjoyable' (Annan 1990).

Bibliography

Anderson, G. (2009). *City Boy: Beer and Loathing in the Square Mile*. London: Headline.

Annan, N. (1990). *Our Age: The Generation that made Post-war Britain*. London: Weidenfeld and Nicholson.

Orwell, G. (1949). *Nineteen Eighty-Four*. London: Penguin Books.

Polk, S. (2016). *For the Love of Money: A Memoir*. New York: Scribner.

Smith, G. (2014). *Why I Left Goldman Sachs: A Wall Street Story*. New York: Grand Central Publishing.

Time Present: Actions Have Consequences

Conclusion to Part II: Actions Have Consequences

The decade from 2010 to 2020 has seen a Great Recession, a Great Debasement and the rise of criminal and crony capitalism. We have witnessed the harsh penalties meted out to those who are not at home in the new global money culture and those on the wrong side of austerity programmes. These have come as rude shocks to a generation who assumed steady material progress and trusted democratic institutions. I have also suggested that these illnesses and deformations of capitalism are among the fruits of our global culture—the culture shared by participants in the global money space. They are among the consequences of the particular and unique ideology that followed the formation of the global money space at the end of the twentieth century and its accompaniment, Money Delusion. Recall that Part I showed how the global money space and society emerged out of the battle of ideas in the twentieth century—ideas that drove actions. The global culture with its liability to Money Delusion naturally encourages an excessive build-up of debt and subsequent collapse. It celebrates money-making without ethics, offers no barrier to the advance of crony and corrupt capitalism and consigns opponents and outcasts to the modern equivalent of Victorian workhouses. It is associated with abuse, addiction, injustice, crime, exclusion and cultural vandalism. Yet governments and central bankers claim that there is nothing wrong with our money that a few regulations and plenty of money creation can't put right. We have seen where that attitude leads—to the bad consequences that have been surveyed in this part, Part II, of this study.

We must also challenge the current consensus on the need to make every human being join the new global society and sign up to its culture. To get everybody to imbibe the present fashionable money culture and give up their own—often the result of centuries of evolution—would be cultural vandalism on an epic scale, as bad as the harm we are inflicting on our natural environment. To be clear, I am not anti-money. It can bring huge benefits. I also have great respect for many of the (often very able) individuals who have served in developing countries as officials of, or subcontractors to, institutions such as the IMF and World bank and other multilateral institutions. They upheld international cooperation and helped to create a global money space—great achievements in their time. Our present form of money is, however, destructive—just as money was in the period between the two world wars, though in a quite different way. Just as people attempted to cling to the old gold standard, not realising how conditions made it unworkable, so governments cling on to twentieth-century ideas of state money along with its aggressive money culture just when we need to break free of them.

Part III

Time Future: Consequences Engender Ideas

We need to re-imagine money—again. The intolerable pressure of events makes this urgent. But it would be a mistake to jump straight to a technical solution. Money only works well as part of a bigger idea. It is that bigger idea that is missing and that we need first. Money is an element in a jigsaw, one of the last pieces to fit in. We need to have an image of the whole picture in our mind first so as to see where the money bit fits in. We cannot yet see the whole picture. But we do know that human beings are creative. So far, they have always come up with new ideas, new visions, to meet new challenges.

Part III discusses ways to start thinking about it, and it aids to help us see money and other technologies in a new way. Before looking at specific issues, I start this part with a short speculative introduction. This is intended to frame the subjects treated in subsequent chapters, to remind us that, given the historical experience surveyed in this book, we should not be surprised if events take a more dramatic turn than most of us currently expect.

Introduction to Part III

Might a new totalitarianism creep up on us and take us unawares? We would have no excuse. The history of the twentieth century shows how easy it is for dictators to hoodwink citizens just for those few months that is all they need to grab power and clamp down on free discussion (would-be autocrats will surely be asking themselves now: what is all this money for if not to bribe voters into giving me supreme power?). Orwell's novel *Nineteen Eighty-Four* is often mentioned. China's example of mass surveillance has only recently caught the headlines. Much as President Trump is widely disliked, for good or bad reasons, many give him credit for alerting the world to the challenge from China. The controversy over the Chinese electronics and communications firm Huawei at least achieved that. No company anywhere could ignore the US Commerce Department order, placing Huawei and 70 of its affiliates on a trade blacklist that barred anyone on it from buying parts and components from US companies without the government's approval first. Trump threatened to cut off intelligence sharing from long-established allies such as the United Kingdom if they contracted with Huawei to install vital components of a 5G system in their countries. Meanwhile, there was much greater coverage of China's incarceration of many of its Muslim citizens for so-called re-education and the apparatus of mass surveillance using technology allegedly stolen from Western sources.

At the same time, the polarisation of American politics brought many previously unimaginable scenarios within the realms of plausibility for the first time. Various polls suggested that a majority of Republicans believe US elections are rigged. A survey conducted in June 2017 asked: 'if Donald Trump were to say that the 2020 presidential election should be postponed until the country can make sure that only eligible American citizens can vote, would you support or oppose postponing the election?' In total, 52% of Republicans said they would support postponement (*Washington Post*, August 10, 2017 cited in Levitsky and Zitblatt, 2018). For the first time, people could conjure up a nightmare scenario where the world's biggest economies, controlling between them a preponderant share of actual and potential global military power would, starting from opposite poles of the political spectrum, both be governed by authoritarian regimes. The world has travelled a long way since the glad, confident dawn of the global space. It seems to be falling into a dark place.

It is not difficult to conceive such a descent being triggered by a monetary shock. Our collective and individual dependence on money networks underlines our shared vulnerability. While the guardians of our systems work to detect and anticipate possible threats, they can never be confident that such defences will hold. The anger festering among Outsiders is another potential threat, as is the political power of extreme private wealth. The nation state, still the most viable political unit, is under siege from global money, its tax base eroded, the confidence of electorates shaken and identity politics threatening to run amok. No bank or business is—or can be—confident they will survive the next monetary collapse.

18

The Jealous State and the Future of Money

The erosion of confidence in state money is far from total—we are a long way from Weimar. But any significant loss of trust in money is a major blow to a society. Money should be a bulwark against uncertainty. Money stored as savings, or just waiting for the right opportunity to be spent, offers comfort, like a blanket on a cold night. As long as inflation is under reasonable control, the money will keep its value as potential purchasing power until the time comes when you want to spend or invest it in some longer-term asset (such as a house or bond or share). Loss of trust removes that comfort blanket. Rapid inflation is one way this can happen. More directly, it is eroded if banks are not seen as safe. Also, people ask increasingly, how much is it costing me to keep the banks safe? If there is a major crisis every decade, forcing governments to rescue banks at significant cost, the blanket gets thin. It starts to feel cold. If it goes on like this, how long will governments—even those of developed countries—keep creditworthy? Government debt of 43 countries monitored by the Bank for International Settlements (BIS) doubled as a proportion of GDP from 30% to 60% between 2008 and 2017. Then, there are all the so-called contingent liabilities—monetary promises the government has made that will be called on in certain circumstances. If there were to be a major crisis every generation, requiring repeated state bailouts, government finances would head into a black hole just as public anger would be at boiling point. Also, the ultra-low or negative interest rates of recent years have facilitated cheap finance for the state while depriving people of a reasonable return on their savings. Retired people have been especially hard hit. The abuse of money and power over money under crony, state, surveillance and other deformations of capitalism damages its basic economic functions. And as the

© The Author(s) 2019
R. Pringle, *The Power of Money*, https://doi.org/10.1007/978-3-030-25894-8_18

previous chapter showed, contemporary money culture is experienced by many people as divisive as well as unpleasantly aggressive and destructive.

Although many people, at least in relatively stable countries, still trust their central bank to maintain a reliable currency, there is also a strong minority view that 'fiat' currency has value only because people have been 'conned' by the central banks into believing this. One day all fiat currency will be worthless. People with this outlook use cash for daily business purposes but hold their savings in precious metals or other 'tangible' assets (real estate, diamonds, etc.). They expect the present system to collapse. And the large proportion of the world's population who live in unstable or corrupt countries have even more urgent and rational reasons to watch their money and find safe havens.

This chapter surveys the future of money from a particular point of view: will it be shaped by the state or by private initiative and the market? It looks at forms of money from the latest to the oldest. We start with bitcoin and libra, before moving to cash (bank notes and coin) and gold. We then briefly touch on rival modern theories—those championing private money on the one hand, and state money on the other.

Why Bitcoin Matters

Bitcoin is our first exhibit. This digital asset was conceived and launched specifically as a challenge to a money system that, its creator said, could not be trusted. It is modelled on gold. Satoshi Nakamoto, an *alias* used by the anonymous creator of bitcoin, heralded its introduction in a paper of October 2008. He said 'a purely peer-to-peer version of electronic cash would allow online payments to be sent directly from one party to another without going through a financial institution' (bitcoins, are in this respect, like cash or gold coins; Nakamoto 2008). Nakamoto commented that commerce on the Internet had come to rely on financial institutions serving as trusted third parties to process electronic payments: 'While the system works well enough for most transactions, it still suffers from the inherent weaknesses of the trust based model…. What is needed is an electronic payment system based on cryptographic proof instead of trust, allowing any two willing parties to transact directly with each other….' He created the first block in the bitcoin blockchain on January 3, 2009, embedding a headline from *The Times* of London of that date that underlined his determination to position bitcoin as outside the existing monetary system: 'Chancellor on brink of second bailouts for banks' (The Times 2009). The blockchain is, in effect, a large accounts ledger, a huge spreadsheet kept simultaneously on thousands of computers across the world. No single entity controls it and all transactions are permanently recorded on it. Ten years later, 17.4 million bitcoins were in circulation, with 3.6 million still to be produced.

Thus a would-be new currency and form of money can arise through private initiative. That's not new in itself. However, few economists would have believed such a phenomenal growth of a non-interest bearing, private monetary asset was possible. True, there were already numerous local currencies, community currencies and so forth, but these used the prevailing national money as their unit of account—they were exchangeable at a fixed rate with the dominant state money. Bitcoin is a privately created, irredeemable electronic asset with money-like characteristics. Bitcoin—and some other virtual assets launched in its slipstream—is important because they could pick up more money-like characteristics. It is true that it has a long way to go. It is accepted only to a limited extent as a medium of exchange/payment for a range of goods and services, it is not viewed as a store of value and it is not a unit of account—a unit in which prices of goods, services and assets may be and, in fact, are expressed. The unit of account function is often seen as the most central and critical quality of money. Unless goods and services are priced in bitcoin, it has to be exchanged into another medium of exchange such as dollars or pounds at the time of payment, adding to the costs of using it. It has not achieved that status. Central bankers are correct to insist it is not a currency.

However, after a roller-coaster ride in 2015–19, its value was again above US$10,000 in mid-2019, slipping to $8000 later in the year. If it had no basis whatsoever as a store of value or money, it should have fallen close to zero soon after its initial launch. Clearly, many people were willing to speculate, risking large amounts of money on the outcome. While monetary experts were virtually united in condemning it, and it made some central bankers and commercial bankers almost apoplectic with anger, the market was giving another message: wait and see. It has some inbuilt safeguards. The design makes it robust against hacking and even the most advanced attempts to create (mine) more coins quickly—the maths puzzles a miner had to solve automatically become more difficult when coins are 'mined' too rapidly. But this is no guarantee against a future successful effort—perhaps by quantum computers—to break its codes and identify the owners. This links to the debate about the supply of bitcoins. Some argue that although it is technically capped at 21 million units, this can be increased if a majority of 'miners' (who add transaction records to the public ledger) agree. From the start, when Nakamoto issued his challenge to conventional money, demand has been fuelled by mistrust of state money. But, some say, due to the way in which coins are created or mined, it could eventually be controlled by a monopoly. Anyway, assuming supply is indeed fixed, its value depends wholly on demand. Many regulators warned of its risks. Benoît Coeuré, a eurozone central banker, described bitcoin as 'the evil spawn of the financial crisis'. It's a classic tug of war. But in the end, the market, people, will decide what forms of money have value and which do not.

Libra Grabs the Limelight

Private digital currencies carry risks but offer useful potential competition for official money. Plans for a mobile phone–based digital payment system launched by Facebook and its associates—the libra coin—in June 2019 immediately grabbed the attention of policy-makers. This was because the sheer scale of the prospective take-up of libra—a monetary asset that would be used to make payments to anybody anywhere at low cost and at greater speed and convenience than through conventional banks and payments operators—held out the prospect of it quickly acquiring a leading role among currencies. Although essentially a payment mechanism rather than a bank, it could transform the monetary system. First, it would represent a digital equivalent of cash at a time when use of bank notes and coin for making payments is declining. Second, people in countries with weak, inflationary currencies might flee their domestic currencies, exchanging them *en masse* for libras (which unlike bitcoins would be backed by a bundle of existing leading currencies). If merchants were to start quoting prices in libras, it would quickly become full-fledged money. This in turn might prompt central banks to offer bank accounts to individual customers. This would enable sovereign money (money issued by the state) to compete with libra and other private forms of digital cash. Such currency competition would also shake up the banking system. As Cœuré has remarked, how we respond to these challenges is up to us: 'We can focus our efforts on ensuring that private payment systems will thrive in a space that respects our common global policy priorities. Or we can accelerate our own efforts to overcome the remaining weaknesses in global payment systems, safe in the belief that only public money can ultimately, and collectively, ensure a safe store of value, a credible unit of account and a stable means of payment' (Cœuré 2019). Another option would be for market-based and public payment systems to complement each other. This would be in the spirit of the approach favoured in these essays, of money as a joint venture between the public and private sectors. They would jointly shape the payments universe in the twenty-first century. Libra has issued a welcome wake-up call to the official guardians of money and is to be taken much more seriously than bitcoin.

The Struggle over the Future of Cash

In the twentieth century, cash was the people's money; everybody used notes and coins. Banks were quite forbidding; until late in the century, only a minority of adults had bank accounts. Until the 1970s, to withdraw cash, you generally visited your branch, which often closed early in the afternoon, where you were greeted by a male bank clerk standing behind four feet of polished timber, his 'banca' or 'bench'. People had bank books in which transactions were entered by clerks in copperplate handwriting. Men mainly did the banking. Few working-class people used banks. Many had tins to keep the money. One tin for bills, another tin for holidays. Having money in one's pocket really mattered. Outside the home, school and workplace, you could do very little without it. Wages were paid in bank notes. Even at the end of the twentieth century, only a small minority of adults in the world had bank accounts. By 2019, this rose to 60%, including 90% of people in developed countries, and others had access to non-bank mobile payment services. Yet bank notes and coins still provided a money that met people's need for an immediate easy-to-use means of final payment. Cash allows two parties to complete a payment without revealing their identities, and it leaves no trace. While it is true that people also use less cash for everyday purposes, many keep larger balances at home than before.

Some politicians, economists and bankers want to restrict the use of cash. On average, it is true that people hold far more bank notes in value than they need for normal transactions. Those who favour tighter state control argue that it is used largely in the underground economy to escape taxes or in criminal activity such as drugs and people trafficking. In the United States, based on Internal Revenue Service estimates, the tax gap—the amount lost to the government in tax revenue because of the use of cash in the underground economy—is around US$500 billion in Federal taxes and another US$200 billion in lost state-level revenue. Small and medium-sized enterprises on average report only half their income—hiding much of the rest in cash hoards. Reducing this by only 10% would yield US$70 billion in larger tax receipts (combining Federal and State taxes). This excludes income from illegal activities. The gap is about 16–25% for southern European countries, between 10% and 15% for Germany and France and perhaps 7% in the United Kingdom. Then, there is the use of currency in the criminal economy. A restaurant can launder cash from crime simply by claiming it serves more dinners than it really does, issuing fake receipts. The leak of the Panama papers revealed hidden offshore accounts of some 140 public officials including a number of former and current heads of state and government. The revelations of the Panama Papers were not just a one-off. Individuals and companies use offshore entities to hide from paying taxes or being prosecuted as criminals. Money laundering probably amounts to 2–5% of GDP a year worldwide. Tax revenue lost through use of cash to evade taxes is estimated to be around 10% of GDP in the EU.

Restrictions on Paper

In an attempt to reduce such evasion, some governments and central banks have stopped issuing large denomination notes and restricted the maximum size of transactions that can be settled in paper money. The Canadians stopped printing the CAD 1000 note in 2000, although, despite requests to turn them in, about CAD 1 million are still unaccounted for. The Singapore dollar S$10,000 note is no longer issued, though remains in circulation. The European Central Bank ceased issuing €500 notes at the end of 2018—the largest denomination note to be issued is €200. However, the €500 note will remain legal tender and can be exchanged for an unlimited period. Sweden, Denmark and Norway all issue 1000 krona/krone notes (worth between US$100 and US$120). France imposes limits of €1000 on cash payments. The largest notes by value still being issued are Brunei's BND 10,000 note (US$7122) and the CHF (Swiss franc) 1000 note (worth about US$1000). The highest denomination note in the United Kingdom is £50 (US$80): this will be issued in polymer form (plastic is a kind of polymer). The Japanese ¥10,000 is worth about US$90. Many bankers favour abolishing large-value notes. But it will be a delicate operation, at best. Heavy-handed interference affecting people's monetary habits can quickly lead to protest. As the following section illustrates, a recent bungled government demonetisation programme shows the risks involved.

India's Shock Demonetisation

On November 8, 2016, the Indian government announced without warning the withdrawal and demonetisation of ₹500 denomination (US$7.50) and ₹1000 (US$15.00) banknotes, the highest denomination notes in India.

From midnight that night, they were no longer legal tender. It was announced they could 'in the near future' be exchanged at branches of the central bank or at commercial banks for new ₹500 and ₹2000 notes. The government claimed that the action would curtail the shadow economy and crack down on the use of illicit and counterfeit cash to fund illegal activity and terrorism. The sudden announcement—and the prolonged cash shortages in the weeks that followed—created significant disruption throughout the economy, threatening economic output. Suddenly, 86.4% by value of the cash in circulation was no longer legal tender. A total of 98% of all consumer transactions by volume in India are in cash. This action caused hardship for hundreds of millions of poor Indians. The new notes would not be ready in sufficient quantity to replace the old ones (22 billion notes in all) for five or six months.

The official reasons for this action were to tackle counterfeiting Indian banknotes, nullify black money hoarded in cash and curb funding of terrorism with fake notes. But, in the event, very little untaxed black money was forced into the open and thus taxed, a one-off benefit, and little of the cash economy moved permanently into the formal financial system. In any case, illegal wealth is not generally held in the form of bank notes in India but in property and other such assets. The better-off citizens have many other ways of hiding from the tax authorities. Holders of the old currency managed to dispose of it; complex money-laundering networks sprang up in the wake of the demonetisation to help wealthy Indians deposit huge volumes of previously undeclared currency without exposing themselves to tax authorities. Such people allegedly sold the old notes, at a discount, to brokers who then dispatched low-income Indians to deposit or exchange them at banks.

This was a misuse of state power over money—a reflection of the attitudes unfortunately often associated with the state theory of money. The reasoning goes like this: if money is only an instrument of the state, then there is nothing objectionable about the state using it to promote whatever object the state finds politically attractive. If people suffer, then it is in the cause of a higher good. This is the mentality of social engineers.

Changing Payments Habits

True, payment habits are changing fast. In the United Kingdom, card payments overtook cash in 2016. People are more willing to use cards for lower-value payments. However, retailers still spent over £1 billion (US$1.29 billion) to accept card payments, and credit card charges remained high. Cash is still widely used. It remains the dominant payment method in the European

Union, with 79% of all transactions being carried out using cash (54% of the total value of all payments) in 2017. Despite numerous articles predicting the advent of a cashless society, people, in fact, rely mainly on cash in most countries. A ban on large notes could be seen as close to a sovereign default; the US$100 bill that is widely held globally accounts for 78% of the value of all US currency. Cash provides emergency reserves for people in countries with unstable exchange rates, repressive governments, capital controls or a history of banking collapses. In the decade after the global financial crisis, not only the eurozone but also Japan and the United States saw a rise in cash in circulation. Many mistrusted banks. Regulators had assumed that their reforms strengthened confidence, but the lack of such trust is borne out by public opinion surveys. For the campaign against cash to succeed, all countries with reasonably good money would need to take part. Yet some, such as Switzerland, will refuse on principle; the Swiss are unlikely to get rid of their CHF 1000 note.

Experience shows that tampering with the money that people are familiar with can cause great unrest. Cash is cheap and efficient. Cash does not need a password and, unlike a bank account can't be hacked, nor does it depend on technology that might and sometimes does break down. An offer of cash is not liable to be rejected as card payments sometimes are. We should also consider the impact banning cash would have on vulnerable groups. To work as intended, everybody would have to have the digital technology and be able to work with it. In reality, many people don't have that technology, and there are many more who would struggle to work with it and/or would be made very vulnerable if they were forced to depend on it. From this perspective, the proposal to abolish cash is simply cruel: it is hard to imagine any other single economic measure that could cause as much human suffering.

Moreover, many people besides the poor rely on cash. Potentially anybody who hasn't adopted the politically correct narrative of normality, ready with proof of identity and two IDs, including a passport or photo car licence. The easy accessibility to cash, especially for the elderly, the socially vulnerable or minors, allows people to participate in society and, for example, allows children to learn how to handle money. When people use cash, they face none of the barriers involved in applying for a credit card or opening a bank account. Cash always works in a way that more technology-reliant methods of payment do not because of things such as network and power failures. Thus, banknotes will retain their place and their role in society as legal tender for a very long time to come. Moreover, printed banknotes will remain the European Central Bank's (ECB's) core business. If there is public demand for digital central bank money, this should only be a technical variant of cash.

Cash is not the biggest factor in enabling money laundering and terrorist financing. The first culprits are the banks. The second is legal services. Cash comes only third. That's according to US evidence. A UK government risk assessment of money laundering and terrorist financing in October 2015 also ranked cash as the third biggest risk factor a little ahead of legal service providers. The accountancy profession is high up the list. If society really wants to stop money laundering, there is no reason to attack the third-ranked risk factor but leave the first- and second-ranked risk factors alone. Going further, both banks and accounting service providers are already heavily regulated—and especially so in the illicit transactions area. The fact that we have had such regulations for a long time now and yet banks and accounting firms are still the main risk factors suggests that this regulation has failed pretty dismally.

The Real Purpose of the Campaign

The real purpose of the crusade against cash lies elsewhere—to clear the decks for central banks/governments to introduce a negative interest rate policy. They could not impose such a tax on money if people had the option of switching into physical cash. This would in effect involve charging the public for keeping cash balances in the form of bank deposits in order to induce them to spend more, and so push the economy out of a deflationary trap. So, many people will naturally conclude, if 'they' can't any longer steal from us by inflation, which was the state's ancient route way of creaming off a slice of our money, they will do it directly by taking money from us—all supposedly in the good cause of making us spend it—or what's left of it. But there are further obstacles to the zero-interest-rate policy other than people's holding of cash. They might respond to a tax on bank deposits by moving back into an even older form of money—gold.

Gold and the State

Most governments and modern central bankers like to hold gold in reserve themselves but don't like their citizens having it. They definitely don't want to tie their national money to a fixed weight of gold. To the rationalist, to want money to have any material substance is a superstitious relic like belief in fairies. Have faith in the Enlightenment! Gold, they say, should not be regarded as money of any kind. It may be beautiful and lend itself to ornamental use as jewellery but there is no reason why money should be beautiful. If gold demand remains especially strong in countries that have suffered historically from episodes of rapid inflation, such as Germany, India, China and Latin America, this is another argument for maintaining good monetary policies. So, what if there have been 50 hyperinflations in the past 100 years and a persistent, worldwide inflation, with prices even in the United States rising 23-fold in the twentieth century? Gold critics say this is further evidence pointing to the case for good, rational central banking. True, we had to learn how to manage paper money, but thanks to the untiring efforts of dedicated central bankers, we now know how to do that.

The official story is that gold as a monetary asset has lost ground throughout the age of State money. When the twentieth century opened, the gold standard was in full swing; when it closed, gold had supposedly been banished from all its official monetary functions except as a residual reserve. From being 50–60% of official reserves in the 1960s, by 2000, gold had shrivelled to 14%, and official holdings had fallen by about 5000 tonnes from the peak to about 33,000 tonnes. A low point for gold was reached in the 1990s, when its demise even as a serious store of value seemed imminent, as it earned no interest, its price had been declining for years and most central bankers regarded it as obsolete. In 1996–99, Gordon Brown, then Britain's Chancellor of the Exchequer, acting on Treasury advice, sold 400 tonnes or one-half of UK's remaining reserves at an average price of about US$300 (or about £200) an ounce. This was later seen as a major error, as the gold price (in dollars and pounds) soared fivefold in the next ten years. Brown's Treasury advisers thought it would make him look smart and modern but he ended up looking like a loser. (In recent history probably only George Soros has cost the UK reserves as much in a single episode—by his successful speculation against the pound in Black Wednesday, 1992.)

The war on gold started after the demise of the Bretton Woods system in 1971. Governments led by the United States did all they could to reduce its role in the international monetary system. Under the new articles of the IMF, pushed through by the United States, members were barred from defining their currencies in terms of gold. The IMF was prohibited from choosing gold as the common denominator of a new exchange rate system. The definition of the SDR in terms of gold was abolished, along with any notion of an official price for gold and all obligations on members to make payments to the IMF in gold. The SDR replaced gold as IMF's unit of account. The Fund also sold part of its gold holdings. Even France, traditionally a champion of gold's role in the system, gave way—transferring its hopes to the euro. Governments came out against gold all guns blazing. But gold would not only survive, it would be one of the best safe havens from the coming inflationary binge.

Gold's Commentary on the Follies of Policy-makers

Issuers of state money hate the gold market, the place where many thousands of individual orders and expectations are reconciled and combine to produce a price, precisely because it offers an objective, impersonal, market commentary on their follies and foibles. When they adopt inflationary policies, the market immediately signals its expectation that prices will rise through the gold market. Other things being equal, the gold price of the currency of the country concerned rises. The gold market sees through the tricks and empty promises of politicians. It is forward looking. It anticipates the effects of policies that will devalue money. But it also sometimes disappoints gold bugs by obstinately refusing to rise when they think it should. In 2018, why was not the gold market responding to the follies of Trump's huge deficit spending and tax breaks? It had its reasons, which can be guessed at but never known for certain. It was doubtless signalling there was little change in the prospects for US inflation. But when in due course there would be a change in sentiment, the gold market would be the first and best indicator, and then President Trump would fulminate against it, and wish to suppress it like presidents before him (including Roosevelt in 1934 and Nixon in 1971).

Gold Always Bounces Back

Though driven out of its official role in money, the price soared. By 2011, the price reached US$1600, six times its low of US$252 an ounce reached after the UK sales in 1999. The foundations for this rally were laid at the end of 1999 when European central banks announced an agreement to limit annual sales of gold for the next five years, an agreement twice renewed (though varying in the details). This in effect put a floor under the price (see Chap. 17 for the inside story). Other causes of the remarkable rally included the central banks' regime of ultra-low interest rates and loose monetary policies; financial market innovations that brought gold buying within the reach of a much larger range of investors; the massive increases in income in emerging markets, notably China, India, Russia and Brazil, which had long had pro-gold cultures; and where people now could suddenly afford to buy much greater quantities for private use, notably jewellery.

However much states promote their money and demote gold, gold always stands ready to serve as money. This is for several reasons, in addition to its long-term purchasing power stability. First, gold is nobody's liability. Using the currency of any nation as the fulcrum of the international monetary system means relying on the faith and credit of that nation, the integrity of its money markets and the prudence of its policies—in other words, its willingness and capacity to keep its currency sound. The history of sovereign default, debasement and currency collapse shows it is foolish to rely on governments' promises. Second, gold is seen as a safe haven. Every adult in the world knows what gold is. Nothing else comes close. For money, trust is of the essence. Third, gold has a market value independent of its use as money. Because such a large amount of gold is willingly held throughout the world for a wide variety of reasons—as an investment diversifier, as jewellery and as a store of value for central banks—the annual flow of newly mined gold is easily absorbed. This occurs naturally through the price mechanism.

If you believe central banks will secure price stability, one attraction of gold would lessen. But central banks do not aim at price stability—in the commonsense meaning of prices neither rising nor falling over the long term. Their aim is an inflation rate of 2% a year—which amounts to a doubling of the price level every 35 years. If central banks had let deflation take its course in the early 2000s, the price of gold would, indeed, have fallen, because this would have been an unexpected shift in policy. But by adopting an inflation target, the central banks made a mighty, concerted and international effort to raise the gold price—at the same time as they were cursing it! Gold pays no interest, but with all the major central banks of the world working on its behalf, that is enough to satisfy most investors.

Just to add one further element in the mystique of gold—something to do with the nature of money. People do not so much own gold as act as trustees of the gold of which they are temporary guardians. Gold connects the past, present and future together in a secure, reliable chain linking generations. This is a feature that good money should have but is beyond the capacity of contemporary money.

Why Gold Is Priceless...

We all talk as if gold has a price. Because it is priced in terms of US dollars in international markets, most people assume that the dollar price of gold is the basic price; if quoted in other currencies, they take the dollar price and then convert the resulting sum into the other non-dollar currency at the current exchange rate. But this can be misleading. The value of gold is determined by global forces of demand and supply for the metal. The price quoted in currencies reflects the outlook for that currency, irrespective of its dollar price. Thus, if people start to expect more rapid inflation in the eurozone, other things being equal, the euro price of gold will rise without any effect on the dollar price. The same with the price of gold in yen, or Kenyan shillings or whatever. The price of gold in Zimbabwe dollars is determined by the Zimbabwe central bank and not by the US Fed. In other words, the true value of gold is gold itself, and its price in any currency reflects the value of that currency against gold. You cannot see or touch the real gold price. Its true value is set by demand and supply for gold, not by any central bank. That is why it acts as an impersonal, objective, silent witness of the fortunes of paper currencies. It is for that reason truly independent; that is why it is such a sensitive barometer. It is a measuring rod and item of adornment that is also ready to be money. That means people who hold gold can exchange it at any time (unless it is embedded in their teeth!). But for generation after generation, more gold has been demanded and the newly mined amount (which only adds a small percentage—usually about 3% a year—to the total above-ground stocks), is easily absorbed. That is why, even though gold has been demonetised, its ghost still hovers over fiat money.

It is true that the value of gold was more stable in real terms when it served as official money, during the days of the gold standard. Demand was steadier when it was demanded as money as well as in other uses. And its nominal price was fixed. Under volatile fiat money, waves of credit set up inflationary and deflationary forces that are naturally transmitted to the gold market. The wide swings in the price (both nominal and real) during the past 70 years were brought about mainly by official policies: it was undervalued in the 1960s when its price against the dollar was fixed while the United States followed inflationary policies. When the fixed price was abandoned, the market price responded in textbook fashion to the inflationary policies of the 1970s, the disinflationary policies of the 1980s and 1990s, and to the ultra-loose monetary policies during several years in 2003–11. These swings were exacerbated in the latter part of the period (1990–2000) by destabilising sales of gold by central banks and governments. The evidence suggested that, in the absence of such destabilising official policies (monetary policies as well as direct intervention in the gold market), the nominal and real price of gold would have been much more stable.

Are we victims of an illusion that our fiat money is the real thing, when in reality it is still a derivative of gold? In the end, our money will be judged by the people; the market that can best reflect that judgement is the market in the best non-fiat money or money substitute available, the gold market. If a currency loses its gold value completely, it will be unable to perform monetary functions even if the government of the day insists on being paid taxes in that currency and says it is reliable and sound.

Other arguments in favour of gold derive from this long-term stability of its purchasing power. People say, its price is determined by the policies of the Federal Reserve. They should say, its *dollar* price is heavily influenced by the Fed. Monetary policies are not the only factor influencing local gold prices—restrictions on imports or exports of gold, for example, can cause a divergence between local prices and the international price. Also, large sales or purchases of gold—notably by central banks—can have a large effect on prices. But its stability in terms of its real purchasing power in the long run for people everywhere (no matter what their currency may be) means that many people still consider gold the best available store of value in the long term.

Private Money: Stable Money?

'In the basic models we use to explain capitalist concepts', says one mainstream economist 'money doesn't matter—what matters is the relative supply and demand of different goods, and hence their relative "prices"' (Portes 2016). (But, you may well ask, 'how is a price expressed other than in terms of a money?' Well, one can imagine that there may be a 'real' price that is not directly observable, over which money lies lightly like a veil.) Others contend that money is a product of a specific aspect of state power, namely taxation: the state creates demand for money by requiring citizens to pay taxes in it (see section on modern money theory below). Economists reflect an old aristocratic tradition in dispensing with money so far as they can—many central bankers, ironically enough, share that outlook, as discussed in Chap. 13. (The Federal Reserve led the way in abandoning use of money aggregates as guides to policy in the 1990s.) But for the rest of us, money is the way we feel economic changes actually impinging on us. The economy, a real entity to economists, is an abstract idea for most people while money, which economics can do without, is real, you can count it and cannot manage without it. Can officials with their secure, public-sector salaries, tax-funded perks and generous pensions ever understand money—really? Some sections of the public have begun to doubt that.

That is what makes the new private money school interesting. It is led by economists such as Kevin Dowd, Gerald O'Driscoll, George Selgin and Lawrence White. Their analysis arises from the case for a free society, including a competitive banking system free of state controls. They explain how the private sector can create monetary stability, protect the banking system from crises and maintain the value of money without the need for a central bank. They typically maintain that the restraints imposed under most central banking regimes increase the vulnerability of the banking system to panics and runs on deposits. They propound a modern version of the theory of commodity money. Firstly, the evolutionary account of money's origins as related by Adam Smith in the eighteenth century (following Aristotle) and fleshed out by Carl Menger in the nineteenth century still holds good. As White describes it, money is a market-born institution. Convergence on one or two commodities as the common media of payment emerged from the actions of barterers seeking more effective trading strategies, without anyone aiming at the final result (White 2017). Secondly, the state theory people have no satisfactory explanation as to why gold and silver became the most popular commodity monies. If money was created by the state, why did rulers choose gold and silver rather than some much cheaper material, such as iron or copper? Because they were aware (like private traders) that such metals had key properties. Thirdly, the creation of money by credit requires trust, and trust grows from repeated interactions and—as Adam Smith himself mentioned—moral sentiments. Not state power.

Adam Smith recognised the role of mutual aid and credit in families and tight-knit communities. Moreover, he understood that the rise of commerce served in turn to reduce the relative importance of ties of kinship and such personal ties, further increasing thereby the importance of monetary exchange. Money was crucial to facilitate trade among strangers.

The Right to Privacy

There is another important aspect to this debate. A principle of classical liberalism is that people have a right to follow their interests and conduct their affairs without being tracked and followed or subject to someone else's accounting as long as they do not interfere in the affairs of others. Too many people say 'If you haven't done anything wrong, what are you worrying about?' This shows naivety about how precarious the structure of our rights is, and they assume the protections we have built into our constitutions will survive a determined attack. We must know the fundamental grounds for the right to financial privacy and be ready to defend them; as the rise of Hitler and of Lenin showed, it can be easy for a ruthless individual to sweep aside restraints—and soon it is too late. The right to financial privacy is a natural and necessary accompaniment of the rights to free speech and to peaceful enjoyment of one's property. Like these two fundamental rights, it serves not only the interests of individuals but also of society, in constraining the tendency for governments to exceed the powers granted to them.

An Ambitious 'Modern' Theory

A contrasting view is articulated by Randall Wray in his interpretation of the state theory of money (derived from Keynes's classic account, which in turn owes much to Knapp). Wray makes large claims for his synthesis: 'To put it simply, we have uncovered how money "works" in the modern economy' (Wray 2012). Governments can, he claims, guarantee full employment by creating enough money; they do not have to worry about going bankrupt or creating inflation. The theory supplies an analytical structure to ideas about money that many people hold. 'The government first creates a money of account (the dollar, the pound, the euro) and then imposes tax obligations in that national money of account' ....other uses of money are subsidiary, deriving from government's willingness to accept its currency in tax payments. Wray often quotes his mentor Hyman Minsky to the effect that: 'Everyone can create money; the problem is to get it accepted.'

Following Keynes, we begin with a money of account, that is, the unit (pounds, dollars, etc.) in which we price the goods and services we buy and well. This is chosen by the state. Then, we choose 'some thing' denominated in that unit of account to use when we buy and sell goods and services. In the United States, Congress has the power 'To coin money'. The term 'dollar' is used to both refer to the unit of account or sovereign currency and the paper or coin issued by the US governments. But Wray restricts the use of the term money to refer only to the unit of account; the term 'money things' is used to denote notes and coins and so on denominated in that monetary unit. The sovereign government alone has power to determine the money of account it will recognise for official accounts, and modern governments alone are invested with the power to issue currency denominated in its unit of account.

Money is a 'general representation of value'. It can buy all commodities—and, when they are sold, commodities 'buy' money. Capitalism is driven by business people's desire to get money (money things) by producing and selling commodities. Money is not merely what we use to measure the value of output, nor is it a veil over the 'real' economy. It is intrinsic to capitalism. Although the state defines what counts as money, monetary 'things' can be privately created. Indeed, banks are the main source of monetary creation through their lending activities. But such private monetary IOUs are written in the state's money of account. Also, if an issuer, such as a bank, promises to convert their IOU to another, such as the state's money, they need to be able to assure holders they will be able to do this on demand. To make this promise credible, they must keep reserves in the state currency or have easy access to it. Banks play a key role in the economy, as they create the 'monetary thing' needed by producers to buy raw materials, sell the finished product and to bridge the gap between these stages of production.

Governments may spend as much as they need to in order to guarantee full employment and other social goods. A state never runs out of money. It isn't a scarce commodity like silver or gold. Its value is determined by the difficulty of obtaining it—something that the state, as monopoly issuer, can decide. The decisions about how to issue, lend, and spend money come down to politics, values, and convention, whether the goal is reducing inequality or boosting entrepreneurship. Inflation can be controlled through taxation, and only becomes a problem at full employment. The state can guarantee a job to any-one who wants one, lowering unemployment and competing with the private sector for workers, raising standards and wages across the board. This extreme version of the state theory is one of a family of similar proposals that became popular in the early twenty-first century—at a time when the state was in many countries indeed resorting to money printing as a means of fending off recession. There were other similar versions, such as various proposals for so-called helicopter money in the form of cash transfers to households.

The extreme claims made for the power of money-creation were entirely fictitious. If governments had really wanted to, there was a much easier way of giving people money—reduce or even abolish taxation. The reason for not doing so was not lack of ability to create money but awareness that to do so would risk pushing inflation and inflationary expectations above a socially tolerable level. The state power to create money at will would not be 'costless'. If it made people hold more money than they wished to it would cause infla-tion which reduces the real value of state debts—and thus the real value of people's investment in state bonds. This is equivalent to a default. There would be no reason to expect it to lead to higher growth or bring more resources into employment beyond what central banks were already able to do through monetary policies. Modern monetary theory (MMT) does not reveal more scope for deficit spending without inflation. As Coats (2019) notes: 'despite its efforts to change how we view monetary and fiscal policies, MMT abandons market-based countercyclical monetary and fiscal policies for targeted central control over the allocation of resources. It would rely on specific interventions to address "road blocks" upon the foundation of a government guaranteed employment program'. He concludes that this is 'an unsuccessful and empty attempt to convince us that we can finance the Green New Deal and a federal job guarantee program painlessly by printing money'. MMT attempts to repackage and resurrect the empirically and theoretically discredited Keynesian policies of the 1960s and 1970s. A 2019 survey of leading economists showed a unanimous rejection of MMT's assertions that (1) 'Countries that borrow in their own currency should not worry about government deficits because they can always create money to finance their debt;' and (2) 'Countries that borrow in their own currency can finance as much real government spending as they want by creating money.'

Yet this theory fits into the mindset of our time. It repackages Keynesian remedies in modern language—and it is no accident that this language is monetary. *The world's problems can be solved by a sufficient injection of money.* This is, in my judgement, a prime example of the mindset that society has to reject: the absurd idea that there is a technical monetary solution available for the state to employ, as easily as waving a magic money wand, for any remaining unemployment—indeed for all our anxieties—to melt away.

Bibliography

Coats, W. (2019). 'Modern Monetary Theory: A critique.' Cato Journal, Vol. 39, No. 3 (Fall 2019).

Cœuré, Benoît (2019). Digital Challenges to the International Monetary and Financial System.

Nakamoto, S. (2008). Bitcoin: A Peer-to-Peer Electronic Cash System, October 31, 2008, from https://nakamotoinstitute.org/bitcoin/.

Portes, J. (2016) *50 Ideas you really need to know about capitalism.* London: Quercus Books.

The Times (2009). Chancellor on Brink of Second Bailout of Banks, January 3.

White, Larry (2017). 'Money Isn't a Gift from the State', Foundation for Economic Education (August 27).

Wray, L.R. (2012). *Modern Money Theory.* Basingstoke: Palgrave Macmillan.

19

The New Sociology of Money

In recent work on the sociology of money, scholars make a number of claims relevant to the search for a better idea of money. From a reading of the relevant research, I have derived the following propositions (expressed in my own words):

A sociological analysis of the nature of money can throw light on our present difficulties in maintaining and managing money.

Conflicts between social interests and classes are always at work in the processes that produce money.

The future of money is always open; money is a part of our broad effort to better the human condition. There is always scope for innovative ideas about money, so long as they address the real issues of the time. Many monetary reformers, often dismissed as cranks, have been influential.

Money can be created by private initiative, though it normally receives the imprimatur of a state or other Authority. Alternatively, money can be created by the state, though it needs to be supported by a market demand. Modern money is essentially a joint venture between the market and the state.

The people—the market—determine the value of money. Money cannot be neutral.

People are not passive receptacles and their behaviour in monetary matters is not necessarily predictable. They mould money to suit their needs.

If such claims can be substantiated, then there is good reason to hope that radical change in our current monetary arrangements can and will come. It is

© The Author(s) 2019
R. Pringle, *The Power of Money*, https://doi.org/10.1007/978-3-030-25894-8_19

true, however, that sociology also shows how difficult it can be to make change happen. If money gains its value from processes at work deep in society itself, including the struggle for power, we cannot just reform it as we wish. We cannot simply apply some abstract ideal of economic and monetary stability. The forces in society that produce present money are too strong for that approach to yield results. That explains, indeed, why many proposed reforms get nowhere. Sociology helps to focus our minds on what might be feasible. I consider these ideas and the scholars mainly associated with them in the order of the above points. I begin with the most outlandish.

Why We Suffer from Money Delusion

For an original, controversial but thought-provoking approach, the prize goes to Noam Yuran of Tel Aviv University. I give him pride of place because his analysis recognises what I have called the virus of money eating away at our social institutions. This is Money Delusion. How does money acquire such a grip over us and our societies?

Yuran tells the story of Robinson Crusoe by Daniel Defoe, often called the prototype English novel. Crusoe is stuck alone on a desert island (Yuran 2014). For him, money is pointless. When he finds some money on the beach, he wonders whether to pick it up. No, he says to himself, it would be quite useless here. Indeed, he swears at it, calling it a drug, pleased to be finally free of it. 'However', Crusoe says in the story, 'on second thoughts, I took it'. Why does he do that? What are the second thoughts that make him pick it up? For economics, its utility is zero. No rational person would accumulate anything of no conceivable use. Economists view money only as a means. Alternative economics starts right here. Individuals are not driven by calculations of gains and loss; the desire for money itself is an economic reality.

Obviously, Robinson Crusoe is under some sort of compulsion when 'on second thoughts' he picks up the money. What is going on? Yuran argues that money and the economy are an impersonal system. It stands outside individuals. It confronts us with its rules. Money 'speaks back' to Crusoe, pressing demands that in some way he has to obey. In other words, money is a social reality beyond the individual's point of view. Money is something that a young person hears about and learns to desire; many of us remember being thrilled as a child when we were given a book token as a birthday or Christmas present. We inherit this thing, this system, blindly. We come to terms with it. Money may have originated in the human imagination, yet nobody can doubt its objective existence.

Yuran dismisses the usual definitions of money. It is not 'an object believed to be money' nor something accepted as money nor merely a means of payment nor store of value. Rather, it is *an object desired as money*. In the myth of King Midas, he is given the gift of being able to turn everything he touches into gold; he is at first overjoyed when he finds he can use this to turn some twigs into gold but is then dismayed when his food and drink become gold as soon as he touches them. What is happening? His desire is transferred to the object desired, which becomes money. By wanting anything too much, it becomes money and so acquires power over you, frustrating your other wishes. Economists err when they see money as a means to an end. Only if desire for money is recognised as part of its nature will its effects be understood.

This insight throws light on Money Delusion which contributes to various pathologies, such as successive crises and the failure of efforts to reform the monetary system. How does the desire for money develop? It emerges, according to Yuran, out of frustration with actually owning anything—since purchasing something necessarily means deferring purchasing anything else with that money. Brand names, as well as alternative investments such as contemporary artwork (see Chap. 22), are sustained by their similarity to money. The brand becomes the product. When Nike trainers became 'must-have' items for certain groups of people, one of its executives said, 'Nike is a marketing company and its product, the trainers, our marketing tool.' Brand names enhance the desirability and exchangeability of products—that is, their similarity to money as objects of desire. The evolution of money itself illustrates this process. When it was gold, desire for it was rational as gold has a market value independent of its value as money. Although it is paper or immaterial, we still behave as if money represents something material. Money has never fully detached itself from a material base. Anything stands ready to be money, but the desire needed to make it money will end in frustration.

When the leading central banks created billions of this material between 2010 and 2017, economies responded sluggishly. Yuran says that this exposed modern money's hollow core; evidently, people did not desire it as they used to or as central bankers think that they should. Money is only as valuable as users of it decide; the public can drain money of its value. Suddenly, in a crisis, everybody focusses on debt and the difficulties of repaying it. Demand for borrowing, for credit, collapses. It is true that money demand in the main currency areas increased in the ten years after the crisis, as measured by the real money stock, but this was engineered only by dint of extreme interest rate manipulation and official creation of money (QE) required to offset weakness in private sector demand and credit creation. Money must be an object of desire, but having it can be traumatic.

The Future of Money Is Open

As I have tried to show in this collection of essays, money has played very different roles in societies over the last 100 years. Yet financial and political elites encourage the view that there are no alternatives to their 'tried and tested' money. Anthropologist David Graeber makes a passionate plea to reject this fatalistic and self-serving doctrine. Do not submit to the logic of debt! 'Nobody has the right to tell us what we owe' (Graeber 2011). History is bursting with episodes of debt cancellation and forgiveness, not to mention default. In fact, default is an essential feature of the system. It is only because of the fear of default that bankers care about who they lend to. Only this makes them allocate credit according to its most productive uses—at least in theory!

Digging the monetary system up by its roots, as Graeber does, shows that the history of money is not pretty. The midwives of our modern monetary mechanisms had bloody hands. The spread of the money economy was marked by horrific violence, slavery, debt peonage, rape and theft. Creditor classes and their allies used any weapons available to enforce their claims on debtors. If you look hard enough, today's global monetary system relies on similar mechanisms—military power, a pervasive apparatus of surveillance, police and the courts, an insistence that the weak pay their debts in full, while the strong do not, and a labour force sucked into positions of inferiority through the money machine.

According to Graeber, the usual story of money and banking is a fairy tale. They did not emerge naturally from voluntary cooperation and barter. Modern money emerged to finance warfare. Central banks represent the institutionalisation of the marriage between the interests of the warriors and financiers. Wars, and the drums of war, pervade all of money's history and present. Nixon floated the dollar in 1971 (abandoning its fixed price against gold) to finance the Vietnam War. The dollar still is backed by US military power. The United States has never hesitated to use its military power to serve its ideology and money interests. The US national debt is a promise to the whole world that everybody knows will not be kept. Countries lend it money that they know will not be repaid. Why? Graeber says they invest in US bonds as a tribute owed to its power. Historically, the main buyers of US treasury bonds have been countries that are or have been under US military occupation, such as Germany and Japan. All countries other than the United States have to repay their debts on the nail or face ruin. The dollar as the dominant global currency is rooted in military might.

The only important global institution is the IMF, which insists that (unless you are the United States) you must repay your debts; a default, it is claimed, could bring catastrophe... Look at the pressure applied recently to Greece. However, there is a big exception. China, the new kid on the bloc, is different. Why is China investing/lending so much to the United States? According to Graeber, China may look as if, like other countries, it is paying tribute to the United States by lending it money—money that it knows won't be repaid. But in reality, China is treating the United States as a potential client state. Its massive investments in US government debt are a way of softening the United States up. They are a substitute for the gifts China used to bestow on client states, before sealing their subordinate status. This has been China's traditional means of exerting its moral and political authority. As is often the case with monetary issues, people do not understand what is really going on beneath the surface of what seems to be an ordinary monetary transaction. The United States does not understand that it is entering into a relationship of inferiority.

The same applies in my view to the way China is using money to open up the world as you might use a tin-opener. We have seen how America used the power of money to establish a new global order under its aegis after World War II. Now monetary resources have enabled China to build up a far-flung presence, and potential military threat, in little more than 10 years. One tactic is to lend countries more than they can afford to service. In May 2019, at least eight countries were reported to be on the brink of default—Mongolia, Montenegro, Pakistan, Laos, Maldives, Djibouti, Kyrgyzstan and Tajikistan. All are being drawn into China's orbit. When Tajikistan's debt needed rescheduling, China reportedly accepted land and minerals instead (Tett 2019). That is typical of its method of using money, political and market clout to build its empire. The Italian, French and other governments have signed up to China's Belt and Road Initiative, part of President Xi Jinping's 'China's Dream', an open challenge for global leadership, and a way to reshape the international system with China at its centre. Italy is considered as part of Europe's 'soft underbelly', easily dislodged from its moorings in the European Union by its need to finance it enormous state debt of 130% of GDP. The Chinese Five Ports initiative could see China taking effective control of Venice, Trieste, Ravenna, and other ports linked together by the North Adriatic Port Association (NAPA). It is employing similar tactics at many other points around the world—often following up with large-scale Chinese immigration and settlement. This would lead to a larger international role for the renminbi, China's currency.

Graeber shows society has at some periods of history been able to control money; ideas and religious beliefs have corrected the faults of an economy of debt and debt slavery. Today, he argues, we should look to political action, morality and new institutions. These can play a role analogous to that played historically in Europe by the Church. Debtors would have more power, in Graeber's vision of a brighter future (making one wonder who would lend to them)… Reformed money would again support a 'human' economy rather than the current, cold commercial economy. Graeber is an angry anarchist, and his vision unrealistic, yet his analysis and historical insight shed new light on our current dilemmas.

Money to Help Us

In *The Social Life of Money*, an ambitious, wide-ranging survey, Nigel Dodd invites us to view money in a more cheerful light. Money is above all an *extraordinarily powerful idea* (Dodd 2014). (This is my view as well.) He vividly describes the diversity of notions of money and the hopes they nourish: good money can transform society. Although reformers from Sir Thomas More at the time of Henry VIII to Karl Marx have often wanted to abolish money, many others have re-imagined it, as a means to improve society. Indeed, Dodd says that there are utopian elements in almost every form of money. Look at the symbols of national or regional unity that often decorate banknotes, the 'famous Brits' whose pictures adorn Bank of England notes, the celebrated Americans featuring on US dollar notes and so on. Dodd has no time for theories of money held by mainstream economists. In his analysis, these support policies that inhibit personal freedom, corrode communities and increase inequality. New theories of money, if dispersed and adopted, could change that. Yes, money has become tainted, but it will be part of the solution. Let us, he says, prove the truth of the saying of Pierre-Joseph Proudhon, a pioneer of anarchist thought, that 'human creativity is at its height when a general bankruptcy is imminent'.

Dodd criticises the state theory of money. True, people cannot easily create new forms of money in the face of established state control of existing money, but they can make it pretty useless, confining it to petty cash. They can blunt its functions as a store of value and unit of account, while keeping it as a means of payment. People can give and withdraw value from money. Like Ingham, he says that the loss of trust has a more debilitating effect on money and on the economy than many economists realise.

Money May Not Need an Issuing Authority

While modern monies are fiat currencies, money can be created without an issuing authority. Sociologically, money's value derives not from the institutions that issue it but from the people who use it. Indeed, nation states had a struggle to establish their money as the only legal tender—using taxes, prohibitions and severe penalties for the use of non-state money. And private monies keep re-appearing, as in bitcoin. By this route, Dodd supports the theory that money develops—or might emerge—spontaneously.

Contrary to the claims of dogmatists of all theoretical schools, there is no single set of arrangements for producing money and regulating its behaviour that is natural. Money can be taken out of the control of states and banks and re-appropriated by users. A gradual erosion of state control over fiat money—which he implies is happening—creates opportunities to give users more control. Money's social function is to serve as a bridge over time and space. In this, it can be compared to the functions of religion as defined by Emile Durkheim, a founding father of sociology. The money reflects a society's culture and in turn shapes it. (That is indeed a main theme of this book.)

Monetary reformers and idealists are often dismissed as cranks—indeed some of them have been. But this is unfair to the majority of them. Idealists who propose ways to improve money should be listened to. It took dreamers, not individual self-interest or the state, to create the very idea of money. Surely, people had to put a distance between themselves and the object desired so as to enable them to compare what they wanted to acquire with other objects, and so form an idea of their relative or real value. Imagination was necessary to do this, that is, create such mental 'distance'. Only a leap of imaginative understanding would enable somebody to see objects from the points of view of other people, and *then to imagine a common measuring rod*. Even today, currencies continue to be dreamt up—look at the euro or bitcoin. We should try to re-imagine money, on a small scale as well as a large scale. Otherwise, this social convention will not meet our rapidly changing social needs. It is too easy to assert that money will just evolve naturally as if it were a species of animal or plant. It is also lazy to presume that the state will provide what is needed. Where Ingham (see below) views money as changing to reflect a social and power struggle, as a joint venture between the state and the private sector, and Graeber calls for revolutionary upheaval to overthrow an unjust order, Dodd looks to individuals and small groups to play their part in re-creating money. Money is a public good—its use by one person does not reduce its usefulness to another—that can be provided by private effort and cooperation.

State Versus Market: A False Dichotomy?

In our efforts to understand the Money Delusion, we can also learn from the work of Keith Hart, another sociologist. In his seminal work of 1986, he asserts that we should think of the state and the market as part of the fundamental dualism through which money is created. In a brilliant insight, he invites us to look at a coin—any coin. It has two sides, Heads and Tails. On the Heads side, you usually find an effigy of the monarch or another symbol of sovereignty. This expresses the connection between money and political authority. It is hierarchical—value flows from the head—the top—down. It shows how much the state says the coin is worth; that is, this is the link to power. The Tails side expresses the coin's function as medium of exchange in the market; value is determined, in the end, by the market—by what people will offer you in exchange for this coin. Here value derives from a horizontal relationship, as the exchange is deemed to be voluntary. The state's assertion that its nominal value should be accepted as a real value is tested every time the coin money is used. Monetary systems oscillate between state regulation and market exchange: 'Oscillations between the two produced both revolutions and institutions designed to contain the contradiction' (Hart 1986). In a later contribution, Hart argues that the predominance of nation states in the production and management of money is ending (Hart 2001, cited by Dodd, p. 307).

Money as a Joint Venture

The lead here was taken by Geoffrey Ingham, of Christ's College, Cambridge, whose book *The Nature of Money* (2004) was a milestone in the rediscovery of money by social scientists. Ingham accords the state a central role—diverging here from the views of some fellow sociologists. Indeed, state action was essential to create the conditions in which early capitalism developed—for example, to remove obstacles to domestic trade in land, capital and labour. Equally important was the formation of a mass consumer market—another social product. The struggle between the state and the new bourgeoisie resulted in the rise of an independent class of entrepreneurs and bankers. They agreed to finance the state's wars as long as these also advanced their interests. This produced a balance of power between the state and the bourgeoisie, and that in turn spread political stability and trust. These were the social conditions that produced the credit money that, in its turn, fuelled the industrial revolution and formed the basis for modern monetary systems.

The key to the creation of money by banks is the promise of repayment. They lend to customers they deem creditworthy—debtors expected to have the will and means to repay. This makes banks able to redeem their promises to deposit-holders. Money is credit—though not all credit is money. Capitalism's dynamic growth is fuelled by the banks' monetisation of debt. It is in the money markets that the merchants of debt assess credit and determine who gets what. The state plays a critical role: to provide law and order and public goods, correct market failures and manage financial crises. This growth of credit in turn is indispensable to the creation of consumer wants. It is not enough to have people imbued with the Protestant Ethic of hard work and asceticism, capitalism also needs consumerism (see Chap. 4). It needs money. Yet, on this reading, money is always at risk—it can vanish. These struggles make money fragile but make capitalism dynamic. 'Money cannot be neutral: it is the most powerful of the social technologies, but it is produced and controlled by specific monetary interests and is also inherently unstable'. Economic theory with its emphasis on the 'real' economy has inverted the actual relationships between the two sides: although income must be generated by the production and sale of goods, 'this takes place in conditions largely dictated by money' (Ingham 2004).

Some economists think that the supply of money should be brought fully under state control. This is not the answer, according to Ingham, as lending decisions would then be wholly political. Nor are there any easy reforms that will make the system more stable, as instability is a necessary part of it. For example, the regime of too big to fail banks may be unacceptable in the sense that it is seen as grossly unfair, leading to costly bailouts and bad banking, but it cannot be ended simply by an effort of political will. Wall Street needs Washington DC (and vice versa), and the City of London needs the Westminster government (and vice versa). These are what Ingham calls capitalism's 'axial relationships'. Each side has an interest in the long-term survival of the other, although the relationship often comes under strain (Ingham 2013). The state, in effect, outsources to banks the right to make profits by producing credit money as a store of value, and underwrites the deal, but that creates moral hazard. The most catastrophic dislocations of modern capitalism arise from this pivotal relationship. The ties between the state and the finance sector in the production of money are symbiotic. The idea they can be cut is unrealistic, as it is precisely the struggle between them that gives money value. Ingham is pessimistic on the prospects for fundamental reform of banking and money. He is scathing about those idealists who claim to have found an ideal money:

First, whatever claim is made to have found the best solution to the question of how, and how much, money is created, we can be certain that it is not the only one, and that it was arrived at after an essentially political struggle for economic existence between two different interests. Second, without such a struggle money cannot have value. (Ingham 2013)

People Mould Money

Last but not least is the sociologist widely recognised as the pioneer of the rediscovery of money by the discipline, Viviana Zelizer of Princeton. She showed that we inhabit a world of monetary pluralism, a variety of different kinds of payment systems and monetary media. To quote: 'Everywhere we look people are creating new kinds of money'; 'Not all dollars are equal'; 'There is no single, generalised, money' (Zelizer 1997). Mainstream economics has paid little attention to the invention of new forms of money and has not recognised that social pressures turn the spending of money into a complex activity: what should money buy? Does the source of the money make any difference to how it is used—saved or spent? Zelizer's work on the social groups she studied shows how people earmark money, splitting it into parcels to be used for different purposes. They mould money to suit their needs. This anticipated the growth of new forms of money in the twenty-first century.

Minsky's Vision

Although with a few exceptions the economics profession has ignored the new sociology, one economist emerges as close in spirit to them—and his major work predated those mentioned in this chapter. This is Hyman Minsky who in 1986 argued for a view of money, banking and financial markets that differed radically from the standard view. He criticised the latter for separating its analysis of how money affects the economy from consideration of how money is created. Economists assume that money is something that can be identified, measured and analysed quite independently of its institutional context and uses:

But in truth, what is money is determined by the workings of the economy, and usually there is a hierarchy of monies, with special money instruments for different purposes. (Minsky 1986)

It is worth pausing for a moment to register this: 'what is money is determined by the workings of the economy'. Money is not always and everywhere the same thing. The economy has a number of different types of money: 'everyone can create money; the problem is to get it accepted' (Minsky 1986). On Minsky's analysis, therefore, as soon as bitcoin is accepted as money, it is money. And according to Yuran, as soon as bitcoin is desired as money, it is money. Neither mentions the State.

Much to Learn

I have learnt much from these authors. From Yuran, we gain a glimpse—though not a complete explanation—of the psychological processes behind the Money Delusion. Money has to be desired, but that desire is bound to be frustrated. From Keith Hart, I learnt that money is not just key to many regrettable aspects of society but will also form part of the way forward, as an inescapable way in which humans express their identities; 'If we hope for a more peaceful and integrated world society, money will certainly play an important role in its recovery from the present impasse.' We are searching for a structure of money that would be 'adequate to humanity's common needs' (Hart 2017).

From Nigel Dodd, who fleshes out Minsky, I learnt of the many specific and distinct *ideas* of money and their influence. The globalisation of finance, the declining importance of banks in favour of managed money and the advance of securitisation meant that there was in principle no limit to banks' capacity to create credit. They needed no recourse to bank capital as interest-bearing securities would be accepted as money. This would be essentially private credit money.

Such diversity of concepts of money is foreign to economic theory. By contrast, take one chapter of Dodd's book—on utopia. Here he sets out 'to unleash the utopian spirit from inside money'—an expression that would only bewilder most economists. They would be at sea in his discussion of the thoughts and reforms recommended by numerous social philosophers and thinkers from diverse fields. Dodd puts the case for pragmatism, notwithstanding his utopian sympathies. Echoing Viviana Zelizer, he favours a 'genuine monetary pluralism' in which a 'full a range of monies is available, circulating in networks that are free to all, for individuals to use according to need and circumstance'. From Geoffrey Ingham I learnt how money gains value through the social processes that produce it and how theories of money are themselves an integral part of the process. His analysis of money as a partnership between the state and the private sector, and of the ways in which the tension between partners lends dynamism to capitalist economies, is fruitful.

So, what's important about this work? I would pick out four points: a view of money as part of a broad effort to improve the human condition; an insight into how Money Delusion works in the human psyche; the idea of money as a partnership between the state and the private sector; and an explanation of how money derives value from society, and specifically from a social struggle. I think all the sociologists mentioned would agree on one conclusion: the future of money is open. While it will be moulded by social demands and pressures, there is always scope for innovation, inspiration and new ideas. We must resist the view that our current monetary arrangements are the best possible and ignore pressure from anybody who wants to close down discussion of alternatives.

Bibliography

Dodd, N. (2014) *The Social Life of Money*. Princeton: Princeton University Press.

Fitzgerald, Scott F. (1931). *The Great Gatsby.*

Graeber, David (2011). *Debt: The First 5,000 Years*. New York: Melville House Publishing.

Hart, K. (1986). 'Heads or Tails? Two Sides of the Same Coin.' *Man* New Series 21(4): 637–656.

———. (2000/2001). *Money in an Unequal World*. London: Profile Books.

———. (2017). Hart, K (ed) *Money in a Human Economy*. New York: Berghahn Books.

Ingham, G. (2004). *The Nature of Money*. Cambridge, UK: Polity Press.

———. (2008, with a new Postscript, 2011) Cambridge, UK: Polity Press.

———. (2013) 'Reflections' in Pixley, J and Harcourt, G.C. (eds) (2013). *Financial Crises and the Nature of Capitalist Money*.

Minsky, H.P. (1986). *Stabilizing an Unstable Economy*. Yale University Press.

Tett, G. (2019). 'Belt and Road Initiative: China grapples with its BRI lending binge' *Financial Times*, May 2, 2019.

Zelizer, V.A. (1997). *The Social Meaning of Money*. Princeton: Princeton University Press.

Yuran, N. (2014). *What Money Wants: An Economy of Desire*.

20

Money and the Decline of Classical Liberalism

Having looked in the previous chapter at the work of scholars who have spent many years reflecting on the nature of money, we turn to intellectuals who may have no claims to expertise in this field but who exercise a strong influence on the climate of opinion. They write the books and articles, edit the journals, direct the plays and films and in a myriad ways shape norms of behaviours, attitudes, outlooks, fashions and trends. The development of the global money space opened up the whole world to the spread of their ideas. They are the arbiters of the ideas—the keystones of the ideological structure—on which the new society is founded. They surely bear a heavy responsibility for its culture and its delusions.

These intellectuals, journalists, writers and artists are not a homogeneous group, but some attitudes are so common among them as to be representative. They typically subscribe to the Enlightenment project, as recently championed by Steven Pinker (2018). This transcends political allegiances and positions on the Left versus Right, free market versus Interventionist spectrum. They believe, in general, that the world is getting better. However, optimism is shadowed by a sense of foreboding and a deep ambiguity. Western culture has great faults. Intellectuals are aware, even agonisingly aware, that their culture has already destroyed or undermined many other cultures. They are therefore beset by guilt feelings. Their concern for the exploited or underprivileged, abroad or at home, is suffused with doubt. The exploited peoples of Africa or Asia or South America must be compensated for what the intellectual's class or country or civilisation has done to them, or not done. Living standards must be raised. But they should not become obsessed with GDP

© The Author(s) 2019
R. Pringle, *The Power of Money*, https://doi.org/10.1007/978-3-030-25894-8_20

growth. Why should these ill-used people be encouraged to entangle themselves further with the 'false values' of Western culture?

In the ages when change could spread itself comfortably over the centuries, cultural diversity, the recognition and even enjoyment of differences among human beings, had a role in psychosocial evolution. Out of this diversity and the traffic between societies many cultural flowerings arose. One need think only of the strands from Greece to Rome and Palestine, and from past Germanic or Celtic society, which have gone to make Europe, or of the interplay of Hinduism, Buddhism and Taoism in the East. The global culture gives little scope for much farther development along these lines. We talk of respecting and encouraging diversity, yet the new global culture has destroyed all possibility of enriching or even varying what is left of traditional cultures. UNESCO has its world heritage sites, but no sociological reservations are feasible in which other cultures could be kept alive just in case they should be needed or for their intrinsic beauty and interest. The victor in the evolutionary struggle will soon be quite alone. Of course, this syndrome goes far beyond the monetary sphere, but money is an active ingredient in the mix. It is working at bewildering speed and its effects are surely irreversible. The problems we encounter with money should be placed in such a wider social context; many of the societies which had learnt how to keep it in its rightful place have been stamped out.

Many, perhaps most, of the intellectuals still believe that governments can take from the modern package—science, technology, monetisation and rationalisation of all aspects of life—what they choose, that they are in control. But deciding on this or that apparently limited issue—an industrialisation programme, say, or expanding primary education in a developing country, or even merely permitting citizens to have dealings with neighbouring societies—leads on to consequences which cannot be limited. The agenda of modernisation is not a menu from which you pick what dish you like. It is more like a *table d'hôte*, with every society expected to go through the set meal to the end.

Lack of Historical Awareness

It is difficult to comprehend or convey how revolutionary this all is because of our lack of awareness of history. We live 'now'—in the immediate present, with one foot 'hopefully' in the future. Few have any deep awareness of, or interest in, the immensity of the human experience that preceded our personal coming to consciousness. Tourism is a major growth industry but also an instrument of cultural destruction and modernisation; its benefits measured by estimating how much money tourists spend. Objective reality is a series of snapshots as it might be projected in a film taken over the span of a lifetime. We prefer not to be reminded how infinitesimal that span is. Because we live so much in and for the present, we grotesquely overvalue its importance in the totality of human experience. We have little sense of our own continuity with the past. Such awareness was always present in societies of the past, whether they possessed historical writings in the modern sense or not. Modern economies powered by science and the higher technology are the products of only the last few seconds on the historical clock, but the typical modern intellectual is interested in what happened earlier mainly to show how much progress we have made.

This is an attitude typical of the great rationalists of the West, who tended to assume that whatever they particularly liked about their age was part of the natural order of things, and therefore safe. Adam Smith was sure that the pursuit of self-interest under the system of 'natural liberty' would be checked by 'sympathy' (See Norman 2018, who calls *The Theory of Moral Sentiments*, Smith's earlier work, a 'paean to politeness, civility and self-improvement'). Similarly, in our own day, the intimate relation between capitalism and freedom, so convincingly argued by Hayek and Friedman, is not a law of nature, but valid only for an independently existing free society where freedom is valued for itself as a moral good. Similarly, again, with Hayek's socialist critics. When the socialist Richard Tawney dismissed Hayek's fears of excessive state power as exaggerated because the state was 'an instrument and nothing more', which 'sensible and decent men will use for ends which are decent and sensible' he was merely *assuming* civilised behaviour, just as Adam Smith and the others before him (Tawney 1927). People say just the same things to dismiss criticisms of our money culture—money is not to blame, it's only a tool; of course, it needs an ethical framework.

The modern intellectual is naive. He or she is not aware of, or prefers not to dwell on, the limitations of the forces they champion as tools of development. One early example of this attitude was Sigmund Freud. Here was another of those European rationalists who both hated their society and were unaware at the same time how much they owed it. He praised 'honesty' to his patients, and readers, but gives no reason why honesty with oneself should inhibit evil. He just assumes that a person will make a right choice because he assumes, without saying so, that the right is the product of reason or science. Freud was chased out of Vienna by people who were being unblinkingly honest in their murderous anti-Semitism and ended his days in London where the humanitarian values that he took for granted still survived.

The new global culture offers an ideal environment for the spread of high-tech, science and rationalism washing at the walls of all the world's legacy cultures. The pre-scientific community is no longer visible, any more than is the pre-scientific human being. We cannot tell what kind of replacement society the new human will make. This could come down to a question of what they will believe in. Intellectuals have to rid themselves of the comforting belief that their present ideology will deliver utopia. It can just as well deliver tyranny and perfect the arts of war. As John Gray, a philosophical rebel, has observed: 'To think that science can transform the human lot is to believe in magic' (Gray 2002). So, what will they believe in?

Technology and Money Don't Make a Society

Until recently, intellectuals expected that people would be content with a uniform, technocratic, rationalised modern culture. Now, at a time of violent protests on the streets of major cities, and bookshops full of titles proclaiming the end of democracy, and the 'age of anger' people who accepted this conclusion should be urged to reflect. What are the roots of our society? This phrase *technology-based society* appears so often in newspaper leaders and the speeches of presidents and prime ministers that it has acquired an air of proven truth. If the expression means that one can hardly pass a day in any country without being made aware of the transformation wrought by technological change the statement is obvious, even banal. But to say that our society is based on science and technology does not follow. The use of mobile phones, email, social media does not make a society. Nor does the possession of modern hospitals, laboratories and, say, vaccines. Nor does 'price and financial stability', even if by some remote chance they were achieved. The protests should remind us of this, make us go back to history and study how societies have been held together. We shall then re-learn that no society has even been held together or based on anything so cold-blooded, so empty of human warmth and feeling, as networks of monetary ties in the service of rationalisation, cost-savings and technological progress.

The essential qualities of human society have nothing to do with such things: they are not quantifiable, or definable, cannot be stored or processed, cannot be applied mechanically or by rote, can only be communicated by custom and tradition, are best adopted my mimesis. Its values, or purposes, lie outside the rational-technological-monetary order, though they may embrace that order. Our faith in advanced communications and monetary networks operating across the global money space and the economy they sustain makes them appear to be unstoppable. Yet such faith cannot itself provide a basis for any of the ways in which humans have lived together. Thus, the search is on for forms of association compatible with them. What forms of human aggregation will be acceptable?

Looking around us, it seems what people actually want is good food and drink, sport, holidays in pleasant places, good music, enough sex and nice children. On this view, we should have no need to ask what their meaning is. The satisfaction they give is their own sufficient justification. So an outcome is quite imaginable in which the global monetary space will service a planetary eudaemonism, assuming or creating a human type devoted to maximising sensory pleasure and avoiding pain. Such an outcome could be attractive, but it is not very likely. The elites whose creativity has been mainly responsible for dragging society up from age-old poverty will surely reject mindless pleasure-seeking as an evolutionary dead-end. Are not recent protests telling us that people generally reject it? 'We are not like that' is what they are, in effect, saying 'We are not driven by monetary motives or a simple search for pleasure.'

This is the answer to thinkers such as Yuval Harari who expect the elite to create a race of super-enhanced humans who will chase after distinctive twenty-first-century goals such as 'bliss' and immortality (Harari 2015). This fails to convince, because all societies have revolved round some principle or principles other than their own survival and self-enjoyment. Belief in something—some mutually held theory, some overview about existence—would seem to be indispensable, even for a society with such a glorious global money culture as our own! (Thinkers such as Dawkins, Harari and Pinker claim to be criticising conventional opinion while actually inviting us to admire it, that is, admire ourselves.)

Whatever Happened to the Individual?

The politics of identity is merely an evolution of the prevailing idea of liberalism long embraced by Western intellectuals. In this form of liberalism, the individual person is merely one item, or building brick, in the physical world; the class, ethnic group and society are larger, more interesting and far more closely identifiable. 'Individualism' was the appropriately ugly word coined by this progressive liberalism for the corresponding political outlook that attaches irrational importance to the mere separateness of the individuals. Under individualism, society may, for its own purposes, choose to concede rights to the individual, but they belong to him or her by express grant (which can be withdrawn), usually by virtue of his/her being identified as belonging to a group, class or minority. They do not inhere in our essential nature. Classical Jeffersonian liberalism saw them as part of our inalienable being. The rights referred to in the American Declaration of Independence, for example, are not favours or privileges that any state, or United Nations charter, or any organisation whatever has in its power to bestow, grant or graciously concede—or take away. They are in us all, already. But to contemporary liberalism, with its colours pinned to the flag of rationalism, this is sheer mysticism or music. Such rights belong to the community, to be granted or withheld as it decides. That is the logic used to legitimate the dominant belief about money—the state theory of money—that, as we have seen, has been the underlying basis of monetary policy and practice for 100 years. That is the assumption also used, for example, to justify invasions of privacy and the campaigns against private money, cash, gold and virtual currencies discussed in Chap. 18.

The impoverishment of the idea of the individual person mirrors the advance of science-based, species-thinking, class thinking. In such an intellectual climate, truth is revealed by, and becomes the possession of, experts. They alone are qualified to discuss it—not John Smith, whose only importance is as a customer. Having lost a clear grasp of these distinctions, notably the gulf separating classical liberalism from its contemporary progressive version, we veer this way and that, drifting with the tides, dragged sometimes in the direction of collectivism, and next towards extreme individualism. This is to open the floodgates to populism in its recent intimate forms and to manipulation by social media moguls. While the conventions are still observed and the individual is still treated as if he/she had rights, on the left and the right the powerbrokers are pulling the strings. As shown in the discussion of crony and state capitalism in Chap. 16, there is not much to stand in their way. Hence, the recent wave of books predicting the end of democracy.

The problem facing intellectuals is to find any position to halt at, any ground on which to make a stand. The loss of belief in a world-behind-appearances places unbearable pressure on the world of the here-and-now. If death puts an end to all the striving and all the careful weighing of choices on which individualism sets such store, then the satisfactions derived from those choices he/she makes, or feelings he/she cultivates right now acquire a preternatural, absolute, significance—because that is all there is, or ever will be. Thus, a radical foreshortening of the landscape occurs. In place of Edmund Burke's enduring 'partnership in every virtue', and in place of a doctrine of the individual that held a balance between his or her rights and duties because they were both seen as part of a larger scheme of things, a restless pursuit of satisfactions ensued—satisfactions that had to be both immediate and of absolute significance.[1] All that was needed, it seemed, was a market in everything and unlimited purchasing power. This is what gives money its hold over technological culture.

The Aggrandisement of 'Society'

People write and talk as though love of truth and pursuit of social justice were somehow implicit in nature and the cosmos. In reality, they are a legacy to them of their society. Meanwhile, a vicious feedback is occurring. To the extent that the individual accepts that he/she is unimportant (except as a customer), possibly a fiction, less and less capable of even relative good and evil and to the extent that moral conduct is predicated solely on the social environment, to precisely the same extent will the claims of society grow larger over all the individuals composing it. Such are the changes of meaning that have occurred, almost unconsciously, in the transition from classical liberalism to the new. It can be seen that the common factor in this process is that the meaning of universal concepts—the individual, truth—has been narrowed. They used to be open-ended in the same sense that each of them contained a door opening on the infinite possibility and variousness of the universe. The possibility may be an illusion, the door a mirage. I am not concerned with this, but only to demonstrate that in substituting a world of closed rationalism for the former metaphysics, we are undermining the foundations of our culture and politics. That has been the work of intellectuals over the past century. They forgot that every enduring social and political outlook is much more than a logical construct, a formula for how people can best be managed or administered; behind it is a view about human beings, the purpose of life and how we should live together. From this angle, social democracy seems increasingly incoherent.

The Dregs of Liberalism

What a mean, vulgar thing contemporary liberalism has become! Its vision of humans as consumers; their occupation, satisfying their appetites; its representative types, the mega-rich, celebrities and dream-merchants; its heaven, an endless creation of unsatisfied wants; its hell, the removal of wants; its enemies, the few outsiders who know why they despise it and sense that something better could redeem it. What may finish off these dregs of our culture is a quality one expects to find in dregs: shallowness. Nowhere is this seen better than in their pervading assumption that economics is the centre of existence. For economics can never do justice to either the good or the evil in any of us. How irritating to be told that there is no such thing as a free lunch, as if that were the purpose of our existence.

Back to Basics

Politically, the techno-money complex is a lobby group as powerful as the 'military-industrial complex' that President Eisenhower warned Americans about. Reformers need an equally strong political force. This is missing. But the environment movement was weak to start with, also. We should take heart from its success and perhaps imitate the methods used by its pioneers. In this book, I have argued that ideas and beliefs come first and that they have great power for good and evil. For good ideas, there is no better person to start with than the Scots eighteenth-century philosopher David Hume, a friend of Adam Smith, who not only articulated the case for classical liberalism but also explained why pressure to create money would doom democracy. Nobody has done either job better.

'The Contemporary Relevance of David Hume'

In 1992, I wrote a paper with the above title for the David Hume Institute in Edinburgh in which I argued that the economic advice being offered to countries of the former Soviet Union as they went through the transition to market economies was incomplete (Pringle 1992). It needed to be complemented by more awareness of the philosophical underpinnings of liberal democracy. Indeed, the settlement of questions of governance was, I suggested, necessarily prior to issues of economic reform and policy. The idea fell on stony ground. Western governments and international institutions maintained their narrow focus on economics and monetary issues, such as the establishment of independent central banks—yet another example of the money culture at work!

In this paper, I show that, at the centre of Hume's justification of liberalism is the process that Hume thought he was engaged in—the pursuit of truth. His concept of liberty is not a demand for personal freedom to pursue his preferences and whims, whether in politics or in matters of personal morality; but rather, he demands what he called *public liberty*, that is, the freedom to publish, proclaim and pursue the truth. Only individuals could uncover the truth and that is why they must be free. At the same time, the benefits flow out into society, just as society has nourished the individual and given him friends and family. The love of truth is the 'first source' of all his enquiries. Whatever his beliefs about ultimate things may have been Hume demands for himself and for everybody else the *public freedoms* to pursue the truth. But these freedoms only derive significance because there is a truth or truths to discover—the freedoms would otherwise be meaningless, the merest absurdity and self-indulgence. The benefits flow out into society; they are not to be monopolised by the author.

Prosperity as a By-Product

Hume sees liberty as surrounded by many enemies, and as needing friends. Philosophy necessarily becomes political if it wishes to preserve an environment where it can be carried on. Economic prosperity is a by-product of conditions established for and justified by other reasons. In general, people appreciate being free to think what they like and say what they think. But he observed how rare it is for them to be free in these ways. To maintain these freedoms, people need to share an understanding of how *public liberties* can be protected and why they should be. Without *the zeal for the public interest*, few will have the guts to resist the enemies of liberty and truth (Hume 1777). We cherish liberty not to pursue our individual pleasure or interests but because of its central importance in the process of scientific and moral progress and public enlightenment. Properly taught, this should still be a message to inspire.

A Case for Rebellion?

The task is to correct our utopian supermarket philosophy before it is too late. Where can we turn? In this part of the book, I suggest three ways in which we could start: rediscovering the true principles of liberalism (this chapter), studying examples of cultures that seem to have a better control over money—I propose the case of Japan (next chapter)—and learning how to 'see' money and other technologies in new ways (Chap. 22). To begin with, we should try to regain some sense of the human condition as it was pictured by the greatest imaginative writers of Western culture. At very least, such an effort might make us stop and think before uttering words and phrases whose original meaning has been lost. It might even give us a fleeting glimpse of what those who built that culture before it was taken over by the monetary-technological complex might have had in mind when they spoke of truth, the individual, freedom and free discussion.

If we want to know why our money is not working well, these are the issues we should be debating. It is far more than a technical problem that can be sorted out by experts. We have the money we deserve.

Note

1. [Society] is a partnership in all science, a partnership in all art, a partnership in every virtue and in all perfection. As the ends of such a partnership cannot be obtained in many generations, it becomes a partnership not only between those who are living, but also between those who are living, those who are dead and those who are to be born (Burke 1790).

Bibliography

Burke, E. (1790). "Reflections on the Revolution in France," 1790, The Works of the Right Honorable Edmund Burke, vol. 3, p. 359 (1899).

Gray, J. (2002). *Straw Dogs: Thoughts on Humans and Other Animals*. Granta Books.

Harari, Y. (2015). *Homo Deus: A Brief History of Tomorrow*. Harvill Secker.

Hume, D. (1777). *Essays Moral, Political, Literary*.

Norman, Jesse (2018). *Adam Smith: What He Thought and Why it Matters*. Penguin Books.

Pringle, R. (1992). *The Contemporary Relevance of David Hume*. The David Hume Institute. Hume Occasional Paper No 34. Available online from the David Hume Institute archive.

Pinker, S. (2018). *Enlightenment Now: The Case for Reason, Science, Humanism, and Progress*. Penguin Books.

Tawney, R.H. ed. (1927). Introductory Memoir to Studies in Economic History: the Collected Papers of George Unwin.

21

What Can We Learn from Japanese Culture?

Early Western visitors to Japan discovered a country unlike any they had previously come across. It obviously had very high standards of literacy and numeracy. By contrast with the almost continuous warfare in Europe, Japan had experienced nearly 300 years of what diplomat Ernest Satow called 'profound tranquillity' (Satow 1921). British lady traveller Isabella Bird, who was the first Westerner to visit many of the places on her route and lived among the people, reported that 'in many things the Japanese are greatly our superior' (Bird 1881). Visitors marvelled at the standards of expertise displayed in sophisticated crafts, the ways in which people of all walks of life would create objects of beauty, write haiku poetry, practise the delicate arts of calligraphy, ikebana, the tea ceremony and many others. They discovered too a society in which money seemed to play little part. When the topic came up, people seemed often to be embarrassed by it.

In this brief chapter, I offer a personal account of certain aspects of Japanese history, society and culture that have made a particular impression on me. I have visited the country regularly over many decades (my first professional visit as a financial journalist was in 1972), interviewed many leading bankers including all recent central bank governors, authored articles on Japan's economic and monetary developments and commissioned papers on Japan's economy and monetary system by leading scholars. For my present purpose, I select the following topics for comment: first, indicators of its business culture; second, the role of money in everyday life; third, the philosophy of business leaders who pioneered the Japanese version of capitalism; fourth, its historic social structure; fifth, I take a brief look at a little-known analysis by a remarkable American reporter who arrived with the US occupying forces after the defeat of Japan in 1945. Finally, I ask, has Japan succumbed at last?

© The Author(s) 2019
R. Pringle, *The Power of Money*, https://doi.org/10.1007/978-3-030-25894-8_21

Business Culture

By many criteria, Japan is special. For instance, consider the amazing longevity of many of its businesses. Of the 5500 or so companies in the world at least 200 years old, more than 3000 are in Japan. Germany is a long way behind with 800 or so, and the Netherlands and France have about 200 each. A few Japanese business enterprises are more than 1000 years old, with businesses ranging from construction to hotels to papermaking.

How many societies have the strength and resilience needed to renew themselves over hundreds of years while keeping their recognisable form and distinctive features and to create business enterprises able to adapt to changing conditions over a thousand years?

Japanese culture and the building blocks of its society, including corporate enterprises of various kinds, show astounding powers of endurance. Many ingredients are in the mix but among them are selfless dedication to service, abhorrence of pecuniary motives, modesty, a ceaseless and untiring search for perfection and endless patience. Even during the long decades when business was bad, somehow they endured as functioning entities. Britain has some proud long-established companies also, but this handful do not play a comparable role in Britain as such companies do in Japan. With 21,000 companies more than 100 years old, these are fruits of a distinct business ethic. Such resilience and endurance did not come from pursuing profit.

Consider the years of training required to become a sushi chef. After years of practice learning how to sharpen knives properly, and then in learning how to prepare rice to the exacting specifications of the master, the apprenticeship may be extended to the correct daily preparation of the fresh ingredients, such as preparing blocks of fish, grating ginger and slicing green onions. Years of training will elapse before he becomes a master—an 'itamae'.

I have personal acquaintance with one such enterprise, one of Kyoto's many schools of ikebana flower arrangement. Like all such organisations, it is headed by an Iemoto, a Master (in this case, a female) who preserves the traditions of the particular school and passes on its own, typically to another family member who has undergone the long training required. This system is also used in Japanese music, the art of the tea ceremony, calligraphy and performance arts such as Noh theatre. As in many other such enterprises, the one I know personally can trace its lineage back to the founder of a particular school or branch—in this case, the Myuki Enshu school of ikebana. This emphasises the philosophical aspects of flower arrangement as expressed by the founder. Each generation since the mid-nineteenth century has kept the tradition alive, while inevitably going through various modifications far too subtle and delicate for the untrained eye (like mine) to fathom. It is not and cannot be entirely static yet maintains a pride in its continuity.

Stubborn Resistance in Everyday Life

In everyday life, there is less emphasis on monetary measures of success than in the West. What matters for the individual's status is the respect in which he or she is held, an asset earned during the course of a lifetime. The efforts that an individual makes to lead a life of high quality—to make a contribution to family, friends, his or her company, university, hospital or other affiliation—so far as within his or her abilities are what earn social esteem. Of course, this is true to some extent universally, but in Japan, they are still particularly prominent. Businesses large and small still aim above all to provide a quality product; people's pride in their work is a pleasure to behold.

Japan has achieved a high standard of living together with social stability, law and order, and low incidence of crime. Surveys show it reports the lowest rate of bribery in the world, with less than 1% of the population likely to pay or receive a bribe. If you leave a wallet in the train, it is likely to be returned to the Lost Property office promptly, with all its contents intact, even if it contained money. I have had personal experience of this too. Japan also remains free of the blame culture—the knee-jerk search for someone to blame when accidents or misadventures happen that has become routine in the West. When disasters or accidents strike, the Japanese do not seek compensation but patiently set about repairing and rebuilding their lives. This philosophical attitude, often called 'stoic' in the West, was exhibited to a global TV audience in their response to the Great Tohoku earthquake in 2011. I was there when it happened—the whole of Tokyo and all the glass in its sky-high buildings started shaking and what felt like a wave swept through the ground beneath my feet. A total of 15,000 people died. From all over Japan, volunteers came to assist the survivors. There were no reports of looting.

Japanese dislike tipping, the idea that one will give or receive a better-than-average service, because one is paid or has paid more than average for it. Such feeling or expectation is unpleasant; it leaves a bitter taste. Value is measured on non-monetary scales. For instance, fleeting or chance encounters are endowed with significance—you never know what they may lead to. Where in the West events, good or bad occurrences (where they do not have an obvious explanation) are put down to chance or God's will, the Japanese will search for their implications; they look for significance in serendipitous encounters. Every meeting is viewed against an awareness of the fragility of life. It may be our last with this person. Even shopkeepers have this at the back of their minds when serving a customer. That is the thought behind rituals such as the tea ceremony: take care, treat the moment with reverence and meditate. Even in the bustle of a modern Japanese city, beneath the similarities with other cities everywhere, the people going about their lives are still different. Often, meeting a friend, they will be silent at times, whereas Westerners feel the urge to fill the space with speech.

People still believe in *bachi*: if you suffer a misfortune, you check first to see what you may have done wrong. It is part of the tradition of Buddhist philosophy shared by many Eastern peoples: 'actions have consequences'. Did you neglect a duty? Conduct yourself badly or with pride? People share the assumption that if you act badly, some form of punishment will follow— though often in unexpected ways. 'How stupid I was!' You never point the finger at others, because you know they will have done their best, still less try to get monetary compensation.

Monetary Attitudes

There are some habits that anybody notices who has spent some time in the country. Money is rarely passed directly from hand to hand. When purchasing an item or service—rather than handing your money to the cashier— you place your payment (whether cash or credit) on the small tray provided. This is where your change will be placed as well. When handed over in non-commercial setting, money is wrapped in high-quality paper. The banknotes have to be clean, fresh and looking like new (bank teller machines sanitise and press notes before issuing them). Open displays of money are bad manners. Paper notes and coins are considered rather dirty; children will be told to handle them with care. Money is prominent as an object to be given on specific occasions. Gifts of money—often quite large gifts that may amount to hundreds of dollars—play a large role (a gift system subject to highly complex rules of reciprocal obligation).

It has required sustained effort, in the trendy language of identity politics, for the Japanese to preserve their cultural uniqueness. If there is a common theme in Japan's encounter with modernity, it is to avoid being taken over by the West—either politically as a colony or in terms of culture. The Japanese idea of/attitudes to money should be seen in this context. In traditional Japanese society (as indeed in many other non-Western societies), money is kept in its place. Money is not a free-standing object that you have and can do what you will with. This is not to say that Japanese resist monetary relations, markets mediated by money or market-determined prices expressed in money. As discussed below, they have used their versions of advanced credit and banking techniques for hundreds of years. But perhaps it is precisely this long experience that has enabled Japan to resist being taken over entirely by the modern outlook. It is still defending itself, while also embracing the latest technologies and pop culture.

Among other factors supporting resistance, I briefly mention three: the historic social structure; the legacy of Bushido; and Japan's brand of capitalism.

The Historic Social Structure

Before the headlong rush to industrialise at the end of the nineteenth century, Japanese society was already in many respects just as developed as were the heartlands of capitalism. Japanese had higher literacy rates and a longer continuous tradition of high culture than Europe. Moreover, people of all social strata had a sophisticated appreciation of aesthetic and literary values and were themselves usually highly skilled in one or more arts or crafts.

Money had always played a much smaller role in Japanese society. True, major Japanese cities and trading centres had developed complex banking systems and trade finance from at least the seventeenth century along with a very active coastal trade (much more efficient than going by road across Japan's mountainous inner regions). But there was no national currency—each province would have its own, as in eighteenth-century Germany—and the use of barter was common. Feudal lords collected sums owing to them mainly in rice. Precious metals were used to decorate buildings and to create works of art. In general, people managed with few possessions. There was no national tax system. In rural areas, rice was the main medium of exchange and standard of value.

In feudal times, Japan controlled the risks of excessive money power accruing to traders by placing merchants as the lowest of all social classes. Above them were the samurai/farmers/peasants/and artisans. This reflected the influence of Confucian teaching, and its view of merchants as non-productive. Indeed, merchants were treated as parasites who profited from the labour of the more productive peasant and artisan classes. They had a separate section of each city, and the higher classes were forbidden to mix with them except on business.

Japan's warrior culture and code—bushido or 'the way of warriors'—had elements in common with knightly codes in medieval Europe and feudal or aristocratic codes in other parts of the world. It was supposed to uphold virtues of loyalty, honour, discipline, self-sacrifice and skills in martial arts. It laid special emphasis on frugality and a disdain for money. It is said that a well-brought-up samurai should exhibit such a low opinion of monetary values 'that he did not even know the price of rice' (when in reality many of them were very poor). As society was rigidly divided into samurai, bureaucrats, peasants, artisans and merchants, this was the tone set by people of the highest status. Scholars trace the origins of the status hierarchy to Confucian teaching. (The popularity of the term 'bushido' in the West dates back to the effort to repackage Japanese culture for Western consumption in the nineteenth century.)

'Father of Japanese Capitalism'

The founders of the Japanese brand of capitalism in the late nineteenth and early twentieth centuries left a lasting legacy. Take, for example, Shibusawa Eiichi (1840–1931). Shibusawa, who came from a humble background and is also known as the father of Japanese capitalism, dedicated himself to a life of business guided by the *Analects of Confucius*. He believed business should not only be competitive and super-efficient but also be guided by a strict ethical code, and a sense of social responsibility. These aspects must work together. A business person should never put personal gain or profit first; however, profit and money were essential for realising a good society. They were not to be viewed as necessary evils but rather as instruments to save the world. Business activities are essential for realising ultimate moral goals. It is a duty to make people wealthy so that society can be. Born as a farmer, with a higher status than that of merchant he knew nevertheless what it was to be treated with disdain. Following his visits to Europe, where he saw at first hand the makings of a new industrial society, he dedicated himself to raising the status of business. He founded Japan's first modern bank and hundreds of other companies. He was closely involved in the modernising of Japan's education system and in an estimated 600 projects related to education, social welfare and business (Fridenson and Takeo 2017). (Shibusawa was only one of dozens of rising business leaders whose work transformed Japan into a strong industrialized economy—I select him to represent this entire group. Indeed, Shibusawa's special status is to be recognised as his portrait will feature on the new ¥10,000 note to be introduced in 2024.)

Having looked at a few of the reasons for Japan's resistance to Western ideas about money, there was still the question of whether it could do anything in practice to protect its culture.

Could Japan's Alternative Be Tolerated?

Between the sixteenth and the mid-nineteenth centuries, Japan's rulers had restricted access by foreigners to Japan. Famously, only five ports were authorised to engage in foreign trade. The Japanese government feared that open access would subvert Japanese society. Japan's rulers restricted access by Japanese feudal lords to advanced Western armaments, and were hostile to Christian missionaries and the commercial ideas that they would bring with them. Christians were persecuted and forced to publicly renounce their faith. The last revolt by Christians took place in the 1630s. During the 250 years of *sakoku* (closed society), foreigners were banned from entering Japan and Japanese nationals banned from leaving the country under penalty of death. But when Japan started to modernise from 1868 on, it was building on foundations going back hundreds of years. These included very high standards of literacy, craftsmanship and its own kind of technology. The Meiji restoration and the amazing speed of Japan's catching-up afterwards were motivated by a determination to avoid the fate of other Asian countries and become a colony. When they looked at a map of Asia, the Japanese observed that almost every country in Asia had been taken over by a Western power. In 1898, the Philippines became part of US territory.

The modern history of Japan is a struggle to reject what Japanese felt to be a foreign virus. In the victory over Russia in 1905, it became the only non-Western country to defeat a major Western power by force of arms. Its defiance would later serve to encourage independence movements in other Asian countries. Indeed, it emerged as a rival. This raised a basic question: could this be tolerated? Might a non-Western country be permitted to join the international economic order as a formidable competitor but keep a unique way of life, if that meant also repelling Christianity and the Judaeo-Christian *Weltanschauung*, including aspects of Western culture?

An Unconventional American View

At this point, I would like to pay my respects to Helen Mears, an American reporter who, in *Mirror for Americans: Japan* (1948), offered an original analysis of Japanese-US relations and misunderstandings which also helps to explain the limited role of money in social life. This is only a brief note on a study that in my view has deep and lasting value.

Mears describes how Japan developed into a sort of controlled society in order to keep the domestic economy functioning. This is not, she says, because the Japanese were (as was often said in the West in the 1930s and 1940s) an 'enslaved' people whereas 'we' Americans are a free people, but because of contrasting histories. As she insists time and again the values and satisfactions of the Japanese are different from 'ours'. For example, the central function of money in American life developed to meet distinctively American needs. To put it in a nutshell: Americans have always been in a hurry; they had a vast continent to settle; let's get the job done. The Japanese, by contrast, were in no hurry and had nothing much to do: 'so their emphasis was not on speed, but on slow motion', and this explains not only their resistance to modernity but also many details of day-to-day life.

The Japanese, Mears said, are naturally preoccupied with tradition, ceremony and ritual. Americans have so much to work with that they can afford waste. The Japanese cannot. They become skilled at conservation. Americans make extravagance a virtue; they make a cult of waste, developing civilisation on the principle of rapid replacement of everything they use in daily life. That explains why Americans encourage individualism and democracy, whereas the Japanese do not; under their conditions, individual initiative 'would have been disruptive'. They subordinate the individual to the group and discourage competition. The aim: a stable society. That explains why America had from the beginning a money economy. Americans have always liked money and admired it: 'The Japanese in their pre-modern period developed a love of money only among a handful of people...' (Mears 1944).

Given such beliefs, values and attitudes, the Japanese did not develop an independent, competitive middle class of businessmen, bankers and professional white-collar workers. People with such skills existed but as hereditary retainers of one of the great families. They did not develop a free enterprise system. The economy was based on sharing (an ethic that remains strong and indeed is growing in the twenty-first century). The farmer produced the wealth—rice—and shared it with the landowners, the aristocracy, who accounted for about 7% of the population. The Japanese developed techniques of intensive cultivation while preserving the fertility of the land. That is how a poverty-stricken economy turned the islands of Japan into 'a beautifully tended garden'.

They solve their problem of limited living space by accepting huddle, by living in miniature houses, by owning few things and by living according to rule. The individual with his pile of money is subordinated to rules set by the family, the community, the clan. In my view, the picture Mears drew in the 1940s remains in many ways valid.[1]

The Money Virus Attacks

However, the money virus would not leave Japan alone. In the 1980s, it attacked again and Japan succumbed. The bubble in asset prices from 1986 to 1991 was one of the most extraordinary in modern economic history. The causes have been endlessly debated. American pressure to revalue the yen played a part—yen appreciation caused a recession in Japan's export-led economy that was combatted by an excessively easy monetary policy. But asset markets could not have reached the absurdly excessive levels they did without the enthusiastic participation of Japanese investors, big and small. So, the Japanese turned out to chase easy money just like everybody else—no surprise to those who have ever visited one of the ubiquitous pachinko parlours where hundreds of punters spend hours mindlessly filling machines with steel balls and triggering a spring-loaded hammer to release the balls that then fall—or more often fail to fall—into one of the prize-winning cups (this market's gambling revenue in Japan was for a time said to be larger than that of Las Vegas, Macau and Singapore combined). Many Japanese were ashamed of this boom and bust, which was followed by the relative stagnation of 1990s and 2000s—a period dubbed the *lost decades* (although, in fact, the standard of living continued slowly to improve).

There is no doubting the power of money in modern Japan, with its inherent liability to financial scandals and its form of crony capitalism (see Carlson and Reed 2018). Dentsu Inc., the world's largest advertising agency, has a strong influence over the media. Ever since World War II, TV advertising has assiduously seduced the population by the dream of a US-style consumer society and the search for an affluent lifestyle. You look in vain for criticism and informed debate of Japan's power structures. The soporific mood engendered by robotic, moronic TV game shows is never disturbed by any controversial news reporting: Japan has a compliant press corps, and reporters nearly always toe the official line. Indeed, this has got worse since censorship was strengthened by the Abe government in the wake of the Fukushima nuclear reactor disaster. Disillusion with the mainstream media has made many Japanese turn to new, more independent, online news sources, some of which, however, have questionable editorial standards.

Cultural historian Christopher Harding says that Japan's struggle with modernity matters more than ever: 'Modern Japan offers a compelling case study in the sort of wrestling that lies behind—and ahead—of us all' (Harding 2019). Many Japanese lament the decline of traditional Japanese virtues. Kazuo Inamori, the founder of Kyocera, an extremely successful and innovative ceramics company based in Kyoto, says 'Japan is pursuing profit without any moral guidelines' and motivation is 'driven by greed' (Inamori 2004). Ishihara Shintaro, former actor and Governor of Tokyo from 1999 to 2012, even described the Tohoku earthquake in 2011 as a 'punishment from heaven' for greed.

By Japanese standards, there has indeed been a rise in corruption. This causes guilt and distress; people blame themselves, not others. The Japanese *Weltanschauung* remains in my view fundamentally distinct. The recent resurgence of a (mostly moderate) nationalism is in this respect positive. Fears of a swing to the extreme Right have thus far proved unfounded. At some deep level, Japan is still struggling to hold onto its identity. Of course, there is much to learn from other great cultures that have weathered the onslaught of modernity, from Islam in its diverse forms to Hinduism. Yet Japan is unique in having reached as high a level of living standards and technological innovation as leading Western countries while retaining strong elements of its age-old culture. Among its other merits are that, in my view, it retains a refreshingly healthy attitude to money. Despite constant attacks by the money virus, its long historical heritage still protects it. Japan has many faults, but those early Western visitors were right to detect something special. In terms of the approach to be discussed in the following chapter, the Japanese still have a different way of 'seeing' money. Japan proves that a Western attitude to money is not a necessary concomitant of achieving and maintaining a competitive economy with world-beating companies and technological leadership in many fields.

Note

1. The book was banned by General MacArthur during the American occupation and is rarely cited by the Western scholars but has been republished in Japan in translation.

Bibliography

Bird, Isabella L. (1881). *Unbeaten Tracks in Japan*. John Murray.

Carlson, M.T., and Reed, S.R. (2018). *Political Corruption and Scandals in Japan*. Cornell University Press.

Fridenson, Patrick, and Takeo, Kikkawa (2017). *Ethical Capitalism: Shibusawa Eiichi and Business Leadership in Global Perspective*. Toronto: University of Toronto Press.

Harding, C. (2019). *Japan Story: In Search of a Nation, 1850 to the Present*. Penguin.

Mears, Helen (1944). *Mirror for Americans: Japan*. New York: Houghton, Mifflin.

Inamori, Kazuo (2004). *A Compass to Fulfilment*, trans. David A. Thayne, 2005. New York: McGraw Hill.

Satow, E. (1921). *A Diplomat in Japan*. Yohan Classics, and Stone Bridge Press.

22

Contemporary Art: Towards New Ways of 'Seeing' Money

Cultural changes alter how people perceive the world. They see it in a new light. They notice certain aspects that did not matter to them before, and pay less attention to matters that had been important, even essential. Modern global culture requires people not only to use communications technologies but also to pay continuous attention to the pipelines connecting them to the worldwide financial network. They are alert to opportunities, risks, dangers and threats when shopping, buying and selling or simply browsing. Where they might have been brought up in a village where what mattered for their livelihood was the next year's crops or the health of neighbours, now their futures are determined more by people hundreds or thousands of miles away clicking on their keyboards and mobile phones. They have to keep up with the new world. They cannot afford to be cut off. Never in human history have so many people had to adjust to such a change in such a short space of time. It has to be traumatic. If the norms of the new society and its culture force new views of the world on us, how do we, in turn, see money? It seems to be everywhere and nowhere. It is invisible. Who controls it? Can they, whoever they are, increase or reduce its supply to me or to my loved ones?

© The Author(s) 2019
R. Pringle, *The Power of Money*, https://doi.org/10.1007/978-3-030-25894-8_22

What thoughts go through people minds can be imagined:

As for me, I do not know where they are. Surely they live and work in New York. Does President Trump control them, the arbiters of my destiny? Will he let me borrow money or will an algorithm decide? Will the algorithms be in a good mood today? Should I offer a sacrifice to induce them to grant my petition—'oh, give me a customer today!' My experience is they are usually grumpy when they first wake up in the morning—if only I knew what time morning is where they live! I must talk to one of my online friends. I look out on the familiar landscape from my home or office, but my mind is far away. I do not really see those birds over here; I am too busy to have tea with neighbours as I might have to answer that critical email I am waiting for. I know the faces of a few of my customers and sometimes they send me images of their families, although there are so many rules about what kind of images are allowed or not allowed that it is better to avoid them; you don't want to have the Internet police snooping around. Thank goodness, I don't live in China, where everything you do is tracked and recorded 24/7. And I am making more money, most of the time, than I used to as a small farmer up here in the mountains. But I am always anxious.

Anyway, you get the general drift of this imaginary soliloquy. Such are the mental processes many of us experience. Nothing like this has ever happened. It is startlingly new and must cause wrenching dislocation in the human psyche as well as in social relations everywhere.

How can such a world be humanised? Unless we view money in correct perspective, we cannot understand it. As a result, we shall not be able to control it. Or rather, we will not be able to counter its inherent desirability (see Chap. 19); in other words, it will control us. When we look out on a landscape, we may believe that to be 'nature' as our parents saw it, but the nature we see is not the same. No matter where we live, pollution has changed the light that enters our eyes. To believe that nature is the same is an illusion. Similarly, the flickering light from computer screens changes our perceptions of reality—what exists out there.

The Teaching of John Berger

John Berger, a pioneering art critic, taught us that how we see an artwork, what it means for us, depends on the assumptions that we bring to it. These assumptions are learnt. We learn our ideas about beauty, truth, genius, civilisation and status from society. We already have these ideas when we look at a painting. But these ideas lag behind reality: these assumptions no longer accord with the world as it is. The past is not 'waiting to be discovered, to be recognised for exactly what it is'. Instead, history is always 'the relation between a present and its past'. As in art, we bring perceptions and assumptions to our uses of money; and as with art, these can get out of sync with reality. We can force change in forms of money as in forms of art. In Part One of this book, I showed that societies can do that. But there are some preconditions; for instance, we have to believe we can do it. I agree with Berger that a knowledge of history helps. By recapturing the past, we recover freedom to act in the future. 'A people or a class which is cut off from its own past is far less free to choose and to act ... than one that has been able to situate itself in history.' That requires 'seeing' it differently (see Berger 1972 for all above references).

The past is not for living in: 'it is a well of conclusions from which we draw in order to act'. This is true of attitudes to money also. The parallels between the stories of art and money stretch back to their origins. The visual arts started as a sacred preserve; so, probably, did money. Art was magical but also physical—a place, a cave, a building in which the work was made. So was the first money we know about, as units of account maintained by priests in ancient Babylon 2000 BCE. The experience of art, which was at first the experience of ritual, was set apart from the rest of life—'precisely in order to exercise power over it'. Later the preserve of art became social, entering the culture of the ruling class. The authority of art was 'inseparable from the particular authority of the preserve' of art. All this can be applied to the history of money. Will the art market develop the equivalent of a central bank charged with feeding the market with just enough liquidity to keep prices nicely firm?

Again, there are echoes of the history of money. Once the preserve of the King and ruling elite it became a means of payment for citizens in ancient Greece and then, with the development of international markets, a means for the dissemination of useful knowledge throughout the then civilised world through commerce. The mystique of money persisted. Society gives authority over money to a small cadre of people. Will technologies such as that underlying cryptocurrencies (see Chap. 18) do for money what cheap reproductions did for art, democratising it while increasing the worth of the original? As in art, in money too we have a new language. Could this language be used, as Berger urged it should be in the world of art, to 'confer a new kind of power'?

Art for the Outsider

Great works of art have always been revolutionary, not in the sense that they stir you to action—that is the function of propaganda—but in what they reveal. They nudge the world as we see it. It shifts on its axis every time an artwork brings a fresh way of seeing. Art challenges conventions. It can arouse sympathy for people disregarded by society—for the outsiders (think of the dwarfs and blind people in Velazquez, Goya's black drawings, the peasant figures in Breughel, Picasso's circus performers and sad, contemplative Harlequins). There are such challenges in contemporary art—symbols, representations and marks that reflect the sensibilities of outsiders. These are the people who, for whatever reason, do not fit in with contemporary society, who reject it or have been rejected by it (see Chap. 17). As discussed later, the market in contemporary paintings may be dominated by the wealthy—but there's nothing new in that.

In view of its domination by Big Money, one might assume that the art market is the last place to look for challenges to conventional ways of feeling and seeing. But keep looking and you will find some. Many of the visual arts over the past century have done more than hint at the existence of something twisted, out of true, about society. It is not an artist's business to explicate his meaning in the language of an accountant finding a discrepancy in the books, but a message speaking of something wrong is what the fragmentation and disorder of images in paint, bronze or stone surely comes to. One thinks of the faces of Francis Bacon's pictures running down into deliquescence, like candle wax, of Anselm Kiefer's grim landscapes and cityscapes of desolation. As has been said of Kiefer's work: 'he does the big embarrassing stuff, the stuff that matters: the epic slaughters of the world, the incineration of the planet, apocalypse then, apocalypse often; the fragile endurance of the sacred amid the cauterised ruins of the earth' (Schama 2007). Personally, I find startling and revelatory qualities in artists such as Gerhard Richter and Anselm Kiefer. As Picasso hoped would be true of his work, some of their work lets me see things that I would not have discovered without them. Sometimes they arouse my human sympathies, or connect me in new ways to my society. Often I see only an abstract passion, an intellectual analysis, a machine of glass and steel like modernist architecture and money. The global culture is reflected as in a mirror.

Anxiety Fuels Demand

One can find in them a kind of terrible beauty. Art pictures the disintegration and desolation left by money's hurricane. Everything is in flux; even property is no longer firm and solid. This makes people anxious.

'Oil painting, before it was anything else, was a celebration of private property', writes John Berger (Berger 1972). Owning it has always been a sign of affluence. The objects portrayed in traditional art—such as still lives, rich fabrics, jewellery, gold—are commodities buyable in a market. To acquire them, you needed money, which was another natural accessory of the Man of Property. Renaissance paintings were sponsored by people with immense fortunes being built up in Florence and other cities. Berger also addresses the subject of money and the consumer society directly. Whereas the oil painting showed what its owner was *already enjoying* among his possessions and his way of life, by contrast, the purpose of publicity is almost the opposite. It is 'to make the spectator *dissatisfied* with his present way of life: Not with the way of life of society, but with his own within it'. The sum of everything is money; to get money is to overcome anxiety:

> Money is life. Not in the sense that without money you starve. Not in the sense that capital gives one class power over the entire lives of another class. But in the sense that money is the token of, and the key to, every human capacity. The power to spend money is the power to live'…Those who lack the power to spend money are nobodies. In contrast, those who have money power become 'loveable'. (Berger 1972, 143)

Where Is the Berger of Money?

Berger's call for new 'ways of seeing' smashed open the doors of the stuffy art world. In revealing the prior assumptions that we bring to a work of art—ideas and prejudices about what beauty is, about truth, genius, civilisation, status, taste—he freed us to enjoy art again. In contrast, despite praiseworthy efforts by many central bankers to talk a language people can understand, the production and management of money still have a dusty atmosphere. The aura of mystification hangs on. Decisions about money's future value are still taken behind closed doors by older people in highly ritualised settings and communicated like tablets of stone to the waiting crowds in approved ritualistic press conferences. Their merits are debated among initiates.

Looking at the rivalry between private ownership and publicly owned spaces in the world of art and museums, similar questions can be raised about the future of money. If the global money space was, to begin with, a product of private sector initiative, perhaps it is time for another generation of private sector innovation. As we have noted, some view bitcoin and/or libra and other new digital currencies as signalling a new season of merry money-making, like the first swallow heralding spring. Does the state need to approve what counts as money? Yes but it may adopt what is already used as money. We are told these new forms are too risky and unreliable; but why not let the public make such judgements? Is not the real reason that the state makes a lot of money simply out of producing money—money it uses to buy things? (For discussion of digimoney, see Chap. 18.)

The state's response has been to regulate ever more tightly the institutions that create most of the money in the economy—the banks; but in whose interests? As public choice theory has shown, it is no use favouring government intervention without also looking at its costs, whose interests it serves and whether (as is likely in the case of money) it will be misused. What Berger said of art galleries is true still of money: 'As usually presented, these are narrow professional matters. One of the aims of this essay has been to show that what is really at stake is much larger.'

A Dirty Market in Hyper-Luxury

The new wave of wealth far surpasses previous waves. It is the growth of finance, more than any other factor, that has driven the new wave of art buying. There are so many *nouveaux riches*, with so much disposable income, that the ambition to show your monetary strength has become increasingly difficult. This creates pressures to create an entirely new class of hyper-luxury goods, well beyond the reach of the merely affluent. Space travel is one such. Acquiring costly artworks is another.

Money links members of the global gilded elite of art, music and entertainment, and it pervades cultural products, some of which pass as currency and are produced in ways that resembled the money printing and money-creating processes. The art world is dominated by mega-galleries and mega collectors trading artworks as substitutes for money. The top ten biggest sales, all in excess of $100 million for each work, took place in the seven years to 2018. Market participants said sales were driven by speculation, competition for status, lust and envy. This was the new global money culture at work. It saturated not only art but also music, entertainment, publishing, sport, higher education and the media. The market quickly recovered from shocks, and there seemed no limit. When $500 million was paid for a (possibly fake) Leonardo, market observers speculated when the $1 billion milestone would be passed. All for a few scratches on a scrap of canvas.

Georgina Adam, an art critic and columnist, paints a dire picture of the art world's excesses, including forgery, rampant speculation, tax avoidance, money laundering and price rigging (Adam 2014, 2018). This is the very opposite of a transparent market, and is a vehicle for all sorts of double-dealing, criminality and deception. Adam does not make this connection, but the vices that she highlights are the natural results of trends discussed in this book; rising income inequality, economic exploitation and staggering concentrations of wealth in the hands of the very few, all of which have enabled activity at the upper reaches to continue unabated despite global downturns in other financial sectors. The nouveaux riches turn to blockbuster art purchases as a means of announcing their arrival at the top of the pile. As one of her interviewees tells Adam, buying a picture, no questions asked, gives you entree to a social world: 'You need to understand this in order to understand why these things happen' (Adam 2018). Rachel Wetzler observes that it's no coincidence that the world's prominent art collectors include those with questionable backgrounds, including Walmart heiress Alice Walton[1]; the Sackler family[2]; Poju Zabludowicz, whose family fortune has its origins in arms dealing; and hedge fund founder Daniel Och, whose firm paid millions of dollars in bribes to government officials in several African countries in exchange for mining rights. 'No doubt they'd rather be remembered for their patronage of the arts than for profiteering off human misery' (Wetzler 2018).

Money, Art and Time

There are other parallels between the two worlds. An enterprising, vigorous society will often be innovative in money as in art and commerce—as has been seen at key moments in history such as the Renaissance. To understand how a society 'sees' its money, it is useful to know how it 'sees' its art. They share many things, including a sensitivity to changing ideas of time. Rachel Cohen has shown that revolutions in painting coincide uncannily with fundamental changes in our perception of time and money. She cites Duccio's painting of the Madonna and child of around 1300 AD in the Metropolitan Museum of Art, New York. Crucially, this depicted the Madonna in a new pose. For the first time in art history, instead of portraying an immobile, monumental image, Duccio shows the Madonna and the baby leaning together as the child reaches out to his mother, as if asking the viewer to imagine a movement, inviting us to wonder what will happen 'next', introducing a dynamic concept of change. This is quite new. This revolution in art—obvious to us, so new then, as for centuries the Madonna and child had always been portrayed in the same motionless image—took place in Siena at the same time as the city's merchants were pioneering the idea of conveying money over distance and time with promissory notes to be redeemed in future at a fixed price.

This artistic innovation was closely followed by a revolution in book-keeping as a way of keeping records of a company's business transactions. Double-entry book-keeping became the basis of modern accounting. This permits a statistical picture to be assembled of a person's or company's financial dealings over time. It lets *people see their business at a glance* (previously each transaction would be recorded on different slips of paper). This was extraordinarily important as a condition of the growth of trade and the early beginnings of the industrial revolution. Time is crucial to the demand for money, as money is a way of postponing a purchase and a means of storing potential purchasing power. Changes in the community's sense of time changed commerce, finance and art forever. Capitalist practice entails continuous calculation of the possible profit in an uncertain future from an investment now compared with keeping the money safe in cash (or short-term loans).

Fast forward a few hundred years to Picasso, developing in Cubism an abstract art form allowing the viewer to see front, side and back of a person/article/violin—a sequence *condensing time*. This occurred at the same time as the financier JP Morgan was not only founding the Met's collection of art but also pioneering new financing techniques—for example, the idea of valuing companies on their price/earning ratios rather than total assets, thus incorporating expectations and *uncertainty about the future*. Then on to Jackson Pollock embodying abstract values; then to today with Damien Hirst's shark, showing that the *very act of buying* an artwork for £200 million or whatever *confers value on it*. Is money giving value to art or is art giving value to debased money? Or, is our debased money—money virtually thrown at us by central banks—merely a reflection of the rubbish (as some people view it) that passes for contemporary art? Is money itself second only to art as the toy of the super-wealthy? Contemplation of such riddles gives us new insights into the deep and quite mysterious links between paintings, finance, money and time.

Art and money are methods of representing value. When value was seen as unchanging, eternal, fixed by God, so paintings were static, lacking in movement—and they could be beautiful. They still are beautiful! With the Renaissance, people began to see the world as changing, but in ways that could be understood, as a story through time. Even the human body in movement or about to move could be beautiful—a shocking thought for Europeans in the Middle Ages. Money changed and so did art. But such changes were gradual; they took time and could be represented as beautiful images of human movement. From the late twentieth century onwards, what matters is the instant; trading of money done in milliseconds, values created and destroyed in the moment. Financiers lose any sense of caring for the longer-term future. Cohen frames the question that many of us ask when financial crashes arrive: 'It may be that our helpless rage at finance comes in part from our sense of bewildered complicity: how did these crazy instant values come to be the realm in which we live?' (Cohen 2013).

Here are further parallels. Consider the moral aspects: money helps us cope with the fear of time and uncertainty; art reveals beauty even in the mundane, the broken down, the lame. Both afford glimpses of order in the disordered flux of experience. Both give us strength in facing the future. Both rest on trust. One must believe that one is facing or dealing with the real thing, that one is not victim of a trick. How can one gain such confidence? Bankers and central bankers often talk about credibility—it matters to them more than almost anything else. How is it established? Both in art and in banking, credibility depends on persuading the client to believe a story—the 'backstory' of an artwork and the 'backing' offered for a money (curious how close the language and words are). In both cases, they talk of the need to 'accept' a note or painting on trust—that claims for its backing, its narrative, are credible. Also like art, a good money is trusted to keep its value, its credit; it may, invested, pay interest but you can never know for certain that it will. (Maybe it is doubt that even the world's least untrustworthy debtor, the US government, will pay real interest on its debt that explains the rise of Bitcoin; the sources of its value are as mysterious as the valuations of some artworks since according to most economists its value should be zero.)

Likewise, a good creative work will 'travel'. Along the way, it will pick up value. To write a book, create a film, artwork or piece of music is like issuing a banknote. They are floated out into the world. In both cases, their eventual value and how long they keep value are decided by the public. Markets in creative works and in money are Darwinian: the fittest survive. Value is given by the public's estimation—what they are worth in real terms is decided in the marketplace. Time may change relative values. You can speculate but you cannot appeal.

Finally, both art and money challenge us. They are difficult. Money can lead us astray and is hard to keep in proper perspective. Great art has often been experienced as puzzling, difficult, even laughable. Look at cartoons of people coming out of the first showing of Van Gogh's paintings in London, in 1912, 20 years after his death. Everybody is portrayed as guffawing, bodies bent double with laughter, jeering at such absurd paintings. Of course, that does not imply that all difficult art is good. But good art is often difficult, coming as a shock, precisely because it asks us to change our habitual way of seeing.

Look Again at Money and Technology

In April 2019, a four-part series on BBC Radio 4 explored 'new ways of seeing' technology. James Bridle, the presenter, an artist and author, discussed ways in which our tools shape the way we see the world. For instance, the Internet makes us see the world differently, in ways nobody has seen it before. The experience of walking down a city street may seem much as it did before, but appearances deceive. Much of the action—what these shops were for—has moved online. So much that was visible is now hidden. Banks, which used to be buildings you walked into where there were people you could talk to, are largely invisible.

That makes it harder to make them accountable. It is hard to see how anything invisible works (Bridle 2019). At the same time, how the world sees us has changed. Artists used to be the image makers of society, but now machines have taken over. Machines gaze at us continuously, taking thousands of images, reading them, scanning them and storing information and using it for—who knows what? The Chinese government is reportedly able to track every individual in China with minute-by-minute precision and accuracy, including all their email and Internet traffic, their friends, calls and associations. But we are all seen by the machine gaze, making it next to impossible to control how this information is used. Defiantly, Bridle insists: 'We can choose the lens through which we see the world' (Bridle 2018). I hope he is right.

If art can help us see technology differently, perhaps it can do the same for how we see money. Then we can look at art to help us lay aside the money lens, as that is perhaps the main instrument used by the culture to shape our view of the world. Wearing a money lens makes us malleable, eager customers, willing citizens of the global money culture. Sellers of investment products want us always to wear rose-coloured spectacles, so that we see their bright promise and not the risks. Good art, like good book-keeping and good scientific theory, helps us locate ourselves in the world, to see and know what really exists. Only then may we hope to control it.

Put another way, reshaping our relationship to technology and thus with the world requires a different way of thinking. A new way of thinking is also needed, if we are to control money. From that perspective, money is just a technology. We have to be free of delusions about technology, including the technology we call money, if nature, technology and money are again to live in harmony. But that may not mean despising it; on the contrary, it may require us to look after it more carefully, just as we in future may look after what we wear, our everyday objects, and even our computers, more carefully, conscious of the resources they have taken from the earth. We should then be newly aware of all the effort that goes to make a banknote, or a digital credit entry, valuable.

Still shocked by the monetisation of art? Cohen puts it well. Pondering on the mysterious forces that drive prices ever higher, she surmises that they must be 'what it is in painting that is beyond banking':

> Their ability not just to represent the hazards of fortune but to let us feel the wind and the turning stars that mark our deepest sense of time and change.

It is for this, she says, that we close up our stalls and carry the canvases to the church. How much is it worth, a moment of surcease? Duccio and Pollock suggest that we will not be able to get an answer to that question:

> There is that within them representable by no sum. It's possible that there is no limit to what bankers will pay for these visual inventions, ones so like their own and yet eluding them all the same. (Cohen 2012)

Notes

1. Alice Walton, listed as the richest woman in the world at the time of writing, is a Walmart heiress. The store chain which has a turnover equivalent to that of the nineteenth largest country in the world, is known and widely criticised for its vast box-like suburban super-stores, its low-grade products, its reliance on cheap labour and the way it has brought ruin to thousands of small, family-owned businesses. It is widely regarded as a symbol of the horrors of the money space invented in the United States.

2. The family made their money out of OxyContin, a drug that reportedly generated some 35 billion dollars in revenue for Purdue, the family-owned company. But OxyContin is a controversial drug. Its sole active ingredient is oxycodone, a chemical cousin of heroin which is up to twice as powerful as morphine. Since 1999, 200,000 Americans have died from overdoses related to OxyContin and other prescription opioids. Many addicts, finding prescription painkillers too expensive or too difficult to obtain, have turned to heroin. See *The New Yorker*, The Family That Built an Empire of Pain by Patrick Radden Keefe, October 30, 2017. During 2019 many museums cut their links with the family.

Bibliography

Adam, G. (2014). *Big Bucks: The Explosion of the Art Market in the 21st Century.* Farnham: Lund Humphries.

———. (2018). *Dark Side of the Boom: The Excesses of the Art Market in the 21st Century.* Farnham: Lund Humphries.

Berger, J. (1972). *Ways of Seeing.* London: Penguin Books.

Bridle, J. (2019, May). BBC Radio 4 series: 'New Ways of Seeing'.

Bridle, J. (2018). *New Dark Age: Technology and the End of the Future.* Verso.

Cohen, R. (2012, November–December). 'Gold, Golden, Gilded, Glittering'. *The Believer*, Issue 94.

———. (2013). *Bernard Berenson: A Life in the Picture Trade.* Yale University Press.

Hughes, Robert (1984). Art & Money.

Schama, S. (2007, 20 January). 'Trouble in Paradise' *The Guardian.*

Wetzler, R. (2018, February 26). 'How Modern Art Serves the Rich' *New Republic.*

Time Future: Consequences Engender Ideas

Conclusion to Part III: Consequences Generate Ideas

This part of the book has tested the thesis that the undesirable consequences of the global money space and its culture would stimulate a search for new ideas. On the whole, the evidence has tended to support this. Interesting monetary innovations have been initiated in virtual currencies, while payment systems are being totally transformed; sociologists have come up with new insights into how money works, how it gains value through social processes, how it holds our attention and why it has to be part of a broad attempt to improve our condition. We argued that intellectuals bear a degree of responsibility for our present crisis, and a few are responding to this. We saw how we could learn from non-Western cultures, how they kept the power of money in check and we discussed how contemporary art might teach us how to 'see' money and other technologies in new ways. What seems missing are any new ideas from economists to match the scale of the crisis, but I have argued that it is unfair to expect too much of them. They cannot decide for society what it wants from its money. Money seems to function well when it is part of a broader, widely shared social philosophy. The great economists of the twentieth century were themselves people with a deep knowledge of culture. They assumed that their successors would share that also. Naively, they expected that education would lift the masses of the people up to their level. Such hopes have been disappointed. Indeed, the culture of which they were proud is criticised as white, male and elitist. Their world has vanished, and nothing adequate has replaced it. Indeed, the financial crisis has shattered confidence in neoliberalism, which, in its original form, was probably the best as well as the most successful of twentieth-century monetary philosophies. Society has to yet to set the direction of travel for the twenty-first century. Therefore, it is unreasonable to expect today's economists to come up with solutions to the crisis of money. Economics is about means, not ends (Robbins 1932; Samuelson 1948).

The Two Levels of Debate

A recurring difficulty is the insistence that there must be a solution, in the sense of a formula that can fix the problem, if only we were clever enough to find it. I believe this is a mistake. I believe it is important to understand why, so I discuss it briefly here.

The pressure to focus on policy has to be resisted, as this is not where the problems arise. In fact, this assumption is itself part of the problem. We are taught to believe that progress comes from solving problems. That is, the scientific-technological-money complex at work. Such technical solutions have their place, but they work only when we have taken the prior steps needed. Politics can be viewed as another device used by the new culture to put us off the track. People look for a solution framed in terms of the familiar Left-Right split, interventionist or free market, state versus private, collective versus individual dichotomies. Readers scan books to see which viewpoint the author favours, liking those that fit in with their prejudices and discarding those that don't. However brilliant, original or profound the analysis, the end result is politicised. Is this merely another trick used by the money virus to distract us while it worms its way into our minds the work of Mephistopheles, the devil who promised Faust all the pleasures he ever dreamt of (and maybe some he didn't!) in exchange for his soul? This is the challenge: we must view the global money culture in a new light and fully comprehend why it has become destructive before we can see its potential and act to release it.

The first step is to make a correct diagnosis. There are two levels at which this can be approached—they may be called 'policy-level' and 'structural-level'.

Level One covers all the areas of monetary policy debate. At this level, I have argued that policies cannot be understood, or their merits debated outside their historical context. As the historical survey showed, it matters which lessons people draw from what happens—and these can change. After the Weimar inflation, German-language thinkers drew conclusions about the case for sound money. German society and politicians eventually accepted that interpretation—a view that eventually found its way via the Bundesbank into the constitution of the European Central Bank. But they did not learn lessons about the proper use of creditor power. A few years later came The Great Depression. At the time, many observers thought this was due to the abandonment of the gold standard by the UK in 1931 and the United States in 1934. The opposite lesson was drawn by later historians: that the Great Depression was caused by attempts to restore and then to maintain the gold standard. The lesson—one that still informs their policy recommendations now—was a denial that capitalism had self-correcting powers and an insistence that active government policies are essential to prevent such depressions.

The inflation of the 1960s and 1970s, viewed at the time as a result of the push of costs, such as the rise in wages due to trade union pressure and the raising of oil prices due to the OPEC (Organization of the Petroleum Exporting Countries) cartel, was later interpreted as being caused by excessively easy monetary policies. The implications for future policy completely changed—instead of policies to contain costs, they switched to containing money and instructions were given to central banks accordingly. Some were given targets for money. But then they found that money was slippery, hard to pin down and define. So central bankers again shifted tack. They decided to focus on controlling inflation through their ability to set policy rates—the short-term rate of interest. The money supply became suddenly irrelevant; some central banks even stopped estimating it. There is still no settled diagnosis of the causes of the financial crisis of 2007–2009. Thus, policies adopted by governments are determined not by theory but by a struggle in the marketplace and politics. When society's priorities change—as seen, for example, in the general shift in mid-twentieth century towards the Left and interventionism—then the policies chosen, and the idea of money reflected in them, have to fit.

Level Two, the structural level, relates to the social roles of money, how different societies come to hold certain ideas of money and not others, how money works in different ways in different cultures. Above all, it goes to what money means to people, how it can be an agent of free will, of personal expression, but also an agent of social control and how money gains value from society. These social processes include societies' values and institutions. They have very far-reaching effects. For instance, I have discussed the routes by which such social processes gave the dollar its leading position and so-called exorbitant privileges (giving the United States privileged access to finance). They explain why the dollar has in recent years become more dominant even as the weight of the US economy declines. We are in a multi-polar world economically, but a unipolar currency world; there is no rival to the US dollar. I would even argue that other currencies are in important respects derivatives of the dollar; they all circulate in its orbit.

In short, money needs a public infrastructure as well as private initiative. Money can be used to oppress, or to set free. It is a delicate plant, but it can grow into a monster. I have used the ideas of money space and money culture in an effort to conceptualise the structural level at which money operates.

Of course, the two levels overlap and interact. I have tried to explore aspects of this interaction. My interest is, however, focused on the second level, as this has been relatively neglected. In the process, I have, doubtless, made mistakes in my summaries—necessarily brief and incomplete, given the vast historical canvas selected—of major episodes of the past 120 years. As Part I showed, my interest in the history is to find out how our present money space and culture emerged as a result of the actions taken by past generations, how these actions were *driven by ideas* as well as material interests and how easily the outcome could have been very different if people had had different ideas, or if those holding different idea had won the battle for survival. In Part II, I discussed some of the *effects*—especially *unwanted implications*—of the global money space and culture that had resulted from actions taken, choices made and not made, through the previous 100 years. Keeping on this structural level, Part III has been about breaking free. What we need here, above all, are new ideas, so the cycle can begin again.

As I write the key issue under debate at Level One is how governments and the monetary authorities will combat the next recession at a time when interest rates are still very low, and thus, there is little room to lower them unless governments are willing to impose negative interest rates—in effect charging people for holding money. Argument rages over whether central banks should strain every sinew to raise inflation sufficiently to allow them to raise rates to 5–8% so as to be sure they have room to lower them by the 3–5% amount sometimes needed from past experience to fight off recession and still keep interest rates positive. This is an important debate which also touches Level Two issues about 'what money is' since if it is regarded as a social convention that should set an unvarying standard, such extreme monetary manipulation—even if feasible, which it probably is not—would be anathema. In my view, given the much greater flexibility in real wages and prices compared with experience in the twentieth century, there is a case for returning to a proper monetary standard. We could and should create a world of money better than the mix of currencies that currently jostle for room in the global money space. That would be an advance.[1] Nevertheless, in the concluding chapter I remain resolutely focused on Level Two.

Note

1. I summarised ways in which money could be tied to an 'anchor' with my own suggestion in *The Money Trap* (Pringle, 2012).

Bibliography

Pringle, R. (2012). *The Money Trap.* Palgrave Macmillan.

Robbins, L. (1932). *An Essay on the Nature and Significance of Economic Science.* London: Macmillan.

Samuelson, P. A. (1948). *Economics.* New York: McGraw-Hill.

Part IV

Concluding Remarks

23

The Money We Deserve

Progress Endangered

The world has made striking material progress. There is no gainsaying the evidence ranging from longer life expectancy to reductions in absolute poverty and rising educational standards; more than 80% of children in low-income countries are at school compared with 50% in 1980. Improvements in the money machine and its global expansion have contributed to this. Yet these achievements are shadowed by disturbing trends. Here I do not refer primarily to such familiar issues as the growth of inequalities or geo-political tensions but rather to a feeling of something fundamentally askew, unnatural and ominous in our condition. Along with rising prosperity goes a widespread sense of loss, accompanied by fear and anxiety. Populist politicians are not the only people to tap into this—novelists, social scientists and commentators also dwell on such themes. Democratic institutions are on the defensive. President Putin tapped into such a feeling when he remarked that liberalism is 'obsolete' and 'has outlived its purpose' (Barber and Foy 2019).

In this collection of essays I have attempted to put money in its broad meanings—the monetary mechanism, financial system, how we govern money, the power of money—into its social, cultural and historical contexts. I have argued that these go far to determine whether money works well for its society. An implication of this approach is that getting money right is not primarily a technical problem. It is more basic: society's needs and priorities, the social and political philosophies that best express those needs, the extent to which they are shared, frame the context in which money functions. Money and associated arrangements then either fit in such a context or they do not. Keynes's genius was to use his imagination to create new ideas of money that were fit for his

© The Author(s) 2019
R. Pringle, *The Power of Money*, https://doi.org/10.1007/978-3-030-25894-8_23

time. That does not imply they would be fit for all time. Milton Friedman ditto. At present, money is out of sync with society's needs. We do not know why or what to do. We cling to old models. Politicians carry on outdated disputes between Left and Right—terms that have little contact with reality.

The crisis of money is at the centre of the crisis of liberal democracy and, I would argue, the whole Western project—which has become the global project. People's bewilderment, anger and dismay have led to the election of dangerous politicians to our oldest and seemingly most secure democracies and to the rise of crony and corrupt forms of capitalism. In the United States, people ask: could Trump's presidency really presage a descent into fascism? 'It cannot be ruled out', declares historian Adam Tooze, though finding it to be 'implausible'.[1] The world's largest economies (accounting together for 80% of world GDP) are China, United States, India, Japan, Germany, Russia, Indonesia, Brazil, Britain, France, Italy, Turkey, Mexico and South Korea. Most of them are led by populists, demagogues and autocrats, with crony and state capitalism being, increasingly, the typical economic models. People cry for protection in a dangerous world of unaccountable money power.

Such power poses as great a threat to social welfare as the environmental catastrophe. They are both relentless, seemingly beyond human control, and both move slowly (albeit punctuated by acute episodes). Neither can be fixed by technocratic formulas. They are both areas where many governments routinely issue empty reassurance that they are addressing the problems. Meanwhile, large private organisations operate seemingly without accountability. Financial networks maintained by leading players, like the communication networks of Facebook, Amazon and other such monopolies, are far more extensive than any state organisation. Political scientist David Runciman views Marc Zuckerberg (aged 35 in 2019) of Facebook as a more serious threat to US democracy than Donald Trump (Runciman 2018). As described later, plausible remedies to both problems—the power of money and climate change—could also share some similar features.

The Backlash Against Liberalisation

How did we reach this position? To pick up the story from the historical sections in Part I, in 1989 the Berlin Wall came down. This was a crucial moment in geo-political history. The dominant Western ideology of the time was one of far-reaching liberalisation. A representative example of the attitudes of the times was a World Bank report that advocated thoroughgoing liberalisation of the financial sectors (World Bank 1989). This is the last illustration I shall cite of one of the main themes of this book—how an idea of money can change the world. The liberalisation agenda did not just appear out of thin air but had a long intellectual ancestry as described in Chap. 6. At a time when governments everywhere were relying more upon the private sector and markets, the financial apparatus was also ripe for change: 'Access to a variety of financial instruments enables economic agents to pool, price and exchange risk', said the report, adding that 'trade, the efficient use of resources, saving and risk-taking are the cornerstones of a growing economy'. It invited readers to consider the poor results of governments' previous efforts to promote economic developments. These had focussed on government action in three key areas: government control of *interest rates*, state direction of the *distribution of credit* and securing *cheap finance for governments*. State intervention in these areas had, said the report, distorted the financial system. The whole top-down, state-led planning approach needed to be discarded. To be fair, the report was careful to note some conditions for successful implementation of reforms and remarked that 'the human and political dimensions of the subject' should be taken into account. But the bottom line was clear: liberalise as far and as fast as you can. This set the tone for the messages that the main international institutions and leading governments would deliver to developing countries and countries moving from Communism to market economies for the next decade. And, as noted, resulting improvements in financial systems did bring many benefits.

Ironically, however, after 30 years of experiment with financial liberalisation, *the same faults that the movement was supposed to banish have reappeared*: many governments again artificially manipulate/suppress interest rates, many states again benefit from cheap or zero interest rates for their own borrowing, and governments are once again under strong pressure to direct credit to priority sectors on the grounds that the market is allegedly failing to do this. Banks do not lend on a sufficient scale to small and medium-sized enterprises, for example. Some countries have set up their own state-run banks. Furthermore, these interventions not only appear to signal a return of the so-called bad old ways of the past, they are accompanied by far more cumbersome and expensive financial oversight by the state than that of the 'bad old days' of the 1950s and 1960s—when bank regulation was in its infancy and government intervention limited mainly to guidelines on credit extension. Yet even such elaborate regulation provides no assurance that we will not suffer further financial crises.

The great financial crisis of 2007–09 proved to be a watershed in terms of both its causes and effects. If, as argued in Chap. 13, the basic cause was not lax regulation, but rather Money Delusion, if people dreamt foolish dreams of money because they were under acute psychological and social pressures, the search for a solution by better prudential regulation is in vain. Proponents dream that it is possible for a saintly, all-seeing central bank guardian or qualified 'prudential regulator' to stand outside the system ready to 'lean against the wind' and raise interest rates to nip a boom in the bud. This makes two big mistakes: first, it ignores the fact that the guardians are under the same psychological, social pressures as the rest of us—plus political ones as well; second, it ignores the lesson of history, which is that once you give officials widespread discretionary powers of this kind, powers to intervene directly in society, then, whatever the hopes of reformers, such powers will be abused—they will be grabbed by sectional interests and used for ends that benefit them only.

What had gone wrong with the implementation of the liberalisation ideas? Two factors. First, those who urged it on governments and on the emerging global money society had a superficial understanding of the neoliberal concept behind it; as shown in Chap. 6, proponents such as Hayek had always insisted on the need for a *constitutional framework* of rules as a precondition for a liberal monetary and economic order—an idea going back to the Scottish enlightenment (Hayek's next book after the *Road to Serfdom* was *The Constitution of Liberty*). Money had to take its place in a system of rules and expected behaviour that people could comprehend and support. This in turn had its roots in a broad liberal philosophy that had lost its hold on the community. These ingredients were missing. Second, the advocates of liberalisation in the 1990s brushed aside the need to adapt policy recommendations to existing cultures—a major theme of several chapters in this book. They insisted that their economics was sound and universally applicable. They were missionaries convinced of the justice of their cause and anxious to convert the heathen. Thus, policy recommendations, however well-meant, were easily felt as a foreign intrusion to be resisted.

The effects of these mistakes in the understanding and implementation of the liberalisation agenda—which was sometimes accompanied by an annoying note of Western triumphalism—have been devastating. True, the legacy of that period has redeeming features, such as the support given by finance to rapid growth and, in terms of monetary management, widespread adoption of central bank operational independence—but we have ended up with many of the disadvantages of the state planning era. Worse than that is the festering public anger at the effects of the crisis. Governments dealt with it in an outrageously unjust way (see Chaps. 14 and 16). People seem determined to punish the elite, the leaders, at any opportunity. Thus, we reach a situation where liberalisation of finance has been put into reverse, regulation has returned, and yet fear of finance and anger at injustice remain festering sores.

As a result, the ideology that animated and was used to justify the liberalisation of finance has lost credibility. We have the framework of a market-based monetary system propped up by the state at public expense without a shared philosophy to justify or legitimate it. This loss has been felt especially outside North America. Some of the countries worst hit by financial crises were those that had embraced the market order most recently and enthusiastically—not only countries of East and South-East Asia, which endured the Asian crisis as well as the great financial crisis but especially the transitional states of Eastern and central Europe. No wonder anti-democratic movements have been on the rise and several authoritarian leaders come to power, such as Hungary's Viktor Orban, Turkey's Recep Tayyip Erdogan, and strong men rule in many former Soviet republics. In the West, meanwhile, outspoken defences of market capitalism are noticeable by their absence. The United States is, as usual, an exception because of its built-in vitality and innovation, and support for free trade appears to have held firm among about half of the electorate despite the Trump effect. Yet even in the United States one rarely sees articles extolling the virtues of free competition and market forces in mainstream newspapers. Look at the response to the development by private initiative and innovation of cryptocurrencies, as noted in Chap. 18. Editorialists compete with central bankers to warn of the risks and the need for regulators to be alert. This wide loss of support for a philosophy that would link competitive finance to social benefit is a major obstacle to attempts to revive liberalism and give finance/money a moral compass.

Don't Blame Globalization

Economists usually discuss these topics under the heading of 'globalization'. They analyse the growing interdependence of economies in terms of expanding trade, rising cross-border investment by multinational companies, the rise of global supply chains, and the effects on income distribution and on jobs. They dwell on the advantages deriving from greater specialisation; the benefits to be gained in terms of lower prices, wider choice and larger markets to be set against job losses experienced by displaced workers; and strains caused by migrant flows, tensions from protectionism, trade imbalances and so on. The benefits of these trends are undeniable and, in the macro picture, they far outweigh the costs. Insofar as monetary issues are mentioned, they typically come under such headings as the international monetary system, exchange rate policies and policies to manage capital flows—nothing in my analysis challenges this picture in any way. I am merely inviting readers to view what has happened and is happening through a different lens, to focus attention on a different angle. In these essays I have therefore employed concepts such as 'global money space' and 'global money society' or money culture in an effort to capture aspects of the fast-changing world that are missed—or, at least are not brought into focus—by the usual treatment of 'globalisation'. The focus on money naturally leads towards adopting the perspective of the individual faced with his or her choices rather than broad economic categories. Just as Milton Friedman showed that individuals would make different decisions about the division of their income into that part saved and that part spent if we imagine that they learn from experience and adapt their expectations, so a focus on money in a global world leads naturally to focus on how it impinges on individual choices, with the emphasis on small firms, on lifestyle choice, on start-ups and grass-roots rather than big macro-economic issues such as 'capital flow management'. A focus on money also connects more naturally to the world as portrayed in movies, novels, personal relationships and an individual's lifechances. That is why throughout these essays I have endeavoured to link money to broader trends in a society's culture and *Weltanschauung*. This approach views a society's money and the specific forms that money takes along with formal and informal rules and ethics that surround it as a product of its culture. It is obviously not at all the case that I see my approach as superior, but I want to argue it is legitimate. There are, however, certain areas where this money-lens approach may lead to different outlooks. For example, it is sometimes claimed that the entire globalisation trend might go into reverse—as a result or example of a trade war or another financial crisis. From the perspective taken in this book, this seems most unlikely; or at least, any such reverse would be short-lived. Monetary and technological networks are so dense and have so much scope for expanding social and economic intercourse—with business, professional and allied services, for example, soon to be easily provided at a distance, electronically—that the likelihood of a permanent reversal of globalization seems vanishingly small. The role of government policies is also put into a different light—as indeed is the entire status of nation states.

Fatalism

People enjoy a wide choice in the modern consumer society with money prices available for a cornucopia of goods and services. But this comes at a cost. Modern money, communications and allied technologies form a package. Advanced communications, digital skills, finance skills, appropriate motivation and the calculating, rational, measuring and maximising mindset are all key elements in it. Nations and individuals cannot pick and choose—it is a *table d'hôte*. Countries and individuals are expected to go through the set meal from beginning to end. It promises more opportunity, but also leads to loss and anxiety. Many people fit well into a money society. But it can be experienced as a threat. It is a matter of survival, of life and death.

That is perhaps why so many of us tend to be fatalistic about money; it just appears to be too strong. In other areas, we face up (though sometimes reluctantly and with delay) to their challenges, such as those posed by social media and, lately, climate change. We are now aware that the way we use the internet determines the amount of information we grant to the likes of Google, Facebook and Amazon. We are becoming aware of the dangers posed by the surveillance state (typified by China) as well as by its private sector version of 'surveillance capitalism'. Social customs are also changing in regard to the environment; we recycle materials in different ways because we have a responsibility to it. This sense of responsibility is quite new. These are all twenty-first-century responses to challenges facing society. However, at the present, when it comes to money people still often feel it's out of their control, too difficult to understand and best left to specialists. This is unfortunate and it is not borne out by history; society determines the kind of money it has and how it works for individuals. As I tried to show in Part I, people have at many points in recent history changed the part money—in the broadest sense of the term—played in their societies. Such fatalism is also dangerous, for as Sir Francis Bacon (1561–1626) pointed out many years ago, 'If money be not thy servant, it will be thy master. The covetous man cannot so properly be said to possess wealth, as that may be said to possess him.'

To help us escape, I have surveyed some ideas being generated from outside economics that might help us reorient our outlook (see Part III). The pressure of crisis, the imminence of a general bankruptcy, is, as the French social philosopher Proudhon observed, a challenge to our creativity. It is time to draw the strands together.

What's Wrong with Contemporary Money

It Is Free for the State, Expensive for Society

The following brief paragraphs sum up my conclusions on themes that have been discussed in several essays in this book.

Zero or ultra-low interest rates allow some governments to borrow at zero or close to zero cost to them. But the costs to society are heavy: these include the costs of regulating banks, the costs incurred by financial institutions obliged to comply with regulations, the subsidy involved in the government guarantee of banks' liabilities (too-big-to-fail), the costs of subsidising mortgage interest and allowing tax deductibility of interest payments by businesses and the damage done by monopolies grown fat on zero-cost capital extracting unearned resources from society. Then there are the costs of sorting out the financial system after each crisis. Finally, there are the costs of all the bad investments made in the overoptimistic mood during the bubble—money spent on capital projects to produce goods or services we do not need or want, expenditure forced on us either by government waste or by the fact that businessmen spend money on capital investments that are not economic for society.

It Favours Insiders

Two features make modern money vulnerable to abuse by private interests, even in well-ordered democracies. First, modern monetary and supervisory policies are *centralised*—conducted by the relevant state or official bodies. These are accountable to parliaments or governments and subject to political direction; even independent central banks are normally given their mandates by a political authority. Second, such bodies also enjoy a large degree of *discretion* in carrying out their functions. They can set conditions for which bodies rely on a large degree of discretion. They are also subject to government direction/guidance/influence. This implies that there are considerable incentives for private sector institutions to influence official regulatory outcomes. The relationship between gamekeepers and poachers is even more incestuous in crony capitalist regimes, now the dominant form of capitalism.

It's Exclusive

Many people remain outside the money system, including people who cannot manage modern technology, people who can only use cash (which many experts want to abolish) and billions of people too poor to interest banks (as shown in Chap. 18). Many other people may have funds but cannot access the system as they do not fit into the modern idea of a corporate state citizen, with two IDs in approved form, a job, approved references and so on. Then there are those who have been cast out of the global money space. Banks can close people's accounts without warning and without giving notice. The ranks of these outcasts are likely to swell as governments use financial information increasingly as weapons of foreign policy, of intelligence, data gathering, with lists of prohibited actions, prohibited individuals and prohibited countries (see Chap. 17). In reality, only certain people are admitted to the global money space. If they are not treated justly, the outsiders may so weaken the moral foundations of the system as to make it lose political viability.

It Tends to Corrupt and Can Spread Disease

As we have noted, monetary diseases spread quickly in the global money space. These threaten traditional ways of life, just as we are destroying remaining wild spaces and downgrading the natural environment (Rajan 2019). People easily believe that the system is working for others but not for them. No wonder it alienates many. The rescue of big finance by the state and the way they generally work together inevitably focus attention on politics as a route to great wealth. As Zuboff has argued, also, what she calls 'impatient money' was at the heart of pressures that caused Google to transform itself into a machine for monetising personal data—an example followed quickly by Facebook and many others. Impatient money 'reflects an interest in quick returns without spending much time on growing a business or deepening its talent base, let alone developing the institutional capabilities that (Austrian economist) Joseph Schumpeter would have advised' (Zuboff 2019).

It Foments Monetary Phobias

That's built into the adoption by central banks of a target of 2% annual inflation rate. This is the modern monetary standard. So whenever actual inflation rises above or dips below target, central bankers and commentators easily panic. If inflation falls—or is expected to fall—below target economists ask, 'Have we got enough ammunition to prevent deflation?' 'Can we print enough money?' 'How can we persuade people to spend more?' Such frequently asked questions show our fear of what money has become and what it might do, or not do. To be sure, individuals can worry about not having enough money—that is quite normal. But it is not normal for society as a whole to be frightened by minor variations in its rate of inflation. Yet central bankers and economists continually scare us by conjuring up fears of uncontrollable deflation or excessive inflation. Many people will be mature enough, sophisticated enough or indifferent enough not to let themselves be scared. But many others will be vulnerable. Yet worry about money at this macroeconomic level is built into the regime.

It's Not Serving a Shared Goal

Money does not work in a vacuum. One lesson of this book is that, on the whole, money works best when it is embedded in (i.e. an inherent and principal element in) a social and widely shared understanding of what makes a society, what its priorities are, what ideas give it shape and purpose, that is, a coherent political and social outlook or philosophy. Since the demise of both socialism and liberalism—at least as living social philosophies commanding widespread support—people are uncertain what social goals our money is supposed to serve. The approach of economics, which is to separate money from society, works well for certain limited problems but is useless for our present purposes.

It Facilitates Arbitrary Power

When in 1695 John Locke wrote a passionate denunciation of a proposal to devalue the British currency through a recoinage (reducing its content of precious metals), he did so to defend the rights of the individual to his property. A devaluation of money would defraud the people who had lent money to others. If the amount of silver in one pound sterling was reduced, the money received by the lender when the borrower repaid the loan would have the same nominal amount of money—for example, bank notes with the same face value—but this would have a lower silver content (be exchangeable for less weight of silver). His insistence on maintaining the precious metal content of money was not aimed at assuring its long-term relative value in terms of consumer prices. This stability in long-term purchasing power of gold is often mentioned as the key advantage of a gold standard. That is indeed one of its benefits. Yet at the time it was introduced, the silver (later gold) standard was defended on different grounds—as part of a constitutional settlement to limit the arbitrary power of the state. For if, Locke argued, the state was allowed to tamper with the definition of money once, it would do so again and again—defrauding people who lent money to it. Knowing this, people would not be willing to lend money to governments. Thus, governments should maintain the fixed link between money and precious metal at all times in their own interests as well as the interests of society. We need to recover Locke's original insight. It must be rescued from the oblivion to which it was sentenced by the totalitarian tendencies of the all-conquering state theory of money.

China's Challenge

China's projection of its economic, monetary and territorial reach in the past 20 years is the most rapid and extensive power grab in recent history. China is not a liberal society. President Xi Jinping has presided over a brutal clampdown on all sources of free expression and instituted a mass surveillance system of unprecedented scope and granular detail. The country incarcerates an unknown number of its citizens—estimates run to two million or more—who have committed no crime. Its economic and political rise has come at a time when confidence in the Western liberal model is at a low ebb. A recovery of confidence will be needed more than ever if we are to make liberalism our main defence against China's claims.

For China's rulers, now and for hundreds of years past, China is and always will be at the centre of the universe. Money is whatever the rulers of China say it is. If liberalism is to have any hope of offering an idea that appeals against this, it must return to a vision of money as a bulwark against arbitrary power. Yet such an idea is absent from modern conceptions of money—even those that call themselves liberal. The majority of economists believe that money is a creature of the state and derives value from the state. How can a *soi-disant* liberal society defend itself when it has forgotten the origins and true properties of its money and shares the same idea of money as its totalitarian rivals?

Money for a Healthy Society

Again, I use the very broadest definition of money.

As individuals, we want money that will let us plan for the future, a money that we can trust, a money that leaves us in peace to think about other things. We want a money that sits still, stops nudging us, stops beckoning to us, a money that will never betray us. We want a money that is what it seems to be, money we can calmly enjoy, while it lasts. Money should be indifferent to our motives, which are always mixed; it should be our friend, on our side; it should not come with a load of prohibitions, warnings, exclusion clauses, hidden traps, or linked to a ubiquitous network of surveillance, facial recognition cameras and form-filling.

Socially, also, we want a money that will let us, our acquaintances and our society occupy ourselves with more important matters and honour other, non-monetary activities that contribute to social well-being. We know that unpaid work is often as valuable, or more so, than paid work. We know that work done for love is often done better than work done for money and makes the supplier as well as recipient happier. We know that envy of other people's money takes away enjoyment of our own; that our habit of measuring everything by money tends to make people envious, distrustful, ambitious, scheming and aggressive. We do not want a money that monopolises, infiltrates and burdens our social intercourse.

We want a money that lets the price system work as it should and serve as a sensitive barometer of demand and supply; money that mediates markets fairly and objectively, so that prices can be set in accordance with the costs of providing the service or product; money that allows profit to be a guide to the allocation of resources, that supports entrepreneurship. We recognise that, as Adam Smith taught, some goods are best financed collectively, by general agreement of the society. We understand that the dividing line between the public and private sector will always be contested. Money should be a neutral medium available for both. Money circulating in competitive private markets is just as good as money raised by taxes for public goods. Money should be a lens that affords us a special window on certain key aspects of social life without distortion.

We recognise the effort required to produce good money. We know that paper monies throughout history have usually been abused by states. They have all lost value. Money is universal. That is why even bad, dishonest monies are hard to get rid of, which is why the temptation to devalue them has proved irresistible to governments as a way of defaulting on their debt. We want a money that can be relied on, money that can be 'the still point in the turning world'. It is no accident that T. S. Eliot was contemplating the nature of time and of beauty when that thought struck him; good money, like good art and literature, and like good scientific theory, brings order into the flux of experience. Like love and religion, money may divide us but also unite us. It is individual and communal. It is a threat and a wonder. It is a public good ready to serve private pleasures. It is a personal asset that promotes collective goals. It must be cared for.

Good money should embody a society's best values and aspirations. It will be non-discriminatory. It should not be 'impatient', biasing us towards the search for a few big quick wins at the cost of many failures. It will keep its real value long term but can experience quite abrupt swings in value in the short and medium term—such fluctuations being of little account so long as people confidently anticipate a return to long-term reliability. It will promote a competitive economy, provide reliable price signals, let long-term interest rates be set by markets; be independent of the political process; be open to all;

be created through a competitive process, respect a need for privacy in a person's financial dealings.

It is best supplied to an unchanging, objective standard in response to the demand of the public. Only then can it again fulfil its proper function as a bulwark of freedom.

Raise Awareness

Money will cease to be a burden when we can see it and its functions in society and human relationships in a new light. This is discussed in several previous chapters and some suggestions made in Chaps. 20–22. We have recent evidence of the power of public opinion, when harnessed to a cause such as global warming. In future it can give expression and impetus to a desire for healthier attitudes to money. That could drive a social movement. We should become more aware of the global money society's dangers, its bias to short-term gratification, its link to criminal and corrupt power and to other dangerous technologies. We should reflect on the way money policies have irrationally rewarded those who already have much and take away from those that have less. The anger is already there. But to be effective, awareness of inequalities and injustices must come with new ideas. That is why the theme of this last part of the book is 'Consequences engender ideas'.

Fight Corruption

In 2017–18 allegations of corruption upset governments in many parts of the world and led to imprisonment for presidents/heads of government in Peru, Romania, South Africa, Argentina, Brazil, Colombia, Guatemala, Israel, Malaysia, Armenia and South Korea. Corruption is as old as politics itself, as are citizens' efforts to root it out. But anti-corruption campaigners have made good use of new tools powered by technology. A new generation of prosecutors and judges drive investigations and convictions. Equally important, however, are public attitudes: fatalism is giving way to resistance and activism. Social media can be a useful antidote. As Anne-Marie Slaughter has remarked, posts, likes and retweets are all things that tell ordinary citizens not only that their voices are being heard, but that their fellow citizens are marching alongside them (Slaughter 2018). Slaughter is an American lawyer and activist.

Let Private Money Compete

The early twenty-first century saw a revival of privately issued monetary assets—this time in digital form. Central bankers said they should not be called currencies and were right to warn society of the risks involved. They should not, however, place obstacles in the way of private monetary innovations. To rival state currency, private currencies not only have to perform the basic functions of money as well as state money does, they also need to possess qualities superior to state money. This is challenging, especially as the costs of changing over from one to another could be very large; so new private monies have to demonstrate substantial benefits. As shown in Chap. 18, they may, however, over time develop some such benefits, so keeping the central bankers on their toes.

Money's Natural Home

As I have argued, money works best in societies where it is one element in a shared overarching philosophy or at least where many people share certain beliefs about the elements of a good life beyond mere individual self-interest. Only in such a society will a monetary regime command the support that will let it endure the shocks and trials that any system will experience. Classical liberalism was based on the idea of inalienable rights seen as part of a person's God-given nature. It had deep roots in the Judaeo-Christian tradition. But writers such as Locke and Hume were clear that society as a whole would benefit from a liberal regime; allowing the individual the liberty to pursue the truth and to hold unconventional or unpopular opinions about the world would bring advantages that would flow out into society. Money, these philosophers held, was a form of property that could and should act as a bulwark against abuse of arbitrary power, not only by the state but also by powerful sectional (or as we would say 'crony capitalist') interests. The gold standard fitted such a philosophy. Money based on gold occupied an important and clearly delimited role. Under socialism and the mixed economies of the twentieth century, money was also harnessed to overriding social purposes. Again, its potentially destructive powers were curbed by the culture of society as a whole with its disdain for purely pecuniary motives and its idealisation of public and professional service. This fitted society's preferences at the time but did not conduce to economic growth or individual autonomy. In the late twentieth century the sweeping liberalisation project—neoliberalism—made sense to a generation confronting the collapse of Communism, bringing disillusion with state planning. There was a widely shared belief that, on the whole, prices set in competitive markets and long-term interest rates free of government intervention would lead to a more efficient economy that would benefit the vast majority of its inhabitants. We have traced the intellectual roots of this idea (see especially Chap. 6). Thus, classical liberalism, socialism and neoliberalism all in their different ways harnessed money's unique powers. We no longer believe in any of these; they are all so twentieth century!

What can replace them? The development of capitalist enterprise that has brought such progress in so many fields in recent centuries was driven by an 'ethic' or 'spirit'. Max Weber and Maynard Keynes agreed on that (Skidelsky 1992); for Weber it was the Protestant Ethic, for Keynes Love of Money, tempered by culture. What source of spiritual energy can unite people and motivate them now? In my view, it has to be an idea that preserves all that is good in a market-based economy and free society with an understanding of the legitimacy and necessity for a rules-based framework and a public sector (as liberals from Adam Smith to F. A. Hayek acknowledged). One option is to re-invigorate liberalism. At a time when we face a daunting challenge from those who champion the unfettered rule of the state—now represented geopolitically by China and in economics by so-called modern monetary theory—this should be attempted. But it is doubtful whether present society has the resources, including philosophical and ethical resources, for the task. Good luck to those who make the attempt, but in my view the conditions are not ready for a rebirth of classical liberalism (the challenges have been discussed in Chaps. 18 and 20); the disillusion following the 2007–09 crash remains too deep and the grip that crony capitalism exerts on many leading countries too entrenched. What is needed is an outlook—a *Weltanschauung*—powerful enough to lead society of its own accord to create the appropriate environment. Social pressures should control the power of private monetary interests and the abuse of public and private power naturally, out of a sense of what is fitting, of decency and proper behaviour. Previous chapters have offered examples of societies that have successfully done that.

There is one candidate that might inspire reform to make money fit for our age, an idea sufficiently powerful and attractive to lift the eyes of men and women to the horizon, above the foreground occupied by self-interest and politics. That is the horizon set by nature. There is no end to the vistas you can see from a ship in the open seas, sea and sky making a whole natural universe. That is what people now care about—the earth, the oceans and the living things they nurture. In his poem, *The Rime of the Ancient Mariner*, Samuel Taylor Coleridge describes the agony of the mariner who stupidly shot the albatross that came every day to his ship. He and the ship's crew are cursed, and the albatross hung round his neck. Only when he discovers a love of nature, even in its most ugly creatures, is he free.[2] The albatross, 'fell off and sank like lead into the sea'. Our Albatross is money. Put it in touch with the natural world and, like the Albatross, it will fall from our necks.

In place of Keynes's Love of Money and Weber's Protestant Ethic, we should embrace a Natural Ethic. Indeed, in time such an ethic could power a global post-capitalist information and service economy. It would allow considerable local variation in cultures, outlooks and *Weltanschauungen*. It would keep money in its natural place. It would work for people in public service as well as for pioneers and entrepreneurial 'disruptors' in private space. It would allow money to carry out its important functions without placing inflated hopes and expectations on it (again, gold was such a link—gold as a marvel of nature).

To put money in its proper place, its natural place, we must lift the dead-weight of current monetary arrangements from our shoulders. We must understand their characteristics, their dangers, how they emerged and why they endure—and why they must be replaced by a superior model, one suited to our times. Society must indicate the general direction of travel. Then we can hand the challenge to economists, to do what they do best, and design the optimal means to an end set by the wider society. Each of these steps needs imagination as well as expertise and technological know-how. Money can and should be linked in a productive and harmonious way with the earth, with nature. The challenge is to make such a link support the natural functions of money and let the market economy work as it can and should do. Then the power of money will hold no terrors. Once society sets the direction of travel, the journey can begin.

I am aware that this idea—of a link between money and the natural world, climate change and the earth's integrity—has already been debated among monetary reformers without making any discernible impression on policy-makers. That is no reason to despair. As I have tried to demonstrate in this collection of essays, many ideas about money and its place in society—including ideas that would become highly influential and even dominant—had to win acceptance against hostile conditions and criticism. Locke's idea of money as an unvarying standard was fanciful in his time—greeted with out-raged incomprehension by contemporaries who believed the monetary standard was inherently flexible; so was the Marxist-Leninist idea of the need to suppress markets and confine money to serve a communist society. The same applied to Keynes's idea of an active monetary policy to combat depression; and to the global vision of a world money space and a rules-based constitutional framework for money held by the European neoliberals of the mid-twentieth century. Scorn and derision were poured on Friedman's view that 'Inflation is always and everywhere a monetary phenomenon in the sense that it is and can be produced only by a more rapid increase in the quantity of money than in output' (Friedman 1970).

All these ideas of money were revolutionary in their time and, in one way and another, for good and for ill, they all changed the world. So will the green revolution—in ways we cannot yet articulate. Interestingly, central banks have begun to take this issue on board.[3] Central banks' interest is at present largely confined to financial stability issues arising out of climate change but, as previous monetary history has repeatedly shown, money has often been influenced in more profound ways by changing social priorities—as it should be. Indeed, in September 2019 the Bank for International Settlements—often called the central bankers' central bank—set an official seal of approval on central bank activity in this area by issuing a green bond fund to meet the demand for climate-friendly investments among official institutions. The green bond fund initiative would help central banks 'to incorporate environmental sustainability objectives in the management of their reserves'. These are to be regarded as 'straws in the wind'. They point to a potentially far-reaching change not only in the public's mood but in its social priorities.[4]

Don't blame money. Although I may be accused in some sections of these essays of anthropomorphizing money, wrongly attributing human characteristics to it, such language is intended only as a short-cut, or as a dramatic device. As Pascal Bruckner, a French man of letters, points out: 'We alone decide to bow down before this demon (of money). No evil genius holds us in his power....Money dictates nothing to us that we ourselves haven't already conceived' (Bruckner 2017). It is wise, he says, to have money and wise to reflect critically on it. Following Benjamin Franklin, Bruckner insists that money is inseparable from ethics. This is presented not as an exhortation but rather as a simple statement of fact; you cannot in practice separate how you use money with the question of how one should. So we should take care of money. Accept that the struggle to make money work well will never end. Do not scorn it. As Galbraith pointed out: 'Nothing so denies a person liberty as the total absence of money' (Galbraith 2000).

A Reset for Money

At one level, money is simply the asset in which goods and services are priced and with which they can be bought.[5] Money in the broad sense I have used the word is more than that, however. This book has been about that "more".

Money in that sense is at the heart of the way we look at almost every aspect of our lives and so we all need to think about it. How we earn money and spend it sends messages out across the fabric of social spacetime not only about who we are as individuals, what our priorities are, but also about the kind of society we want. When markets are working as they can and should, each such action influences how resources are allocated across the whole of society. Money relates us to others. It gives us the ability to choose what we want from what is on offer, subject to our budget. From other people's point of view, it is an instrument available to induce me to serve their interests, by offering me incentives to produce what they want, at the price/pay rate offered on the market. It is both liberating and a binding constraint, a tool that I use to get what I want, and a means to induce me to do what others want. Although our modern money has lost its bearings, it can and should be reset.

Notes

1. Tooze (2019).
2. 'O happy living things! No tongue
   Their beauty might declare:
   A spring of love gushed from my heat,
   And I blessed them unaware' (Coleridge 1960/1798)

3. To cite one sign of this, see an 'open letter on climate-related financial risks' of April 17, 2019 which stated that 'as financial policymakers and prudential supervisors, we cannot ignore the obvious risks before our eyes' of the catastrophic effects of climate change:

   > That is why 34 central banks and supervisors—representing five continents, half of global greenhouse gas emissions and the supervision of two-thirds of the global systemically important banks and insurers—joined forces in 2017 to create a coalition of the willing: the Network for Greening the Financial System (NGFS) (see Carney et al. 2019).

4. For further reading on this topic, Nigel Dodd provides an overview in Chap. 8 of *The Social Life of Money* (Dodd 2014). See especially his account of the approach of the late Richard Douthwaite, which he finds 'intuitively appealing', notably Douthwaite's insistence that different monetary forms meet different social needs. Douthwaite uses a chosen scarce resource—energy, as opposed to labour or time, for example—to underpin the value of money. His work and that of others in this field is being carried forward by feasta—the Foundation for the Economics of Sustainability (www.feasta.org). Warren Coats proposes to anchor the value of the SDR to a basket of commodities

(Coats 2011, 2019; (https://works.bepress.com/warren_coats/25/). Leanne Ussher has suggested reforms updating classic proposals for a commodity reserve currency. This remains, in Ussher's view, a realistic if also futuristic goal for reform rather than a leftover from an outdated era (Ussher 2009). An original approach is pioneered by Joseph Potvin in his proposal for an Earth Reserve Assurance (ERA). This is a framework for valuing assets, including currencies, in a multi-currency system with no central reference unit of account. ERA does not itself create a currency unit. It is a new type of primary commodity reserve system. The method of valuation is designed to mirror the long-term capacity of a currency region to produce primary commodities. It uses practical and measurable factors such as topsoil volume, fertility and distribution, fresh water availability, quality and regularity, various ores for metal and minerals, species populations, genomic diversity and integrity, the extent and condition of local, regional and global habitats, essential biogeochemical cycles, and other indicators of sustainable productive capacity. Assurance of this capacity in the form of Earth Reserve deposit receipts—audited by independent certified authorities, and issued by banks—would serve as collateral for a market in these receipts. Each currency obtains its own Earth Reserve Index. As the index accorded to each currency changes, a participating currency becomes more expensive or cheaper depending on whether ecosystem integrity and resource availability are worsening or improving within each currency zone. A currency becomes more expensive as the Earth Reserve is undermined in the areas where it is used. A currency becomes more affordable as ecosystem integrity and resource availability are enhanced in areas where it is used. Potvin argues that this would create a dynamic force in global trade that is the opposite to what occurs presently. Income and jobs will generally migrate towards regions that enhance the Earth Reserve (Potvin 2019). For easy-to-read summaries and background on proposals for international monetary reform, see Larry White's blog at lonestarwhitehouse.com https://lonestarwhitehouse.blogspot.com/

5. I owe this formulation to Warren Coats (private correspondence, 2019).

Bibliography

Barber, L., and Foy, H. (2019). Vladimir Putin: liberalism has 'outlived its purpose' June 27. *Financial Times*.

Bruckner, P. (2017). *The Wisdom of Money*. Harvard: Harvard University Press.

Carney, M., Villeroy de Galhau, F., Elderson, F. (2019). 'Open letter from the Governor of Bank of England Mark Carney, Governor of Banque de France François Villeroy de Galhau and Chair of the Network for Greening the Financial Services Frank Elderson'. 17 April. See Bank of England announcement at https://www.bankofengland.co.uk/news/2019/april/open-letter-on-climate-related-financial-risks.

Coats, W. (2011). 'Real SDR Currency Board'. Central Banking Vol. XXII Iss. 2 (2011). Available at: http://works.bepress.com/warren_coats/25/.

———. (2019). 'The IMF should adopt a Real SDR'. *Central Banking*, August 2019.

Coleridge, S.T. (1960/1798). *The Poems of Samuel Taylor Coleridge*. London: Oxford University Press.

Friedman, M. (1970). *The Counter-Revolution in Monetary Theory*. First Wincott Memorial Lecture, IEA.

Galbraith, J.K. (2000, April 13). Interview in *The Progressive*, by Amitabh Pal.

Potvin, J. (2019). 'Earth Reserve Assurance: A Sound Money Framework'. Pre-submission request for comment, Version 0.5. Dissertation article in partial fulfilment of a Doctorate in Administration (Project Management). Université du Québec. Canada. ResearchGate, pp. 1–22. https://doi.org/10.13140/RG.2.2.21652.86402.

Rajan, R. (2019). *The Third Pillar: How Markets and the State Leave the Community Behind*. London: Penguin Press.

Runciman, D. (2018). *How Democracy Ends*. Basic Books.

Skidelsky, R. (1992). *John Maynard Keynes: The Economist as Saviour, 1920–1937*. London: Macmillan.

Slaughter, Anne-Marie (2018, May 24). 'Social media can help fight corruption one 'like' at a time'. Financial Times.

Tooze, A. (2018). *Crashed: How a decade of financial crises changed the world*. Allen Lane.

Tooze, A. (2019). 'Democracy and its Discontents' *New York Review of Book*, June 6.

Ussher, Leanne (2009). 'Global Imbalances and the Key Currency Regime: The Case for a Commodity Reserve Currency'. *Review of Political Economy* 21 (3):403–421.

Weber, M. (1918). 'Science as a Vocation' in Gerth, H.H and Mills, C.E., *From Max Weber Essays in Sociology*. London: Routledge & Kegan Paul, 1948.

World Bank (1989). *World Development Report*.

Zuboff, S. (2019). *The Age of Surveillance Capitalism*. Profile Books.

Index[1]

---

[1] Note: Page numbers followed by 'n' refer to notes.

© The Author(s) 2019
R. Pringle, *The Power of Money*, https://doi.org/10.1007/978-3-030-25894-8

62240038R00177